T0274863

Miloš Pojar

T. G. Masaryk and the Jewish Question

Translated from the Czech
by Gerald Turner

Karolinum Press 2019

KAROLINUM PRESS is a publishing department of Charles University
Ovocný trh 560/5, 116 36 Prague 1, Czech Republic
www.karolinum.cz

Originally published in Czech as *T. G. Masaryk a židovství*, Prague:
Academia, 2016
Czech edition reviewed by
Dr. Otto Dov Kulka (Prof. em. Hebrew University of Jerusalem)
Dr. Martin Kučera (Institute of History, Czech Academy of Sciences)

For their generous support of this English translation,
Karolinum would like to thank the Forum 2000 Foundation,
Avraham Harshalom, David Hercky, Hugo Marom, Rita Spiegel,
and the Israel-Czech Republic Friendship Association.

Cover illustration: T.G. Masaryk on the Temple Mount in Jerusalem

Editor Richard Vašek
Cover and design by Zdeněk Ziegler
Set and printed in the Czech Republic by Karolinum Press
First English edition

Cataloging-in-Publication Data is available from the National Library
of the Czech Republic

ISBN 978-80-246-3879-9
eISBN 978-80-246-3880-5 (pdf)

Contents

Preface

SHLOMO AVINERI

Kde domov můj? (Where is my home?) – the hauntingly beautiful opening line of the Czech national anthem – could be seen also as encapsulating the challenges facing Jewish people in the Czech lands in the second half of the 19th century. Political equality granted to Jews in the Austrian part of the Habsburg monarchy in 1867 ran parallel with the emergence of the Czech national movement. In the cauldron of the changing realities in the multi-ethnic empire, the very identity of the Jewish community was thrown into the dramatic, new and unprecedented context of the struggle between German and Czech speakers that totally transformed their social and cultural existence: now the Josephine *Toleranzpatent* could not adequately address challenges which were no longer issues of merely religious tolerance.

The main virtue of Miloš Pojar's *T.G. Masaryk and the Jewish Question* is in weaving Masaryk's life story integrally into the history of the Czech national movement both in the waning years of Habsburgian rule and the first Czechoslovak Republic. In a memorable comment Pojar states that Masaryk's leadership redeemed Czech nationalism from serious strains of anti-Semitism and re-formed it in the mold of a humanistic, tolerant and inclusive movement, eventually making post-1918 Czechoslovakia into the only post-Habsburgian successor state which not only established a consolidated democracy but whose ideology, policies and institutions were free from anti-Jewish discrimination which marred, in one way or another, its inter-war neighboring countries.

This was a remarkable achievement, as the beginnings were not auspicious. Masaryk was initially burdened with two sets of legacies which made Czech relations with the Jews in their midst problematic. By Masaryk's own admission, the countryside in which he was born was infused with anti-Semitic prejudices, en-

(7)

couraged by the church and society in general. But beyond this, Masaryk also encountered a Czech national movement which looked with skepticism if not enmity on the Jewish population and saw it as part of the German-language hegemony fostered by the Austrian authorities against which it was fighting to assert its own identity and culture.

The reasons for these suspicions against the Jews were rooted in the circumstances of Jewish emancipation after 1848. While many members of the Jewish intelligentsia participated in the Czech revolution of 1848, for many Jewish people the road to equality went through integration into the hegemonic German-speaking culture, especially in the cities with their mixed German-Czech populations. For many Czech nationalists this led to opposition to Jewish emancipation and occasionally turned anti-German demonstrations into anti-Jewish pogroms.

Masaryk's road away from these prejudices was not immediate. The first step took place when he moved from the countryside to Brno and later Vienna and came in touch with members of the educated Jewish bourgeoisie, in whose households he occasionally served as a tutor; some of his university teachers were also Jewish. It was there that he realized that the issue of Jewish equal rights was immanently linked to the future of society in general and had to be de-coupled from the theological heritage of the Christian approach to Judaism as a religion: it was a civil and moral challenge, not a religious disagreement.

Unsurprisingly, during his Brno and Vienna student days, when Masaryk developed his views on the Czech national movement, some of his first publications focused on polemics against Ernest Renan's views on Judaism and Gobineau's racist ideas. On a theoretical level he sometimes agreed with Renan but argued that they were irrelevant to the issue of Jewish rights in modern society. He recognized that the Jews have national characteristics which may be different from those of the majority population, but they have a right to maintain and preserve them: the principle of emancipation leads to self-determination, and in Masaryk's' vision of a tolerant Habsburg empire the Jews deserved to be integrated: the Herderian cultural principles apply to them as to all other groups. As for Gobineau's theories of race, Masaryk argued that there are no "pure races" and this applied to the Jews as to any other group.

With Masaryk's appointment, first as a *Privatdozent* in Vienna and then as a professor of philosophy in Prague, his views gained a pulpit which he used not only in his lectures but also in his numerous publications, both scholarly and popular.

These views were integrated into his first major work on Marxism, which addressed not only Marx's philosophy but was also a response to the Austro-Marxists who tried to square their Marxist principles with the reality of the multiethnic Habsburg empire and especially the challenges of a multilingual proletariat in some of its major urban centers, as in Vienna and Brno, where ethnicity and class could not be easily separated from each other.

Masaryk recognized Marx's immense contribution to social and economic thinking, yet he differed from him on a major premise: materialism. He recognized the enormous importance of economic factors in human history and social analysis, but insisted that there were other interests apart from them which cannot be ignored and cannot be reduced to merely economic considerations. Masaryk's book became one of the first seminal, positive-yet-critical assessments of Marxism in general and tried to present a kind of socialism based on a broader ethical and cultural foundation.

Masaryk's extensive study of Marx confronted him also with Marx's notorious essay *On the Jewish Question* which equates Judaism with capitalism. Quite interestingly and significantly, Masaryk strongly disagrees with this position for a number of reasons. Sarcastically he admits the force of Marx's rhetoric, but writes that it is poor on social analysis and exhibits ignorance on the reality of Jewish life: not all Jews are capitalists, says Masaryk, pointing out that in Poland, Galicia and Russia most Jews are poor and there is a vast Jewish proletariat in Eastern Europe.

Yet Masaryk's critique of Marx's essay goes deeper: Marx, according to him totally ignores the fact that there are national dimensions in Jewish life, that Jewish identity is not just religious. By ignoring the national aspect of the Jewish question Marx thus is unable to adequately address the issue. Regardless of the complex historical relationship between Judaism and Christianity, the fact of the matter is, according to Masaryk, that in recent times the emergence of Zionism suggests that Jews are returning to history, and the fact that so many Jews support socialism is another indication of their positive role in contemporary society.

Writing in this vein in the late 1890s provides extraordinary insight into the novel dimensions of Jewish life at the turn of the century, and the fact that it comes in the context of a polemic with Marx is quite significant.

But Pojar rightly points out that all these writings were, after all, basically academic: the great defining moment in Masaryk's contribution to changing the discourse of Czech nationalism away from the anti-Semitic tones which characterized it at the time came with the Hilsner Affair in 1899, when a Jewish man was accused in Polná with the ritual murder of a Christian young woman. It was his public role in denouncing the Polná blood libel that identified Masaryk's name with a courageous battle against anti-Semitism. That the Polná Affair took place at the time the Dreyfus Affair shook French politics helped cast Masaryk in a role comparable to that of Emile Zola.

Initially Masaryk was reluctant to get involved in what appeared a messy and nasty provincial murder case, and his first responses – when asked by Jewish students to raise his voice – were tentative and focused on some of the questionable forensic details used falsely to condemn the Jewish defendant. Yet when the murder case became transmogrified into accusations of ritual murder which were supported by the Czech press and some of the Czech student organizations, Masaryk realized – as he wrote – that this was not just a question of the fate of an individual but a battle for the soul of the Czech national movement.

It was not an easy position to take. His lectures were disturbed by radical Czech nationalist students; his pamphlet on the trial was banned by the authorities because it questioned the decisions of the court which condemned Hilsner to death; his lectures at the university were temporarily suspended and some of the Czech papers accused him of treason and being a lackey of the Jews and the paid agent of Jewish capitalists.

But because the issue – a blood libel in the relatively liberal and tolerant Habsburg monarchy at the threshold of the 20th century – gained international press coverage, Masaryk's name became known across Europe and also in the United States, where Jewish organizations got involved in Hilsner's defense. Shrewdly Masaryk later commented that his fame as the defender of an innocent Jewish victim of a medieval anti-Jewish myth helped the Czechoslovak national case during World War I as many

Jewish newspapers and financiers supported the movement in recognition of his role in the Polná case.

Hilsner's verdict was not overturned, though Emperor Franz Joseph commuted his death sentence to life imprisonment. But the visibility of the public debate initiated by Masaryk helped to change the discourse within the Czech national movement, and Masaryk's subsequent election to the Vienna parliament underlined the significant change in the direction of Czech nationalism towards a tolerant approach to the Jewish question which then became the foundation of the new Czechoslovak Republic.

Pojar's description portrays the confluence of Masaryk's intellectual and moral authority in shaping the policies of Czechoslovakia regarding its Jewish population after 1918. This was not free from structural problems originating in the legacy of the Czech national movement and was certainly further exacerbated by the differences between the highly secularized and urbanized Jews in the Czech lands and the mainly Orthodox Jewish communities in Slovakia and Sub-Carpathia, many of them living among the rural and religiously conservative Catholic population; the political forces opposed to Masaryk's approach were not negligible.

Pojar does not overlook some of the internal tensions in Masaryk's own position. His valiant stand in the Hilsner Affair was paradoxically accompanied by some of the ambiguities inherent in his general theoretical approach to the core issues of nationalism. On the one hand, his Herderian background led him to view the Jews as a nation, not just a religious community, hence encompassing self-determination, part of which meant that they were entitled to the preservation of their distinct culture. This led Masaryk to a sympathetic understanding of Zionism, especially in its cultural version as expressed by Ahad Ha'am and Aharon David Gordon. On the other hand, this also caused him to maintain that Jews could not easily become members of the Czech nation, and his support of equal rights for the Jews did not agree with the premises of those Jews who saw in assimilation – especially radical assimilation – an ultimate and desirable goal. It is for these reasons that he viewed Zionism not leading primarily to emigration to Palestine but as a vehicle for a Jewish cultural renaissance within Europe generally and, after 1918, as a distinct ethnic group within a pluralist Czechoslovak democratic republic. It was not an easy position to take, and neither Jewish assimilationists nor Zionists were wholly happy with such a differentiated position; nor were radical Czech nationalists.

These ambiguities appeared to be evident also during his visit to Palestine in 1927 – the only European head of state or major statesman to visit the country during the inter-war period. In Jewish and Zionist memory this came to be viewed as an historical event, to be feted and recalled for decades to come, as testified by the numerous streets and squares called after him in contemporary Israel, as well as in the symbolism involved in naming a kibbutz – Kfar Masaryk – in honor of his visit.

But the event itself – he visited Jerusalem, Tel Aviv, Rishon le-Zion, the first kibbutz as well as a kibbutz founded by immigrants from Czechoslovakia – for all the enthusiastic reception granted to Masaryk by the Jewish community, was a much more complex affair.

The visit was part of what can be called a traditional Grand Tour of the Orient: it started in Egypt, for whose culture Masaryk always had deep respect and admiration; in Palestine he was hosted by the British High Commissioner and met with the leadership of the Moslem Arab community, headed by the Mufti of Jerusalem Haj Amin al-Husseini. He lodged mainly in Christian hostels, primarily Franciscan establishments, and visited the Christian holy sites in Jerusalem, Bethlehem, Nazareth and around the Sea of Galilee – and made sure that these aspects of his visit would be publicized.

Yet there is no doubt that his most extensive exposure was to the Jewish community of the country, and his visits to the Jewish National Library – then headed by the Czech-born philosopher Hugo Bergmann – and the nascent Hebrew University were the most visible aspects of his interest in Jewish matters and his fundamental support for Zionism; so was his deep interest in the kibbutz idea. But the visit also brought to the surface – in private communications, not in public statements – the very ambiguities which characterized his complex approach to Jewish phenomena. While admiring the progress – economic, scientific and cultural – Zionism brought to the country, he was somewhat pessimistic whether the Jewish immigrants would be able to find an understanding and a *modus vivendi* with the Arab majority population. He was equally skeptical that the Jews could become a majority in the country, without which their political aims could not be achieved. Not surprisingly, his visit to Palestine – symbolic and significant as it certainly was – strengthened his support for the cultural, rather than political aspects, of the Zionist project. Just as in the Czech case, so in the Jewish case, Masaryk was centered much more on the cultural rather than the purely political. While Pojar does not say so, in both cases he eventually turned out to be wrong, though because of reasons totally outside of his control.

Masaryk was a true son of the liberal legacies of the 19th century; the 20th century turned out to be much more cruel. Yet both the Czech nation and the Zionist project survived, but not without paying a heavy price for their respective achievements.

***

Let me end on a personal note.

I grew up in Herzliya, at that time a small agricultural village north of Tel Aviv. In the critical and difficult months of the Israel War of Independence in early 1948, the first serious arms the Jewish self-defense force (the *Haganna*) received were supplied by Czechoslovakia, and they were crucial in saving the Jewish community from the Arab onslaught. I was at that time a high school student, a member of the Youth Brigades of the *Haganna*, and when the first deliveries arrived at an abandoned airstrip near Herzliya, I was among the teenagers called up to help unload them. For us, members of the small and beleaguered *Yishuv* – the Jewish community in British Mandatory Palestine – these were historical moments, and I still remember the thrill we felt in unloading and unpacking the machine guns and rifles flown in by Czechoslovak military pilots.

Many decades later, in June 1990, I was a member of an international group of observers to monitor the first free post-Communist elections in Czechoslovakia. The delegation included Madeleine Albright, and her presence added a symbolic dimension to the historical occasion, which to me was combined with the memories of the Czech arms deliveries to the nascent Israel on 1948. That my ancestors came from Moravian Třebíč, where they had found refuge in the 18th century after being expelled from Vienna, added a further historically significant dimension.

(13)

More than one circle was thus closed for me. And to the perennial question of "Where is my home?" the only adequate answer is that it is both the world at large and one's own land: *tertium non datur*. Masaryk with his humanist patriotism would in all probability agree.

Shlomo Avineri
(Professor of Political Science at the Hebrew University
of Jerusalem,
author of *The Making of Modern Zionism* and *Herzl's Vision:
Theodor Herzl and the Foundation of the Jewish State*)

1. Childhood, youth, studies; University of Vienna (1850–1882)

...all my life I've gone out of my way not to be unjust to Jews.
Talks with T.G.Masaryk, 1927–1931

T.G.Masaryk was born on 7 March 1850 at Hodonín, one of the centres of Moravian Slovakia (Slovácko). At the time of his birth 65 Jewish families (215 Jews) were resident in Hodonín. They were mostly merchants, innkeepers, artisans, as well as a physician, a cantor and a teacher, and belonged to the better-off section of the population. A synagogue had existed in Hodonín since 1863 and a Jewish school building stood alongside it. When the school was abolished Jewish children attended the public German school.[1]

The history of the Jews in Hodonín is documented since the first quarter of the 17th century but dates back much earlier. The cemetery in Hodonín was founded in 1620 and closed down in the 1970s under the Communist regime. The estate of Hodonín had been owned since 1762 by the Empress Maria Theresa, who had already expelled the Jews from the town in 1744 and abolished their community.

By 1753, after they were permitted to return, there were 109 Jewish families in Hodonín, and by 1783, during the reign of Emperor Joseph II, a further 13 families had moved there. By 1910 the Jewish inhabitants numbered 976.[2]

---

1) O. Donath. "Židé na Masarykově cestě životem." In *Thomas G. Masaryk and the Jews, a collection of essays*, ed. E. Rychnovsky. New York City, 1941, pp. 125–127.
2) O. Donath. "Židé na Masarykově cestě životem," p. 122. For a detailed history of the Jewish community in Hodonín, see G. Treixler. "Die Gödinger Judengemeinde," *Zeitschrift des deutsch. Vereins für die Geschichte Mährens u. Schlesiens*, 21, 1917, pp. 23–58, 239–262, 335–368.

Masaryk's father hailed from Kopčany, not far from Holič,[3] which is located in Slovakia, east of the river Morava. The Holič estate had been purchased in 1749 by Francis of Lorraine, the husband of Empress Maria Theresa. Thus both estates, Holič and Hodonín, became in turn the property of the imperial family. There were Jewish communities in both Kopčany and Holič.

For several generations the family of Masaryk's mother were settled in Hustopeče[4], where the Jewish community had been revived in the mid-19th century. The reconstructed original Jewish synagogue still stands, but the cemetery was closed down in the 1980s.[5]

In course of time Masaryk's parents moved with their children from Hodonín to Mutěnice and then back to Hodonín. The family then lived from 1856 to 1862 in Čejkovice, and then in Čejč in 1864.[6]

Jewish communities existed in two other towns in Slovácko, namely, Břeclav and Strážnice. The latter community was older, dating from the beginning of the 15th century; by the middle of the 19th century Jews represented 10% of the population and resided in eighty of the houses.

Masaryk started to attend school in Hodonín, but soon after transferred to the village schools in Čejkovice and then Čejč. From 1861 to 1863 he attended the Piarist two-year Realschule in Hustopeče and in 1865 he passed the entrance examination for the prima grade at the Piarist Gymnasium at Strážnice. That same year he was admitted to the *sekunda* grade at the German Gymnasium in Brno

As a child Masaryk had ample opportunity to encounter Jewish families, including those settled in the villages and those in the larger settlements such as Hodonín, and Strážnice.

Masaryk described his impressions from his first encounters -with the Jewish community in his autobiographical fragment

---

3) "I think I'm a pure-blooded Slovak." T. G. Masaryk. "Slovenské vzpomienky." In J. Doležal. *Masarykova cesta životem*. Vol. 2. Brno, 1921, pp. 19–25.
4) "Mother was German". "Běh života." In J. Doležal. *Masarykova cesta životem*. Vol. 2, pp. 1–8.
5) Z. Nejedlý. *T. G. Masaryk*. Vol. I/1. Praha, 1930, pp. 71–73. For details about Masaryk and Hustopeče see A. Janšta. *Masaryk a Hustopeče*. Hustopeče, s. d., pp. 3–24.
6) Z. Nejedlý. *T. G. Masaryk*. Vol. I/1, pp. 75–81.

"Náš pan Fixl" (Our Mr Fixl): "In the fifties (of the last century – it sounds so bygone and distant) every little Slovak in the Hodonín district was inculcated with anti-Semitism, by the family, by the school, by the church and by society as a whole. Our mother forbade us to have contact with the Lechners, telling us that Jews need Christian blood, the blood of children. I therefore always gave the Lechners' house a wide berth, as did all the boys I was friendly with in Čejkovice. I would always be hearing admonitions against the Jews in sermons and also at school. When he was in a very good mood the curate would ask the schoolmaster to play the "Jewish one" – an imitation of Jewish praying, in the style of some hackneyed old song. We lived next door to the schoolmaster and when the curate paid him a visit I would wait on them, so I got to hear that "Jewish one". In the manner of rural music lovers, the curate would mumble some text purporting to be Jewish: "taiterl-taitrrl-tai-terlai" – and he himself would laugh his head off at it!

The supersitition about Christian blood also took hold of me so that every time I happened by chance to find myself close to some Jew – I never deliberately came close to any of them – I'd eye their fingers to see if some blood remained sticking to them. I kept that stupid habit up for a long time.

And yet I liked Mr Fixl in those days, 'Our Mr Fixl' as we used to call him at home. Only now as I reminisce do I realise that our family's anti-Semitism conceded one absolutely philo-Semitic exception; but as a child I didn't realise that Mr Fixl was also a Jew. Mr Fixl was a door-to-door pedlar from Hodonín; Mother bought cloth from him and house linen of every kind. Mr Fixl would call on us from time to time and we would all look forward to his arrival; he would spread out piles of his wares in front of us, telling us where each one came from, from which factory, and to whom he had already sold of bit of that or that, and how much; he would tell us all the latest lively and interesting news from Hodonín and the surrounding villages. And naturally in the process he would let drop a bit of gossip – in strict confidence, of course. And in the end I would always be given a bit of pencil (which we called *plevajz*). In short we were very fond of Mr Fixl. And he was 'our' Mr Fixl.

Blood was forgotten as a result of acquaintance, coexistence and a mutual economic relationship – the superstition applied only to those Jews we didn't associate with, and in general every-one who held to the ritual murder superstition had or has their own Mr Fixl. The Jewish children had their own school and their own teacher, so we grew up apart from each other, strangers and alienated one from another. They had their Jewish ghetto, we had our Christian one.

It was at the Realschule in Hustopeče that I first had a Jewish classmate. But I would avoid him, and look at his fingers... We would all torment him quite a bit, in an unchristian fashion, and yet he was a thoroughly decent lad; he wasn't clever and was a slow learner, and all in all he truly confounded all our Jewish psychology. And that Jew and classmate became the Damascus moment for my anti-Semitism. We once went on an excursion to the Pálava Hills (we didn't call them mountains). On the way back we lingered over supper at an inn in Dunajovice; wine and beer were drunk and the schoolmasters indulged in banter with us, and the butt of their jokes was "Leopold". (I can well recall his face, but I've forgotten his surname; I only know there were some esses in his name.) The sun had gone down – Leopold disap-peared from the table, and eventually it was decided to send out a search party; they found him, they said, standing outside the gate praying with his straps on his forehead. The boys ran out to see and they teased him even while he was praying. I also went to look. I've never forgotten how I was taken aback by Leopold: he was standing outside the gate in a squalid spot, probably to avoid being seen, thinking that no one would look for him there. He was bowed down in prayer. I suddenly had no taste for mock-ery. We scampered around and Leopold did not neglect his pray-ing. From that instant my anti-Semitism was undermined. Maybe it wasn't yet overcome, but it was undermined in a religious sense.

My parents managed to return to Hodonín that time and I had a chance to acquaint myself with the Jewish town and with a large number of Jews. My experience demolished the ghetto of prejudice and through contact and comparison I came to realise that there are Jews and Jews, just as there are Christians and Christians. Acquaintanceship gave rise to friendship – good, faithful friendship. My circle of Jewish acquaintances grew – in Brno and Vienna. Prejudices disappeared even though my child-ish habit surfaced from time to time; habit is a powerful and dreadful thing.

Younger generations now growing up together in national schools cannot feel the anti-Semitism that we did. Here the tendency is to philosophise about the economic difference between us Christians and Jews; people read the theories of Wagner, Nietzsche, Lagarde, and Gobineau. Our anti-Semitism was simply superstition and essentially clerical.

Isn't it odd that we Czechs have no theorist of anti-Semitism? In the Hilsner affair it was the old, primitive and somewhat barbaric anti-Semitism that came to the fore, and a considerable section of the intelligentsia fell prey to it. More than once, in those days, did I recall Leopold behind the gate at Dolní Dunajovice – hopefully I atoned for all the nastiness that I was led into by my former anti-Semitism.

The younger generations no longer have any ghettoes, they assimilate more easily and grow together. Assimilation – I recall the Lechner children who were taboo for us children, whereas Mr Fixl was ours. The ghetto has fallen – but a Jew cannot become a higher ranking military office, cannot become a higher judge and we don't vote him mayor, etc., we still simply have our Fixls, our Mr Fixls. Assimilation?..."[7]

Masaryk would repeat that reminiscence in an abbreviated form to Karel Čapek in *Talks with T.G.Masaryk*: "as for Judaism, well, I was afraid of Jews: I believed they used Christian blood in their rituals. I would go several streets out of my way to avoid Jewish houses. Jewish children wanted to play with me because I knew a little German, but I refused. It was only later, at the Hustopeče school, that I more or less made my peace with the Jews. Once on a school trip to the Pálava Hills we were cavorting about after our meal at the tavern when I saw one of our Jewish schoolmates slip away. I was curious and followed him. He was kneeling behind an open gate with his face to the wall, praying. For some reason I felt ashamed to see a Jew praying while I played. I was loath to admit that he prayed as fervently as we did and had remembered to say his prayers even in the midst of our frolic.

Anyway, all my life I've gone out of my way not to be unjust to Jews. That's why I've been said to favour them. When did I get over my "folk" anti-Semitism? Well, maybe never on an

---

7) T. G. Masaryk. "Náš pan Fixl", *Besedy Času*, 24. 2. 1914; J. Doležal. *Masarykova cesta životem*. Vol. 2, pp. 37–39, 69–76,151–152.

emotional level, only rationally. After all, it was my mother who taught me the superstition about the Jews' making use of Christian blood."[8]

In the years 1865–1869 Masaryk attended the German-language gymnasium in Brno. At that time the Moravian metropolis was German in character. In 1857 Brno's population stood at 58,809 or 59,819 depending on the source. In 1880 it numbered 82,660, comprising 48,591 Germans and 32,142 Czechs (according to their native tongue). In 1857 Jews in Brno numbered around 2,230, and in 1880, 5,498. In 1863, 68.7% of the students at the Technical University were Germans and 30.1% were Czechs, and 11.1% of the total were Jews.[9]

Jews had been living on the territory of Brno since the 13th century. In 1454 they were expelled from the city (and from all other royal boroughs in Moravia), the synagogue was demolished and the cemetery closed. Admission to the city was still made difficult for them in the 18th century; they were not allowed to spend the night there and they could enter the city only on certain days (for markets and court hearings), and until the Edict of Tolerance they had to pay a special toll to do so. In 1797, 12 registered Jews were living in Brno, in 1834, 135, in 1848, 445, in 1857, 1,262 (a different figure from above), and in 1869, 4,505.[10]

Permission to establish a Jewish community was not granted until 1859, and the first rabbi commenced his ministry there a year later. The first synagogue, known as the Great, was built from 1853 to 1855 (it was demolished by the Nazis). The first Jewish school with religious teaching opened in 1861.[11]

At the gymnasium Masaryk had several Jewish fellow-pupils in each year he was at school, most of all in the second grade. It is not known whether he had closer relationships with any of

8) K. Čapek. *Talks with T.G.Masaryk*. Trans. D. Round, ed. M. H. Heim. North Haven, 1995, p. 49.

9) *Die Juden in den böhmischen Ländern. Vorträge d. Tagung d. Collegium Carolinum in Bad Wiessee vom 27.–29. November 1981*. München – Wien, 1983, tables on p. 331 and subsequent.; P. Weber. "Brněnská židovská obec." In *Židovská Morava – Židovské Brno*. Brno, 2000, p. 22.

10) According to T. Pěkný. *Historie Židů v Čechách a na Moravě*. Praha, 2001, p. 404.

11) P. Weber. "Brněnská židovská obec", p. 22.

them.[12] He did not gain any greater knowledge of Judaism, or study it in any way while he was at the school. He read Greek and Latin authors, and German and French literature, and he was interested in Darwinism and philosophy. He also read anti-religious authors. As he later told Karel Čapek "... I couldn't avoid pondering on books like Renan's *Life of Jesus* and the like... "[13]

In 1869 Masaryk transferred from Brno to Vienna and started to attend the sexta grade at the Akademisches Gymnasium.

Masaryk attended the gymnasium in Vienna from 1869 to 1872, when he passed his final examinations. Among the 50 pupils in his final year there were 23 Jews, many of whom later rose to positions of prominence in Austrian public life, chiefly as lawyers, judges, industrialists, professors and actors. Masaryk was subsequently in contact with some of them. There is also no evidence from Masaryk's studies at the Vienna gymnasium that he started systematically to take an interest in Judaism or the so-called "Jewish Question". An important factor would seem to have been the Jewish salons that the came into contact with when he moved from Brno to Vienna with the Le Monnier family as tutor to their son (Chief of Police Le Monnier was not Jewish). These salons flourished in the families of the Jewish bourgeoisie in the era of liberalism in Austria. He also became a tutor in the home of the rich Jewish family of the Sterns, where the lady of the house held a salon attended by the cream of Viennese scientific and artistic life. Later Masaryk also coached Alfred Schlesinger, son of the Director General of the Anglobank in Vienna.[14]

---

12) O. Donath. "Židé na Masarykově cestě životem", p. 149, in note 28 there is a quotation: "... My circle of Jewish acquaintances grew – in Brno and Vienna. Prejudices disappeared even though my childish habit surfaced from time to time." There is a reference to Doležal (*Masarykova cesta životem*. Vol. 1, p. 38) and Donath (*Masaryk a židovství*. Brno, 1920, p. 23). See also Z. Nejedlý. *T. G. Masaryk*. Vol. I/1, p. 177.
13) K. Čapek. *Talks with T.G.Masaryk*, p. 74.
14) Concerning Masaryk's gymnasium study see his Curriculum vitae, which was a source for Z. Nejedlý. *T. G. Masaryk*. Vol. 1/1, pp. 195–219; O. Donath. "Židé na Masarykově cestě životem", note 1, p. 134–138; S. Polák. *T. G. Masaryk. Za ideálem a pravdou*. Vol. 1 (1850–1882). Praha, 2000, pp. 124–146 and subsequent.

Masaryk would later speak of his situation in the family of the banker Schlesinger as follows: "In the circle of their family and friends I came to know how the rich live. They are not happy: their wealth is a wall cutting them off from others, which often leads to follies and perversities."[15]

From 1872 to 1876 Masaryk studied classical philology at the University of Vienna, attending lectures in classical philology and Greek philosophy given by Professor Theodor Gomperz. Gomperz came from a Jewish family in Brno and he had a great influence on Masaryk, introducing him, among others to the writing of John Stuart Mill, whom he translated, and also of Comte. Masaryk also attended lectures in other disciplines, including the grammar of Sanskrit. Disillusioned, on the whole, with the study of classical philology, Masaryk turned to the history of philosophy, and above all to Plato, the aforementioned J.S.Mill, and Auguste Comte. There followed Bacon, Pascal, Vico, Descartes and Rousseau, the *Encyclopédistes*, Leibniz, Lessing, Herder, Kant, Hume, as well as Darwin and Marx, whose *Das Kapital* he read during those years.[16]

Masaryk completed his studies in Vienna at the beginning of 1876 with his doctoral thesis "Plato and the Essentials of the Soul" and passing an oral examination in philosophy and classical philology, whereby he was awarded the degree of Doctor of Philosophy. After a visit to northern Italy, Masaryk arrived in Leipzig with his ward Alfred Schlesinger on 15 October of that same year to attend lectures in philosophy.

During Masaryk's stay in Leipzig in 1876 and 1877, an event occurred that would be decisive for his private life: he met there an American, Charlotte Garrigue, and after closer acquaintance, fell in love with her. They became engaged and were married in America in 1878. In Leipzig, he attended lectures in philosophy and psychology, which he did not find very rewarding. He gave a lecture on suicide to the Philosophical Society, which was essentially an earlier essay of 1875, but was more extensive and intended for publication. The Leipzig lectures were also attend-

---

15) K. Čapek. *Talks with T.G.Masaryk*, p. 88.
16) For details of Masaryk's university studies in Vienna see Z. Nejedlý. *T. G. Masaryk*. Vol. I/1, pp. 219–263; O. Donath. "Židé na Masarykově cestě životem", footnote 1, pp. 138–142; S. Polák. *T. G. Masaryk. Za ideálem a pravdou*. Vol. 1, pp. 146–229.

ed by a much younger student, Edmund Husserl, a Jew from Moravia, born in Prostějov. Masaryk remained in contact with him later in Vienna and they corresponded after the war. Influenced by Masaryk, Husserl studied the New Testament and subsequently converted to Protestantism.[17]

In his earliest period in Vienna, i.e. before his arrival in Prague, when he was studying and coming to terms with the issue of progress and development in connection with the suicide rate, and later regarding the question of human races, Masaryk encountered the phenomenon of the Jews and their role in the development of humanity. At the end of his study *O pokroku, vývoji a osvětě* (On progress, development and public education)[18], devoted to the problems of human progress and public education, Masaryk admits the possibility of humanity's annihilation as a result of "unforeseen radical changes" and the possibility of public education being destroyed by some barbaric nation. He says in this connection that he has in mind races that have contributed to education and concedes that there are nations that have done little for education. Although the preceding passages do not relate to the Jews, he immediately states: "It is well known that the Jews regarded themselves as the chosen people; nowadays the Indo-European race declares itself to be the elect..."[19] Concerning nations, he states that none of them is pure and unmixed. And he continues: "What we call a race has no historical validity, so there can be no question of races being chosen."[20]

In 1877, Masaryk returned to Vienna from Leipzig and two years later he successfully defended his thesis on suicide. That same year, 1879, he was appointed a private Associate Professor at the University of Vienna. In his first major work, the sociolog-

---

17) V. K. Š. "Edmund Husserl a T. G. Masaryk." In *Masarykův sborník*. Vol. 3. Praha, 1929, pp. 367–368; Husserl's letter to Masaryk was printed Jan Patočka's afterword to the Czech translation of Husserl's Cartesian Meditations: *Karteziánské meditace*. Praha, 1968, pp. 162–163.
18) T. G. Masaryk. *O pokroku, vývoji a osvětě*. Wien, 1877; subsequently published in J. Doležal. *Masarykova cesta životem*. Vol. 2, pp. 198–217; most recently in T. G. Masaryk. *Juvenilie. Studie a stati 1876–1881*. Praha, 1993, pp. 48–68.
19) T. G. Masaryk. *Juvenilie. Studie a stati 1876–1881*, p. 65.
20) Ibid, p. 66.

ical treatise *Sebevražda* (Suicide), Masaryk first commented more extensively on Judaism.[21]

"In order to understand modern civilisation, one must know the Greek, Roman, and Mosaic-Oriental culture that rests at the base of our culture; these secondary influences of the ancient Orient can remain unmentioned here because of their slight significance."[22]

After dealing with Greek and Roman culture, Masaryk notes that at the time of Christ's birth the pagan Roman world was in complete dissolution. "Mosaic theism, with its law and ceremonial, also could not take hold of man's destiny and rescue him; the Jews themselves were weak and in need of deliverance. In this time of general longing for a saviour and deliver, Jesus appeared, the Messiah, and his life and his teachings did rescue mankind."[23] Masaryk examines Christian teaching, whose belief in God and pure monotheism, in common with Judaism and Islam, "is inimical to the suicide tendency". In his teachings Jesus restricted himself to the Old Testament.[24]

Masaryk says the following in relation to the Jews: "What is valid for the Christian peoples also holds for the non-Christian peoples, especially those who participate in the modern labour of civilisation. The non-Christian peoples are also happy and enjoy life if they have a unified world-view, if their intellectual cultivation is in harmony with their inner life, if they are, in a word, religious. This depends not so very much on the goodness and elevation of the religion as it does on the degree to which religion is really an object of feeling and is a genuine means of satisfaction and fulfilment for the people. A faithful Jew or Mohammedan finds just as strong a support in his faith as the faithful Christian. All three find peace for their souls amidst gloom; the

---

21) Masaryk's first published work came out in German under the title *Der Selbstmord als sociale Massenerscheinung der modernen Civilisation*. Wien, 1881. Published in English translation as *Suicide and the Meaning of Civilization*. Chicago, 1970.
22) T. G. Masaryk. *Sebevražda hromadným jevem společenským moderní osvěty*. Praha, 1930, p. 163. Regarding Masaryk's attitude to the Orient see, inter alia P. Poucha. "T. G. Masaryk a jeho vztah k Orientu", *Nový Orient*, 5, 1949–1950, pp. 142–143.
23) T. G. Masaryk. *Suicide and the Meaning of Civilization*, pp. 152–153.
24) Ibid., p. 154.

effect of all three can be the same despite the qualitative differences of the effective causes.

"Let us first consider the Jews. The philosophers, no less than the common people, have long racked their brains over the 'cosmopolitan race' of the Jews, and yet the history of this most remarkable people has not yet been written. We are interested here only in the living faith in God of this people. The Old Testament reveals how strongly theism was planted in the hearts of the Jews by those responsible for their intellectual and moral leadership. It is quite amazing how these people amidst their terrible troubles – there is hardly any more unfortunate people than the Jews – always found new hopes and new faith in their God.

The Jews have endured many oppressions to which they have been exposed as a result of their religion, which, as Gibbon has rightly remarked, is wonderfully adapted for defence but has never been directed to conquest. Persecuted and despised, the Jewish people cling to the religion of their fathers and have distinguished themselves by a joy in life and a practical optimism which does not allow the development of the morbid suicide tendency. Their great moderation also has a favourable effect in the same sense.[25]

But religious indifference, scepticism, and unbelief are also prevalent among the Jews, especially among the educated. And it cannot be otherwise; living with and among you irreligious Christians, they take an active part in modern intellectual activities, and therefore show, especially in the cities, the same characteristics as the Christians with respect to religion. Heine, the poet of naked scepticism, was a Jew."[26]

---

25) Masaryk added the following footnote: "Suicide appears among the Jews, as an exception to the general rule, during times of severe persecution. In their sacred literature, which includes a history of more than 10,000 years, there are found 10 examples of suicide at most."

26) T. G. Masaryk. *Suicide and the Meaning of Civilization*, pp. 214–215

2. Masaryk's study of the Jewish question (1882–1914)

...as a nation the Jews really are less mixed than the European nations.
T. G. Masaryk, *Sborník historický*, 1883

JEWS IN THE CZECH LANDS
FROM THE MID-19ᵀᴴ CENTURY TO 1914
1848/49

The attempts of the Jews in the Czech Lands to align themselves with the Czech nation, expressed, for instance, in Siegfried Kapper's Czech-language poetry collection, were disparaged by Karel Havlíček Borovský. He told them that Jews are a nation and therefore could not become Czechs. He spoke somewhat unkindly of the Jews. He also counselled them to stick to German, whereby he caused many of them to embrace Austrian liberalism. The Moravian Jews did not take much persuading; they were always influenced by Vienna and Austrian culture and were much more inclined to accept German culture and the German language than those in Bohemia.

In the states of the German Confederation in the period leading up to the revolution of March 1848, many Czech Jews took an active part in the struggle for a new social order. Representatives of the Jewish intelligentsia, journalists, doctors, industrialists, bankers – and subsequently politicians too – would take part in the Kremsier (Kroměříž) Parliament, the Frankfurt Parliament and in the preparations for the March revolutions in Prague and Vienna, as well as in the St Wenceslas Committee, and as commanders of the student legions. The revolutionary events in Vienna, Prague, Pressburg (Bratislava) and Pest (Budapest) were followed, of course, by anti-Jewish riots, pamphleteering and street fighting, as a result of which many Jews emigrated or were prosecuted for their political activity.

Although the revolution was defeated, the revolutionary year 1848/49 brought about further changes in the status of the Jewish population, chiefly as regards freedom of movement, free choice of abode, and access to civil service employment, including teaching posts in state schools. The Familiants Law, the Inkolat, the ghettoes and the tolerance tax were abolished. Although the reactionary Bach regime put a brake on the liberties proclaimed, they were not reversed. In 1861 Jews were permitted to own or rent land without restrictions. As a result of all these measures Jews moved en masse from the ghettoes to villages or smaller towns. In a later wave Jews left for the industrial and commercial centres of the Czech and Moravian cities from which they were previously excluded.

Jews eventually achieved complete equality in the Bohemian Kingdom through the December Constitution of 1867, which granted them state citizenship and civil and political equality before the law, the right to vote and to be elected, as well as the right to relocate freely, to acquire real estate and carry on any trade.

Hand in hand with emancipation, the process of Jewish assimilation steadily progressed in the 1870s and 80s. In particular the Jews who had moved to rural areas and small towns started to send their children to primary and secondary schools, and after 1882 to the Czech university in Prague. These people adopted the Czech language and thus there emerged a Jewish intelligentsia that spoke and wrote in Czech and started to strive for Jewish assimilation into Czech society.

Gradually a whole number of associations and institutions came into existence that supported assimilation, including Spolek českých akademiků Židů [The Association of Czech Jewish Academics], 1876, Spolek pro vytvoření české jazykové základny pro náboženské a veřejné obřady [The Society for the Creation of a Czech Linguistic Foundation for Religious and Public Ceremonies], known as Or-Tomid [Eternal Light], 1883, Národní jednota českožidovská [The Czech Jewish National Union] (which published Českožidovské listy [The Czech Jewish Press], 1893. Some Jews rejected assimilation, however, regarding themselves as neither Germans nor Czechs. They had no desire to be caught up in the conflict between Czech and German nationalism, and they opted for Zionism. This section of the Jewish population (including Hugo Bergmann, Felix Weltsch and Max Brod) strove to create a Jewish culture and nationality. 1899 saw the founding of the Zionist student organisation Bar Kochba, and in 1907 the Zionist weekly *Selbstwehr* began publication, and continued to appear up to 1938.

The size of the Jewish population grew steadily. In 1850 7,459 Jews lived in Bohemia in 347 localities. In 1880 half of the Jews lived in towns with over 5,000 inhabitants, mostly in German-speaking areas of Bohemia. In 1890 there were 94,529 Jews living in 197 localities. In 1910 a third of the Jewish population in Bohemia was concentrated in Prague[27]. By the end of the First World War the Jewish population in Bohemia numbered 97,777, and in Moravia 37,989[28].

Anti-Semitism was rife in Bohemia and Moravia at the end of the 19th century. It had spread particularly from the Austrian lands (Schönerer's Christian Social Party), and culminated in 1899 in the infamous Hilsner affair, in which Masaryk intervened (see Chapter V). Anti-Semitism was totally incompatible with his attitudes. He wanted both to take action against mass fanaticism and to defend the honour of the Czech nation, which had been adversely affected by anti-Semitism. Masaryk studied

---

27) Numbers of Jews in Prague 1880–1930

Year	Jews	Percentage of Jews in the Czech population in Prague	Percentage of Jews in the total number of Prague inhabitants
1880	20 508	21.7	6.52
1890	23 473	24.8	5.91
1900	27 289	29.4	5.31
1910	29 107	33.9	4.72
1921	31 751	39.8	4.69
1930	35 463	46.4	4.17

28) "Die Stadt ist ganz und ganz Čechisch; es berührt sehr unangenehm deutsch vornemlich von Juden und abtrünigen Čechen zu hören." T.G. Masaryk to E. Boeck 17. 9. 1882 (AÚTGM) as quoted by S. Polák. T.G. Masaryk. *Za ideálem a pravdou*. Vol. 2. Praha, 2001, p. 17, note 8.

thoroughly the literature about ritual murder superstition as well as the facts of the murder at Polná, which he visited.

Masaryk was subject to a vile witch-hunt, whose tone was set by a coalition of clericalists, Young Czechs, the National Social Party and the radical constitutionalists. He was defamed in the press as a traitor to the nation who had sold out to the Jews, and fanaticised students demonstrated against him at the university and outside his apartment. It is no secret that he even contemplated leaving Bohemia.

Masaryk's protest against Hilsner's conviction and his opposition to anti-Semitism in general played an outstanding role. It spurred a moral regeneration of the Czech nation, which started to extricate itself from narrow provincialism induced by the nationalist policies pursued by the National Party ("Old Czechs") and later by the National Liberal Party "Young Czechs". Masaryk's campaign against anti-Semitism had a cleansing effect among broad sections of Czech society and was decisive in ensuring that the Czech nation entered the 20th century as one of the nations least burdened with anti-Semitism in Europe, relatively speaking.

MASARYK'S ARRIVAL IN PRAGUE

In 1882 T.G.Masaryk took up the post of Reader of Philosophy at the new Czech University in Prague. Soon afterwards Masaryk's three extensive reviews of works by the French historian, religionist and orientialist Ernest Renan (1823–1892), renowned for his books on the life of Jesus and the origins of Christianity, were published; they concerned nationality, Judaism in national and religious terms, and science in Islam.[29] Masaryk criticised Renan on the grounds that national questions called above all for a sociological approach; he could not agree with the view that "the nation is a soul" or "a moral conscience". Regarding Judaism he rejected Renan's assertion that "the Jews are no less mixed than other nations", and in the matter of the Jewish religion Masaryk's view, unlike Renan's, was that Jewish monothe-

---

29) T. G. Masaryk. "Ernest Renan o národnosti, Ernest Renan o židovství jako plamenu a náboženství, Ernest Renan o vědě v islamismu", *Sborník historický*, 1, 1883, pp. 36–42, 120–127 and 288–290. For more recent publication see *Masarykův sborník*. Vol. 1. 2nd edition. Praha, 1934, pp. 57–76.

ism did not become a world religion and that Christianity was not based solely on Judaism. At the end of the review he repeats that "Renan's proof that Jews are just as mixed a race as other (European) nations seems utterly mistaken to me." [...] "All that is clear from the instances that Renan himself finds, is that to-day's Jews are an ethnological mixture of various Semitic tribes, but not Semitic-Indo-European." [...] "That all goes to show, I believe, that the Jews are truly less mixed as a nation than the European nations."[30]

Regarding anti-Semitism, Renan "touches on it only indirectly" Masaryk states, "but it would seem that his proof that the Jews are as mixed a nation as other nations is actually in order to defend them somewhat." Masaryk concludes that this does not end the controversy, that it is necessary to recognise the differences between non-Semites and Semites, what character traits they find mutually offensive, and after recognising their mistakes and deficiencies, to seek what they have in common.[31]

In 1882 Charlotte Masaryk published several articles in *The Sun*, the New York newspaper. Her article of 7 November 1882 concerned the Jews, and was entitled "The Persecution of the Jews".[32] Written undoubtedly in cooperation with her husband – and possibly incorporating some of his own wording – the article deals with the Jewish question within the Austrian monarchy. It cites a series of anti-Jewish clichés – The Jews' fear of manual labour, "a deficiency of ideality", "a love of gain", all of which "is illustrated by their relation to the languages of the various nations represented in Austria [...] The moment Hungary became politically free they hastened to master the Magyar tongue [...] In Bohemia, where the Bohemian element is conquering some of its political rights, they are energetically endeavouring to master

---

30) *Masarykův sborník*. Vol. 1. 2nd ed., pp. 70–71.

31) Masaryk's opinions are examined extensively by J. Opat. "Masaryk – kritik rasismu." In *Hilsnerova aféra a česká společnost 1899–1999*, ed. M. Pojar. Praha, 1999, pp. 36–41. See also J. Franěk. "Jindřich Kohn." In *Masarykův sborník*. Vol. 11–12. Praha, 2004, p. 259: "Masaryk reacted negatively to the pamphlet by the French philosopher Ernest Renan proving that the Jews are not a separate nation."

32) The English text was published by S. Polák. "Příspěvky Charlotty Masarykové do deníku The Sun (New York), r. 1882." In *Masarykův sborník*. Vol. 9. Praha, 1997, pp. 159–173.

the Tchechic [sic] tongue." The author considers assimilation to be the only way to solve the Jewish problem. Jews must change their laws and permit marriages with Christians. The author knows Jewish parents who are considering having their children baptised as a way of "taking them away" from Jewish materialism. "The Jews of their own free will must break down the iron wall which separates them from the people of every other nation," and the "Jewish Church" must allow intermarriage. The turns of phrase in the article clearly indicate that they are the view of Masaryk: the Jewish question must be solved by assimilation. It also shows, as Stanislav Polák adds, that Masaryk criticized the Jews for not ridding themselves of many prejudices, and there was no question of his being a philo-Semite.[33]

Masaryk tackled the issues of human races and nationalities at the conclusion of his lectures on political philosophy in the winter semester of 1884–1885. The lectures were entitled "Practical Philosophy on the Basis of Sociology".[34]

Masaryk was well aware of the differences between races and nations; these would always mix with each other and give rise to new nations; the Jews also mixed to a great degree with other tribes and nations. Masaryk's views were diametrically opposed to the racial theories of J.A. Gobineau expressed in his treatise *The Inequality of Human Races*. "Masaryk's entire approach to the question of nationality was anti-racist and anti-nationalist. He ruled out the blood aspect in it."[35]

Masaryk's concept of the nation was positive through and through – nations must struggle for ideals, for the "yearnings inherited from forefathers". "Every nation must regard itself as the chosen one if it is to survive; if it doesn't... it has no right to exist."[36]

After his lectures in practical philosophy Masaryk no longer paid such close attention to Judaism; he was looking for solutions to questions of an essentially political character at that time. At the end of 1894, or the beginning of 1895, Masaryk made the acquaintance in Vienna of Professor Isidor Singer and Heinrich Kanner, who belonged to a group associated with the

33) S. Polák. "Charlotta Masaryková – dopisovatelka listu The Sun", pp. 111–116.
34) For an analysis of the lecture see J. Opat. *Filozof a politik T. G. Masaryk 1882–1893*. Praha, 1990, pp. 75–99.
35) J. Opat. *Filozof a politik T G. Masaryk 1882–1893*, p. 98.
36) Ibid., p. 98.

Viennese liberal weekly (and later daily) *Die Zeit*.[37] They allowed him to publish articles in its pages, particularly at the time of the Hilsner affair.

In 1894 and 1895 Masaryk published two seminal works: *The Czech Question* and *Our Present Crisis*.[38]

In 1895 Masaryk started to take a political interest in Judaism. There was growing discontent with the Liberal Party among Austrian Jews, and Masaryk wrote about it in *Die Zeit* and *Naše doba*[39] in a report entitled "Jews versus Liberalism": "A widespread campaign has been launched among Jews in Vienna and Galicia in favour of a separate political organisation. Mr Landau, a well-known author and authority on Jewish history presented his views on the matter in issue 25 of *Die Zeit*. They are quite noteworthy. His thinking could be summed up briefly as follows: "The Jews supported liberalism, but liberalism was not straight with them, but covertly anti-Semitic. During the Taaffe premiership there were 13 Jewish members of parliament, but they did not stand out as Jews. That liberalism was de facto anti-Semitic is evident from the very fact that out of 817 court officials in Austria only 16 are Jews, namely 2%, whereas they represent about 6% of the population of the empire (excluding Hungary). In Galicia they represent about 12%, but there only 4% of court officials are Jews. Indeed Jews are unable to attain to the higher ranks of the civil service. As far as political power

---

37) *Die Zeit* was founded in 1894 by Dr. Heinrich Kanner, who ran it as a weekly until 1903 and then as a daily until 1917.

38) T. G. Masaryk. *Česká otázka. Snahy a tužby národního obrození*. Praha, 1894, is one of Masaryk's pivotal works, in which he expounded his views on the Czech national revival and set out the tasks of the Czech national programme. He divided the work into five chapters: – the eras of Dobrovský, of Kollár and Jungmann, of Palacký and Havlíček, trends and yearnings of our time, and Humanity. Masaryk does not mention the Jews. T. G. Masaryk. *Naše nynější krize. Pád strany staročeské a počátkové směrů nových*. Praha, 1895. *Our Present Crisis* describes the causes of the crisis of Czech society in the 1890s and the emergence and development of the progressive movement of that period; it characterises the journal Nové proudy, the first literary organ of that movement; it addresses the fundamental issue of reform or revolution and favours reform; and it charts the future tasks of the Czech student body. Masaryk mentions the Jews and anti-Semitism very briefly in relation to his critique of historical materialism and Marx, as well as of liberalism and Christian Zionism.

39) *Naše doba. Revue pro vědu, umění a život sociální*. Praha, 1893–1914.

is concerned, Jews have a complete majority in 8 towns and two chambers of commerce in Galicia. In the first two Viennese districts they hold the balance of power; in urban districts in Moravia they make decisions in favour of the Germans – but they do not act as a mature nation should. They are giving their 6 seats in Galicia to the Poles and work with them against the Ruthenians; in Moravia they agitate against the Czechs; and in the two aforementioned districts in Vienna, the eight members of parliament favour the liberals. In conclusion, Mr Landau quotes Lassalle, who, as early as 1840 was telling his fellow-believers that they do not deserve a better fate, and gave the Jews this slogan: 'The Jews not only must defend their rights they must first win those rights. They need no protection from any party. The Jews must win their rights as citizens of the state. And if they are not given them, they must fight for them.'"

Masaryk paid closer attention to the "Jewish question" in his work *Karel Havlíček*.[40] He described there the argument between Siegfried Kapper and Karel Havlíček Borovský about the Jews in Bohemia. Kapper was a poet and author born into a Prague Jewish family, who wrote in both Czech and German. He stressed the patriotism of Czech Jews and urged the Jews to achieve emancipation and assimilation into the Czech nation.[41]

Karel Havlíček Borovský wrote that as Semites, the Jews were a separate ethnic group and therefore could not be Czechs. Whoever wanted to be a Czech must cease to be a Jew. The Jews could change their ethnicity and join the Germans. He thus rejected outright Kapper's views.[42]

After the Jews obtained equality under the imposed constitution in 1849 Karel Havlíček revised his attitude to them, because, as Masaryk said, they were "unsustainable", and "Havlíček changed his opinions into a much more moderate anti-Semitism."[43] Regarding the emancipation of the Jews,

---

40) T. G. Masaryk. *Karel Havlíček. Snahy a tužby politického probuzení*. Praha, 1896.
41) See his poetry collection *České listy*. Praha, 1846.
42) *Česká včela*, 6.–20. 11. 1846. Reprinted in: *Moje setkání se židovstvím. Sborník přednášek z cyklu Vzdělávacího a kulturního centra Židovského muzea v Praze březen 2004 –leden 2006*, ed. M. Pojar. Praha, 2006, p. 131.
43) T. G. Masaryk. *Karel Havlíček*, pp. 444–450. Jiří Brabec comments on this: "We must first contradict Masaryk, who called Havlíček an anti-Semite on the

Havlíček declared: "What is certain, and we will not deny it, is that the great majority of our people are opposed to this emancipation of the Jews and disapproved of the equal rights that the Jews obtained through the imposed Constitution of 4 March ... nevertheless, after careful, rational and honest consideration of the entire matter, as liberal people fighting for equality we cannot be against the Jews... When ... we reflect on the situation of the Jews, it becomes immediately obvious that their former subjection and their lack of equal rights with us resulted in their present level of customs and behaviour, and they bear only little or no responsibility for their present debasement. Earlier governments generally exploited the Jews and demanded such high taxes of them that it was truly impossible to bear such a burden in an honest fashion... moreover, the Jew was excluded from the most important human rights, was not allowed to buy estates or land, or to engage in certain trades, and he even had to buy the right to marry for an enormous fee; and at the same time he was subjected to the worst kinds of humiliation and ostracism... There is nothing odd about all of this, and as far as the Jews are concerned: They are what you made them..."[44]

In 1896 Mrs Berta Hartmann, the widow of the Jewish politician Moritz Hartmann, helped Masaryk by arranging for him to

---

basis of his critique of Kapper's *České listy*. It would seem incontestable that Havlíček's radical rejection of assimilation and his stress on 'a separate Semitic nation' alien to the Czechs derived from his concept of nationalism, not from an anti-Semitic aversion. After all, in the same article the author states that he as much respect for 'a true and upstanding Israelite as for anyone else, and much more than for a bad Czech.' I therefore do not see such a great contradiction, as if often claimed in literature on Havlíček, between the critique that I have mentioned and the article 'The Emancipation of the Jews' in *Slovan*, where Havlíček points out the causes of the Jews' behaviour that arouse negative reactions among country people and the urban population. 'As liberal people fighting for equality we cannot be against the Jews... Every nation is both honourable and dishonourable.' The appeal here is to both sides: Czechs and Jews." See J. Brabec. "Podoby českého anti-Semitismu před první světovou válkou." In *Na pozvání Masarykova ústavu*. Vol. 1. Praha, 2004, pp. 13–20.

44) K. Havlíček Borovský. "Emancipace Židů" (*Slovan*, 12. 10. 1850). In *Moje setkání se židovstvím*. (A collection of lectures from the educational and cultural series at the Jewish Museum in Prague, March 2004 – January 2006, ed. M. Pojar). Praha, 2006, pp. 132–133.

give private lessons and to continue giving philosophy lectures for two years for a "circle of young ladies". Masaryk also lectured in the family of his teacher, Professor Gomperz.

Masaryk's appointment as regular professor as of 1 January 1897 had been assisted by the librarian of the Vienna parliament Siegfried Lipiner, who was asked by Gautsch, the Minister of Education, to supply a special memorandum on the matter. Lipiner drew it up with Josef Svatopluk Machar and delivered it to Gautsch; he forwarded it to the Emperor, who approved the appointment.[45]

In his major study on *Faust*[46] Masaryk also devotes several paragraphs to Heine, stressing that they were comments and not intended as literary history. He considered that, as a whole, Heine's oeuvre was of "considerable significance". Like *Faust*, Heine "plunges into the depths of sensualism – not philosophised sensualism, but one that was original, racial, Semitic." Heine did not outdo *Faust*. "Heine's revolution was always more negative; he lacked the heart for positive reform and true faith." Heine managed to foresee the era of deeds that was supposed to succeed that of philosophising, but he was incapable of leading it. Lassalle seemed to him to be the messiah of the 19th century. In his later idealisation of Judaism he developed a liking for James Rothschild. "...as a Jew, Heine never forgot all the humiliations he had suffered in his youth at the hands of both Christians and Jews..."[47] So much for Masaryk's comments on Heine, about whom he subsequently said very little.

As a member of the Vienna parliament in the years 1891–1893 and 1907–1914, Masaryk lived through the "Jung-Wien" [Young Vienna] epoch of modernism, that designated a whole series of artistic trends, including Symbolism, Impressionism, Decadence, Secession and Expressionism.

---

45) According to O. Donath. "Židé na Masarykově cestě životem." Regarding Gautsch's memorandum to the Emperor see *Masarykův sborník*. Vol. 2. Praha, 1927, pp. 353–359. The memorandum stressed that Masaryk was not the nationalist that he was regarded as, and it also cited anti-nationalist statements from his newspaper articles and books.
46) T. G. Masaryk. "Goetheův Faust: Nadčlověk III", *Naše doba*, 5, 1898, pp. 585–599.
47) Ibid, pp. 585–586.

It was a period of outstanding writers, such as Arthur Schnitzler, Hugo von Hofmannsthal, Peter Altenberg, Hermann Bahr, R. B. Hofman, Jakob Wasserman, Alfred Polgar, Karl Kraus, Robert Musil and Georg Trakl, and painters like Egon Schiele, Gustav Klimt, and Oskar Kokoschka. Many of them had Jewish origins, including Martin Buber, Otto Weininger, Hugo Bergmann, Ludwig Wittgenstein, Otto Bauer, Abraham Adler and Sigmund Freud (who published his *Interpretation of Dreams* in 1900).[48]

Rudolf Steiner was founding Anthroposophy there, Johann Strauss and Richard Strauss and Arnold Schönberg were composing music and Gustav Mahler was conducting the Vienna Opera (in 1910 he conducted his 8th Symphony in Vienna); Otto Wagner, Adolf Loos and Josef Hoffmann were the leading spirits in architecture.[49]

Theodor Herzl was a regular contributor to the *Neue Freie Presse*, and in 1896 he published his seminal work *The Jewish State* in Vienna.

Vienna was the city not only of Herzl's Zionism but also of the anti-Semitism of its mayor, Karl Lueger.

Masaryk lived amidst all this intellectual ferment of every kind. We only know his reactions to Freud's psychoanalysis and to Freud in general – both were unfavourable. The two men were too different; their personal development had been too disparate for them to be able to react in a similar way to the state of affairs in which they found themselves. As someone with a strong religious belief Masaryk could hardly accept Freud's concept of historical pessimism or his sceptical attitude to faith and religion.[50]

During the period 1899–1900 Masaryk was involved in the so-called Hilsner Affair – see Chapter 5.

---

48) On the situation of the Jews in the Habsburg empire see W. O. McCagg Jr. *A History of Habsburg Jews 1670–1918*. Bloomington – Indianapolis, 1989.

49) See J. Kroutvor. *Egon Schiele*. Praha, 1991; S. Zweig. *The World of Yesterday*. Lexington, Mass., 2011; C. Sengoopta. *Otto Weininger: Sex, Science, and Self in Imperial Vienna*. Chicago, 2000.

50) See M. Petrusek - N. Narbut. "Jak znal Masaryk své sociologické současníky?" In *Masarykův sborník*, Vol. 14. Praha, 2009, pp. 345–346.

3. Masaryk and the social question; Marx and Masaryk; the Jewish question

Marx was the most brilliant thinker of the 19th century.

Every single national economist has studied Marx. I myself learnt a great deal from him. He had an enormous impact. Marxism has forced reforms. Social reforms are the achievements of Marx's ideas. Marxism has influenced everything from spiritual currents to government policies. Everything follows the slogan of socialisation. Everyone accepts social movements. The new trend is evident in the churches, in art and in philosophy.

There is also a reactionary movement, but it is futile. Socialist ideas are emerging and breaking through everywhere. Agrarian, small-business and other parties are a sign of that, although those organisations demand help from the state. Marx's significance lies in the fact that his teaching assisted that development and social ferment.

T.G.Masaryk, from the series "The development of modern socialist teaching."
Nová doba, 30. 1. 1907

MARX AND JUDAISM

Karl Marx, the German economist, philosopher, sociologist and political theorist (1818–1883) was born in Trier on 5 May 1818 into a Jewish family. His forebears on both sides belonged to several generations of rabbinical families. Marx's paternal line was originally called Mordechai (Markus, Marx) and came to Trier possibly from Bohemia, because his grandfather Marx Levi (Mordechai ben Samuel Halevi) was probably born there. He was rabbi in Trier, as also was his eldest son Samuel, Marx's uncle. Marx's grandmother on his father's side also came from a rabbinical family, which had emigrated from Lemberg [Lwow] in Poland in the 17th century. Her father, Marx's great-grandfather, Moses Lwow, was also rabbi in Trier in the years 1764–1768, as also were his great-great-grandfather Josua Heschel Lwow (1693–1771), renowned in the Jewish world of that time for his erudition, and his great-great-great-grandfather Aron Moses Jecheskel Lwow († 1712). Merle Worms, Marx's great-grandmother on his father side was a daughter of the Trier rabbi Isaac Aron Worms and granddaughter of Joseph Israel Worms († 1684), both of whom were rabbis in Trier. Marx's ancestors also included outstanding Jewish scholars, such as Joseph ben Mordechai Gershon Ha-Kohen a representative of the Talmudic school in Kraków († 1591), Meir ben Isaac Katzenellenbogen, the head of the Talmudic yeshiva in Padua († 1565), and Jehuda ben Elieser ha-Levi Minz, rabbi and professor at the University of Padua (1408–1508). This centuries-old rabbinical tradition of the outstanding Talmudic erudition, spirituality and deep piety was broken off by Marx's father Heschel Marx (1777–1838), a lawyer at the higher appelate, and later district court of Trier. Heschel Marx was the first in a long series of ancestors who became both religiously and culturally alienated from Judaism and adopted the traditions of Enlightenment philosophy, becoming an avid reader and devotee of Leibniz, Voltaire, Lessing, Kant and Schiller. He had few qualms in abandoning the Jewish faith when faced with the threat of being unable to pursue his profession following a decree in 1812 excluding Jews from public office in Prussia. He therefore converted to Protestantism sometime between April 1816 and August 1817, adopting the Christian name of Heinrich. He opted for Protestantism in Trier, a Catholic city, because he regarded himself as a Prussian patriot and monarchist, and Trier had become part of the Prussian state in 1815. (Some four thousand Jews similarly converted to Protestantism in Prussia between 1812 and 1846.)

Marx's mother Henriette Pressburg descended from a Hungarian Jewish family that had settled in Holland. She was born in Nijmegen as the daughter of rabbi Isaac Pressburg, himself a descendant of generations of rabbis. She spoke Dutch better than German and cleaved to her Judaism. Whereas her six children, including Karl Marx, were christened in 1824, she hesitated for a whole year before following suit. Nevertheless she felt herself to be Jewish up to the end of her life. The only possibility Marx ever had to absorb anything of his Jewish heritage was during his early childhood from his mother. The Swiss philosopher Arnold Künzli maintained that Marx identified his mother with Judaism and that relation was "traumatically burdened" so that

Marx unconsciously rejected Judaism in that early phase.[51] The heritage of two rabbinical dynasties with roots in the distant past undoubtedly influenced Marx, and some of his characteristics and abilities can be seen as the inheritance of an extensive array of intellectual activity and the brilliant erudition of highly-educated scholars, such as his outstanding gift of association, his quick wittedness, his exegetic competence, his polemical prowess and ability to think dialectically. Georg Adler, for instance, emphasised "the natural perceptiveness of Marx's mind", and his "disposition for abstraction, deduction and construction". He has been ranked by many scholars, particularly Jews, among the Old Testament prophets.

Marx grew up in a family that had strong links with the father, not the mother. His father projected onto him his own aspirations, convincing him that he was one of the "elect", fostering in him hypersensitivity, egocentricity and even egoism. His contacts with his siblings were not good and it eventually resulted in his alienation from his own family.

Thus Marx received no Jewish education and never learnt Hebrew. His family did not keep Jewish holidays and did not read the Torah or any other religious literature.

When Marx was growing up the atmosphere in Trier and Prussia in general was markedly anti-Semitic. Even converts were targeted and there was a resistance to mixed marriages (in 1843 Marx married a Christian, Jenny von Westphalen); Marx's reaction to that hostile environment was to develop an attitude of so-called "Jewish self-hate" – a reaction typical of sensitive individuals who turned away from Judaism within themselves. Marx spent the rest of his life denying his Jewishness and sought to be a non-Jew for his entourage, often identifying with anti-Semitism in a self-destructive fashion. Many converts ended up hating Jews in this way, regarding Judaism as worthless and trying to extirpate every trace of it in themselves – mostly without success. And so Marx, albeit a convert, was constantly the object of anti-Semitic attacks (in utterances by Ruge, Proudhon, Dühring, and Bakunin). His own anti-Semitic statements had the effect of arousing the anger of Jews, on the one hand, and

---

51) For Marx's origins see A. Künzli. *Karl Marx. Eine Psychographie.* Wien – Frankfurt – Zürich, 1966.

served to bolster the anti-Semitism of his non-Jewish supporters, on the other.

During his university study (in Bonn and Berlin, receiving his PhD in 1841 in absentia in Jena, where Schiller, Schelling, Schlegel and Hegel taught) Marx acquired no knowledge of Judaism. He noted only one lecture related to the topic, a lecture on Isaiah given in Bonn by Bruno Bauer, which took an atheistic and anti-Jewish position. It is not known whether, in addition to Bauer's books *Die Judenfrage* [The Jewish Question] and *Die Fähigkeit der heutigen Juden und Christen, frei zu werden* [The Capacity of Present-Day Jews and Christians to Become Free] (both from 1843), Marx was acquainted with any other seminal works on the Jewish question. In 1842 Marx joined the editorial board of the *Rheinische Zeitung*, becoming editor-in-chief on 15 October of that year (the following year the newspaper was banned by the censor). He was planning to contribute a major article on the Jewish question but did not get round to it. In a letter to Ruge in March of 1843 he mentions that he had been requested by the Jews of Cologne to draw up a petition for them: "However much I dislike the Jewish faith, Bauer's view [that the Jews can only be emancipated if they become atheists] seems to me too abstract."[52]

MARX AND HIS CRITIQUE OF JUDAISM

In the autumn of 1843, Marx started work on his only major essay on the Jewish Question. It was published in 1844 under the title *Zur Judenfrage* in Paris, where Marx settled in October 1843. It appeared as part of the *Deutsch-französische Jahrbücher* [German-French Annals], published jointed by Marx and Arnold Ruge.[53]

Marx sought to encapsulate the Jewish Question in the following way: The Jews survived in history not in spite of history, but precisely within history, and by means of history. They owe their survival to the decisive role played in the world by money. Judaism is in fact simply an epithet for market relations, and in

52) *Collected Works of Karl Marx and Friedrich Engels*. Vol. 1. New York, 1975, pp. 398–399.
53) *Collected Works of Karl Marx and Friedrich Engels*. Vol. 3, p. 146.

that sense the whole of Christian Europe is Jewish. Judaism is simply a religious reflection of a bourgeois mind-set. Bourgeois Europe is being assimilated into Judaism. The ideal remains the emancipation of the Jew and the Christian from the bourgeois way of life. Is this emancipation possible? "For us, the question of the Jew's capacity for emancipation becomes the question: What particular *social* element has to be overcome in order to abolish Judaism? For the present-day Jew's capacity for emancipation is the relation of Judaism to the emancipation of the modern world. This relation necessarily results from the special position of Judaism in the contemporary enslaved world. Let us consider the actual, worldly Jew – not the *Sabbath Jew*, as Bauer does, but the *everyday Jew*. Let us not look for the secret of the Jew in his religion, but let us look for the secret of his religion in the real Jew. What is the secular basis of Judaism? *Practical* need, *self-interest*. What is the worldly religion of the Jew? *Huckstering*. What is his worldly God? *Money*. Very well then! Emancipation from *huckstering* and *money*, consequently from practical, real Judaism, would be the self-emancipation of our time. (...) In the final analysis, the *emancipation of the Jews* is the emancipation of mankind from *Judaism*."[54] Thus Marx merged Judaism with capitalism. Jews were the product of capitalist society. But where did that leave the Jewish proletariat? Or Jewish socialism? Did it mean that Jews did not exist before capitalism? The entire essay demonstrates Marx's helplessness in the face of a problem that he could not grasp with his dialectical materialist method. It is not surprising that no one referred to it in subsequent study of the Jewish question, and it is not even cited in the seminal works.

Marx continued to grapple with Judaism for the rest of his life, however. In Paris, in 1845 he published jointly with Engels *The Holy Family, or Critique of Critical Critique. Against Bruno Bauer and Co.,* which contains three more extensive sub-chapters by Marx devoted to the Jewish question, albeit simply a polemic with Bauer that followed the publication of Marx's *Zur Judenfrage.*

In the *Holy Family* Marx essentially repeats the views he expressed in his pamphlet *On the Jewish Question*, but omitted

---

54) K. Marx. *On The Jewish Question.* https://www.marxists.org/archive/marx /works/1844/jewish-question/.

a number of anti-Jewish statements. Marx endorses the views of those of Bauer's critics who called for the emancipation of the Jews from the bourgeois state. But Marx regarded himself not only as the sole person dealing with the Jewish question but also as the only one who had "solved" it, having released Jewry from its religious masquerade and revealed its "empirical, worldly, practical kernel". "Herr Bauer therefore explains the real Jews by the Jewish religion, instead of explaining the mystery of the Jewish religion by the real Jews. [...] Herr Bauer has no inkling that real secular Jewry, and hence religious Jewry too, is being continually produced by the present-day civil life and finds its final development in the money system. He could not have any inkling of this because he did not know Jewry as a part of the real world but only as a part of his world, theology; because he, a pious, godly man, considers not the active everyday Jew but the hypocritical Jew of the Sabbath to be the real Jew. [...] The emancipation of the Jews into human beings, or the human emancipation of Jewry, was therefore not conceived, as by Herr Bauer, as the special task of the Jews, but as a general practical task of the present-day world, which is Jewish to the core."[55]

In his *Theses on Feuerbach* (1845) Marx criticised Feuerbach for having failed to understand the significance of revolutionary activity, he conceived and defined practice only in its dirty-Jewish form of appearance "only in its dirty-Jewish form".[56]

After 1848 Marx spoke about Jews almost solely in terms of a reactionary and financial race. "And as for the Jews, who since the emancipation of their sect have everywhere put themselves, at least in the person of their eminent representatives, at the head of the counter-revolution – what awaits them?"[57]

Marx systematically failed to study the living conditions of the Jewish masses and relished describing the wealth and power of the Jewish financiers. From about 1848 Marx essentially adopted the position of Greater German nationalism when he divided nations into "reactionary" and "revolutionary".

---

55) K. Marx. *Holy Family*. https://www.marxists.org/archive/marx/works/1845/holy-family/ch06_3_b.htm.
56) K. Marx. *Theses on Feuerbach*. https://www.marxists.org/archive/marx/works/1845/theses/index.htm.
57) *Neue Rheinische Zeitung*, 145, November 17, 1848, http://www.marxistsfr.org/archive/marx/works/1848/11/17a.htm.

Marx's fundamental work *Capital* contains only a few references to the Jews, which is odd, because if he was really so convinced about their power and influence, he had plenty of scope in the book to deal with it.

Marx's anti-Jewish statements are scattered through a number of his other works, as well as in newspaper articles and his extensive correspondence.

Only in two newspaper articles did Marx express sympathy with the Jews: regarding the living conditions of Jews in Palestine and persecution of Jews in Vienna. Marx also never raised his voice against the major pogroms in Russia, such as in 1881.

MASARYK AND SOCIAL ISSUES

Masaryk's childhood, the wretched conditions that he observed around him on the estates where his father worked, his own situation as a blacksmith's apprentice, his student years, these all served to develop within him a powerful social awareness. He himself was not a proletarian, but during his childhood and youth he mixed with the rural poor.

While studying in Brno he attended Sunday meetings of the Catholic Union, at which the priest Matěj Procházka would preach Christian social principles, and lecture on socialism, the situation of the working class, and the teachings of Karl Marx.

At university in Vienna he acquainted himself with "Katheder Sozialismus", i.e. the economic teachings propagated by the lectures of professors Menger, Schäffle, and others, and also with the writings of the French utopian socialists, particularly Proudhon and Fourier.

"I've been interested in socialism all my life. In Brno I observed Christian Socialism, and in Vienna I read Marx and the Catholic Socialists. Schauer wrote his first articles for a journal run by a prominent Christian Socialist by the name of Vogelsang.

During the 90s I started having practical contact with socialism. I spent a lot of time with working people and gave talks to them. [...] I proposed a Workers' Academy, where labourers and the newspapermen who wrote about them could you get a political education. [...] I accepted socialism insofar as it coincided with my humanitarian programme. Marxism I did not accept.

Nevertheless my *Social Question* was meant to be a critique of Marx."[58]

Judging from *The Social Question*, Masaryk would seem to have been the first Czech to have read Marx's *Capital* as early as 1873, in its second edition that was published in 1872. "When the second edition of Marx's *Capital* came out [...] I plodded through it conscientiously, back even then I couldn't accept his Hegelian philosophy and materialist view of history."[59]

"I found economics fascinating too and, as I've said, attended lectures by Menger in Vienna and by Roscher in Leipzig; as a student I dipped into the second edition of Marx's *Capital*."[60] During the 1890s Masaryk was gradually formulating his own opinions on socialism, reacting to articles by Eduard Bernstein revising Marx's doctrine and inclining towards Bernstein's revisionist concepts. They were years when he concentrated his studies on social issues, studies which would eventually give rise to one of his major works *The Social Question*.

In the first book publication of *Our Present Crisis* in 1895 Masaryk expressed his views on Marx and the problem of revolution. Reflecting on the state and state power, Masaryk emphasised why he differed from social-democratic doctrine about the state, according to which the state was based on power or force. "I disagree with the doctrine that this state degenerated from a stateless organisation of society and do not accept the view that the present state – and with it all modern civilisation – has essentially an economic significance. I would also like to say something about this concept of the state in respect of *anti-Semitism* and all present economic movements."

The materialistic concept of the state, Masaryk continues, tends to promote a materialistic concept of society as a whole, and of its entire life. But society is not based solely on the economy, it also evolves on the basis of other activities. Man is not simply an egoist; he has other interests apart from the economic ones. The various forms of economic activity evolved from a culturally abundant social life. Thus Masaryk does not believe that society is organised solely by economic management, or capital-

58) K. Čapek. *Talks with T.G.Masaryk*, p. 161.

59) Ibid., p. 89.

60) Ibid., p. 153

ism. "I do not share ... Marx's theories, and likewise I don't share the doctrine of his opponents [...] "Although I do not agree with Marx, I am not blind to the fact that our workers are oppressed."[61]

In the fourth chapter of "Reformation or Revolution" Masaryk also deals with the problem of violent revolution, declaring: "all prudent leaders of social democracy reject violent revolution". He refers to Engels' introduction to Marx's articles *The Class Struggles in France, 1848 to 1850*, in which Engels writes inter alia that "the mode of struggle of 1848 is today obsolete from every point of view"[62] and it was impossible in 1848 to win social reconstruction by a simple surprise attack; the defeat of the Commune had transferred the centre of gravity of the European workers' movement for the time being from France to Germany, resulting in the growing strength of social democracy there, proving that it was possible to make use of universal suffrage, with social democracy able to count on over two million votes. "Rebellion in the old style, the street fight with barricades, which up to 1848 gave everywhere the final decision, was, to a considerable extent, obsolete."[63] Engels pointed to the progress in weapons development, the growth of the urban populations, and the role of railways in transporting troops, which increased the advantages of the "rulers" vis-à-vis the "rebellious".

"If the conditions have changed in the case of war between nations, this is no less true in the case of the class struggle. The time of surprise attacks, of revolutions carried through by small conscious minorities at the head of unconscious masses, is past. [...] But in order that the masses may understand what is to be done, long, persistent work is required, and it is just this work which we are now pursuing, and with a success which drives the enemy to despair. In the Latin countries, also, it is being more and more recognized that the old tactics must be revised. Everywhere the German example of utilizing the suffrage, of winning all posts accessible to us, has been imitated." In France it was being realised that it was first of all necessary to win over the mass of the peasantry. "Slow propaganda work and parliamenta-

61) T. G. Masaryk. *Naše nynější krize*. Praha, 2000, pp. 197–198.
62) K. Marx. *The Class Struggles in France, 1848 to 1850*, https://www.marxists.org/archive/marx/works/1850/class-struggles-france/intro.html.
63) Ibid.

ry activity are being recognized here, too, as the most immediate tasks of the Party..."[64] Engels expresses his conviction that by the end of the century German social democracy will grow to be a decisive force in the country.

Masaryk welcomed Engels' introduction and states that Engels in this instance "... came out very clearly and emphatically against violent revolution."[65]

In an article in *Naše doba*[66] from 1895 he also speaks about social democracy. "What Herder was to our first revivalists, Marx is to our labour leaders! [...]However, as far as the main principles of social democracy are concerned, I have already stated on several occasions that I do not accept the philosophical and sociological basis of the social-democratic programme. The theoretical basis of the socialist politics and philosophy are a materialist philosophy and historical materialism. [...] I am a resolute opponent of the materialist world view. [...] I make a distinction between the various points of the social democratic programme and its philosophical principles. [...] I regard the individual political and social demands as fair. [...] The critiques of Marx and the socialist theorists are justified in respect of economic issues, and they are by and large correct. Their positive theories are of no greater value than other sincere and well-considered theories." "I can take no pleasure in the fact that social democracy is turning Marx into an inviolable authority."[67]

Masaryk dealt with the same issues in another article in *Naše doba* in 1895. Writing about Engels' introduction to the Marx's articles *The Class Struggles in France, 1848 to 1850,* Berlin 1885, in which Engels expands on political tactics and contrasts

---

64) Ibid.

65) T. G. Masaryk. *Naše nynější krize*, p. 247.

66) As successor to *Athenaeum*, the monthly magazine *Naše doba* (1893–1949) was first published on 20 October 1893. During the first three years of its existence its publisher was Josef Laichter; in 1896 his brother, Jan, took over. Originally, František Drtina, Josef Kaizl and Tomáš Garrigue Masaryk nominally shared in the editorship, but it was Masaryk who, from the beginning, assumed the main workload, and, from October 1894 until the outbreak of World War I, held the post of editor-in-chief.

67) T. G. Masaryk. "Časové směry a tužby", *Naše doba*, 2, 1895, pp. 16–37, 110–124, 193–212.

modern parliamentary activity with old-fashioned "revolutionary tactics", Masaryk calls it a "humanistic tactic".[68]

Masaryk's obituary of Frederick Engels was a positive assessment of Engels' activity as leader of social democracy after the death of Marx.[69]

Masaryk's *Social Question* was foreshadowed by his lecture in December 1897, which was published a year later.[70]

MASARYK'S CRITIQUE OF MARX'S VIEWS ON THE JEWISH QUESTION

In 1898 Masaryk published his *Social Question* with the intention of explaining in it "the significance of Marxism as a philosophical and sociological system".

"In this study I want to show that socialism, and Marxism in particular, is an experiment in an entire philosophical system, that Marxism is not simply related to national economies..."

"Marxism is much more important for our times, and particularly for all social questions, than has been thought heretofore."

"This study will benefit both Marx and Engels, albeit I reject their method and philosophy."[71]

In the second part of *The Social Question* Masaryk makes a detailed analysis of Marx's attitude to the Jewish question in the light of Marx's articles *Zur Judenfrage* and *Die Heilige Familie* (1845), which are polemics with Bruno Bauer's *Die Judenfrage* [The Jewish Question] and *Die Fähigkeit der heutigen Juden und Christen, frei zu werden* [The Capacity of Present-Day Jews *and* Christians *to Become Free] (both from* 1843).

Masaryk reviews the entire polemic and concludes with his own critique: "This article about Marx is stylistically interesting – showing us the young Marx and his predilection for powerful antithesis. Marx's ideas are largely no more than a sharper version of the Feuerbach's conclusions about the egoistic mono-

---

68) T. G. Masaryk. "Sociální demokracie proti revoluci", *Naše doba*, 2, 1895, pp. 891–897.
69) T. G. Masaryk. "Friedrich Engels", *Naše doba,* 2, 1895, pp. 1054–1055.
70) T. G. Masaryk. "Vědecká a filosofická krise současného marxismu", *Naše doba*, 5, 1898, pp. 289–304.
71) T. G. Masaryk. *Otázka sociální. Základy marxismu sociologické a filosofické*. Praha, 1898, p. VII.

theism of the Jews (Bauer similarly characterises the Jews according to Feuerbach).

"Marx's conclusions are dazzling but unconvincing. Frankly speaking they are cleverer than is appropriate to a genuine solution of a serious question; to see in Judaism the apotheosis of Christianity – surely not; to conclude that Christianity has returned to Judaism – that is truly an all too impertinent reversal of the Hegelian lance of negation. Were there not Jews before Christianity? To say that Christians reared their Jews is true only up to a certain point."

"Marx ignores the national, tribal aspect of the Jewish question – and yet it exists. The Jews are a nation of their own, even if they have lost touch with their spoken language. But language is not the only or most important mark of nationality."

"Marx also has an incorrect assessment of the religious question in general, and hence also of that aspect of the Jewish question, which is de facto also religious, albeit to varying degrees in different countries. The Galician and Russian orthodox Jews are certainly no Spinozas or Mendelssohns."

"There is an element of truth in Bauer's notion that the Jew represents a lower stage of development, and so it is worth reflecting on whether and how a Jew (and there will probably be differences depending on the country), not having undergone the Christian stage, will enter a super-Christian – not Bauer's anti-Christian! – stage along with a Christian. One can counter Bauer by noting that a considerable number of Jews took part in the general development, although this does not apply to all Jews, of course."

"It is also here, and particularly here, that Marx's materialism obstructs him. Because of his materialist bias he reduces the essence of Judaism and Christianity to egoism. Of course one can regard Jews to a certain extent as an organ of universal greed, a sort of lightning rod of all greed, but it is only partly true. Marx did not sufficiently analyse the characteristics of the Jews and therefore fails to distinguish between the good and bad aspects of their character."

"And likewise he fails to investigate the good and bad qualities of Christians (of different countries). For that reason his judgement on the Jews does not differ greatly from Stirner's condemnation. But after all, the Jewish nation is not typified solely by swindlers but also by Jeremiah, Spinoza, as well as Christ. But of course Marx could not use for his materialism the powerful Jewish messianic sense. And yet this messianism is explained by a good deal of Jewish – and Marx's – behaviour.

Marx did not even understand the historical and cultural aspects of the Jewish problem. Christianity's reception of Judaism, and above its reception of the Old Testament, is certainly a very important fact. Marx is right in saying that Christians were Judaized, but that was not only to their detriment but also to their benefit; indeed the Reformation was largely reception of the Old Testament and Judaism, and, I repeat, to the benefit of the modern nations. So it is not fortuitous that in Catholic and Christian Orthodox countries the Jewish question is more acute than in the Protestant countries."

"I do not mean to say, of course, that it is possible to receive a necessary and good part and create a living and creative synthesis with what we receive. That is the point – we are a long way from that!"

"But that is a task that Jews must undertake, as well as Christians."

"But that solution is not the current widespread anti-Semitism, or even Marx's anti-Semitism. Marx's formula is utterly insufficient, because de facto it simply ignores the question. Marx's formula is not even sufficient for the Marxists themselves; thus just recently Bernstein accused the Englishman Bax of anti-Semitism."

"Besides in one very anti-Bauerian passage he explains that if a Jew recognises the pettiness of his practices and tries to overcome them, then he is working for the emancipation of the humanity as a whole."

"I consider Zionism to be part of this revivalist activity. I don't mean emigration to Palestine – Jews can happily remain where they are; but they must understand that their moral character and their entire attitude to the world need to be remedied. It is not enough to blame the Christians – that is mostly just an empty excuse. Today's Jews lack the self-criticism of the prophets; they are burdened by a specific objectivism, which was also Marx's national dowry. [...] Out of fear of the majority Jews are afraid to question their own consciences. Of course the Christians are equally at fault, but only equally so. The Jew's major

(49)

fault at the present time is that they are too self-satisfied. Of course the same applies to anti-Semitic Christianity."

"The attachment to socialism of many Jews is understandable – its revolutionary aspect is congenial to people who are socially and politically oppressed. In Germany Heine wrote for the proletariat and extolled its revolutionary spirit; Lassalle and then Marx became leaders of German socialism and almost of socialism as a whole. Heine saw in Lassalle the Messiah. He definitely felt himself to be a Messiah, like Marx – that's a Jewish trait; but Marx's messianism suffers from the fault that he himself ascribes to the Jews – Marxism is too practical, too objectivist, and too materialist."[72]

"Our clericalists do not declare socialism to be the fruits of Protestantism and liberalism alone, but also the fruits of Judaism. They point to Lassalle and Marx and other Jews among the socialists [...] but socialism is not Jewish. There was theoretical and practical socialism before Marx and Lassalle. The philosophical foundations of Marxism are to be found in Protestant Hegelianism and Feuerbach. Marx was not the only one to formulate Marxism; the Protestant Engels also had a decisive influence on it."

"There are, however, several reasons why quite a lot of Jews support the socialist party. Above all Jews aren't all wealthy – in Poland, Galicia, in Russia, and also in our country, there is a large Jewish proletariat. Socialism must be attractive to the Jews because it is concerned about the oppression of all; and finally, socialist nationalism and materialism appeals to educated Jews. The reason that Jews are also involved in socialist journalism is the same as why they are involved in journalism in general."[73]

In his *American Lectures* of 1907, in the section about liberalism and socialism, Masaryk refers to Campanella, Saint-Simon and his treatise *Nouveau Christianisme,* as well as to Proudhon, Lassalle, and, most extensively, to Feuerbach, whose ideas about religion were adopted by Marx and Engels, "who founded scientific socialism. This science-based socialism has no religious basis; like Feuerbach, both Marx and Engels regard religion as an illusion. And of course Marx and Engels' socialism is an at-

72) T. G. Masaryk. *Otázka sociální,* pp. 173–184.
73) Ibid., p. 210.

tempt at an overall view of the world. You must not think that socialism in general is merely an economic system; no, it has an opinion about the world and life in general."[74]

Masaryk devoted himself to Marxism in general and Russian Marxism in particular in his next essay *Rusko a Evropa* [Russia and Europe], in paragraphs 157–166 in Part II of the second volume. He also included a footnote referring to his published magazine articles about the question.[75] However, he made no reference at all there to the Jewish question.

In 1924 Masaryk published an article on the occasion of the election of Ramsey MacDonald's government in Britain and the death of Lenin in Russia: "In England social democracy was victorious without a bloody revolution, in Russia a bloody revolution was victorious. Lenin and his followers declared that theirs was the only correct tactic and that it complied with Marx's teaching. That it was not the only correct tactic has now been proved by the English example; and it must be clear to anyone who knows Marx and Engels that Bolshevism (as a Marxist tactic) is not solely Marxist. Marx was in favour of revolution, in the sense of bloody revolution, in the revolutionary glow of 1848. But he later adopted as the main and decisive tactic of socialism Parliamentarism, revolution by the ballot paper. Engels stated this before he died with a certainty that excluded any doubt in discussion. Thus not only in Russia, Marx's tactic was also victorious in England, but it was a victory of the more mature Marx, a socialist and Marxist Marx, and it was achieved in a non-Marxist way." That same year Masaryk drew attention to the inaccuracy of a response to his article published in *Rudé právo*.

A passage from Čapek's *Talks with T.G.Masaryk* seems to sum up Masaryk's thinking about Socialism and Communism: "I accepted Socialism insofar as it coincided with my humanitarian program. Marxism I do not accept. My *Social Question* was meant to be a critique of Marx..."

---

74) T. G. Masaryk. *Americké přednášky.* 2nd ed. Praha, 1929, pp. 25–30 (1st ed. Chicago, 1907).

75) T. G. Masaryk. *The Spirit of Russia.* Vol. 2. London, 1919, 1955, 1961, 1968, pp. 317–362. The note referred to here is on p. 317 of the 1968 edition.

"My socialism is simply a matter of loving your neighbour, of humanity... Loving your neighbour is not old-style philanthropy; philanthropy only helps here and there. A real love of humanity seeks to amend conditions by law and deed. If that is socialism, I am for it.

I do not believe in equality, absolute equality, that is. There is no equality in the stars or in man. There always have been and always will be individuals who by their own gifts and a combination of circumstances can and do achieve more than others; there will always be a hierarchy among people. But hierarchy means order, organization, discipline, knowledge and obedience, not the exploitation of man by man. That is why I do not accept Communism. No sooner did Lenin take power that he called for leaders. The longer I live, the more I realize the role played by the individual in the evolution of humanity, but I repeat: more talent and more of what is known as luck do not justify the exploitation of the less gifted and the less fortunate. I do not believe that all private ownership can be done away with. The personal relationship – the *pretium affectionis* – that binds an owner to his property is good in that it promotes economic progress. Communism is possible, but only among brothers, that is, in the family or in a religious community or close circle of friends; it can be maintained only by true love. I do not accept the principle of class war. There are social estates and social classes, there are degrees of difference among people. But that does not mean war; it means the organization of natural inequality resulting from historical circumstance, it means levelling, growth and development. I am not so blind and simple-minded as to fail to see injustice and oppression, and I know that individuals, estates, and classes must protect their own interests, but it does not follow that *homo homini lupus*, man is wolf to man, as was said long ago.

As for Marxism, it is an economic theory and philosophy, a philosophy of history in particular. Economic theory, like every science, is a matter for investigation, revision and improvement, and Marxism, like any philosophy, must be open to criticism and free deliberation. That is why revisionism arose and will continue to do so. Every revision of a creed or program is painful, but without the pain there can be no progress. I have no ready-made social doctrine in my pocket. [...] I am always for the workman and working people in general, often for socialism, and rarely for Marxism.

"My views of socialism derive from my concept of democracy. A revolution or a dictatorship can occasionally abolish bad things, but it never creates anything good or lasting..."[76]

76) K. Čapek. *Talks with T.G.Masaryk*, pp. 162–163.

4. Masaryk and religion

In religion one senses and becomes aware of one's relationship with the world and with people. To put it another way: in religion we confront the mystery of eternity as a whole. Eternity would be a handy word to describe our problem. The problem of eternity is something you find in the elements of all religions, and it is indeed the essence of religion. And the way one answers that question determines how one formulates one's religion.
American Lectures, 1907

Caesar or Jesus – that is the watchword of democratic Europe...
The Making of a State, 1925

I'm not a materialist, I'm not a monist, I'm neither pantheist nor panentheist. I'm not a dualist. I'm a pluralist; for me, the universe is a harmonious system. So that's my metaphysics for you, all in one go.
Talks with T.G.Masaryk, 1927–1931

Masaryk was a child of the mid-nineteenth century. In Austria the Catholic faith was paramount; after all, scarcely half a century had passed since the Patent of Toleration. Masaryk's pious mother liked to attend church, but most importantly she would read prayer books, and as a child Masaryk would look at the pictures. They didn't read the Bible at home – there wasn't time for that. Masaryk could not even conceive that there might be any other faith apart from Catholicism. As time went by he learned about the orthodox faith in Russia, visited the Protestant (Calvinist) chapel in Klobouky, and encountered Jewish children. He was scared of Jews – see Chapter 1. For him, religion was folklore and superstition, and the entire year was subordinate to it. At school he attended religious (i.e. Catholic) instruction and was already experiencing a conflict between science and belief "intensively, albeit without tribulations". So he grew up as a believer, having no doubts about God or theology. He later said he could not imagine someone growing up ignorant of Jesus and his teachings; "a knowledge of the Old Testament is basic to the cultural heritage of every European".[77]

Interest in religion, politics and nationality issues led him to read poetry and belles lettres, as well as books on art, history and philosophy, and that was while he was still at Gymnasium, first in Brno and then in Vienna, where he completed his secondary studies in 1872. That also certainly included acquiring knowledge of the Bible – the Old and the New Testaments. His studies of the Classics at the university in Vienna – including Plato, Aristotle and Socrates (whom he compared to Jesus) let him to an awareness of the importance of Judaism and Antiquity for our civilisation. Later he was to say: "...Greek philosophy, science, poetry, and art sprang up in the midst of nature and primitive life – a revelation, much as the Old and New Testaments are a revelation of the Palestine desert and primitive Judaism. While we are on the subject of Greeks and Jews, think of the influence these two small nations have had on the whole of civilized humanity. The Greeks gave us art, philosophy, science, and politics, the Jews theology and religion. [...] All Europe is still living off the legacy of the Greeks and Jews..."[78]

The religious question was successively the central theme of the following works by Masaryk: *Slavonic Studies, The Czech Question, Comenius, The Social Question,* and *Russia and Europe.*

Masaryk focussed on religion in the following works: *In the Struggle over Religion, The Intelligentsia and Religion, Modern Man and Religion,* and *American Lectures.*

An important stimulus for his deeper study of Judaism and Christianity was undoubtedly Ernest Renan's *Life of Jesus,* which was first published in French in 1862, and three years later in Czech. It would seem that Masaryk read it when he was still attending the Gymnasium during the years 1865–1869. When a student at the universities of Vienna and Leipzig (1872–1879), he studied everything he could in order to understand the emergence of Christianity – the Old and New Testaments, patristics,

77) K. Čapek. *Talks with T.G.Masaryk*, p. 63.
78) Ibid., p. 107.

and sources for the history of the time. In Leipzig he concentrated on Protestantism, which did not particularly enthuse him. He made the acquaintance of Charlotte Garrigue, and their subsequent marriage possibly heightened Masaryk's interest in the Old Testament, which was particularly favoured by his wife, as a Unitarian.

Thus from 1877 Masaryk produced a number of works concerning the Jewish religion, or the influence of the Jews on the history of civilisation, often in comparison with Christianity or the person of Jesus, which would later become central to Masaryk's reflections, his exemplar, and his ideal.

In his article "On Progress, Development and Science" from 1877 he says: "Humanity did not arrive at the idea of *universal progress and the development of mankind* until the most recent period. The concept gradually evolved, and initially from *Christianity*."[79] Christianity contributed the idea that humanity is one. The old law must be replaced by a new teaching. Christianity spread the concept of cosmopolitanism. In practice this all gained ground slowly, and the teaching of original sin tended to indicate the deterioration rather than the improvement of mankind.

Masaryk addressed the idea of progress, which was the belief current in the 18th century. In Germany it was preached by the writer and dramatist Gotthold Ephraim Lessing, whom Masaryk described as a follower of Leibniz. In his work *Erziehung des Menschengeschlechtes* [The Education of the Human Race] Lessing maintained that revelation was for mankind what education was for the human individual. Masaryk continued in his interpretation of Lessing: "At first the Jews knew only the True God, Christianity informed us about the teaching of the soul's immortality, which is only superficially hinted at in the Old Testament, because reason was not yet prepared for such a profound teaching; in those days mankind was still a child; by the New Testament it was already a youth, and by now it is a man and needs new textbooks."[80] Moses Mendelssohn[81] disagreed with Lessing's idea of

---

79) "O pokroku, vývoji a vědě." In T. G. Masaryk. *Juvenilie. Studie a stati 1876–1881*, pp. 50-51.

80) Ibid., pp. 54-55.

81) Moses Mendelssohn (1729–1786), Jewish scholar and philosopher, a friend of Lessing. Although Lessing was not a Jew, he reflected on the Jewish question

progress, being unable to understand that humanity could go on progressing endlessly.

In Chapter 5 of his seminal work *Suicide*, published in German in 1881 and in Czech in 1904, Masaryk discusses the influence of the Greeks, Romans and Jesus on civilisation. The whole of sub-section 5 of that chapter is devoted to Jesus Christ and Christianity. Masaryk writes: "The pagan Roman world had experienced, despite its culture, complete dissolution at the time of the birth of Christ, and was weary of life to the depths of its soul. Philosophy and culture could not free or rescue man; the remnants of a renewed formalism and ritualism could not still the hunger of the soul. *Mosaic theism, with its law and ceremonial, also could not take hold of man's destiny and rescue him; the Jews themselves were weak and in need of deliverance.*" [My emphasis M.P.]

At that time Jesus appeared, the Messiah as a saviour and deliverer at a time when the Roman world was in state of serious decline. Masaryk stresses the basic pillar of Christian teaching – pure monotheism, belief in a just and holy God, the creator and preserver of the universe, and of human beings in particular. Christians entrust their lives to Providence, and believe in a wise and powerful God and the immortality of the soul. People are brothers from one father. "Christ gave a new command of love [...] which should extend to enemies [...] There is a soothing balm for the sufferings of Job in this holy love." This system of theism founded on "the mediation of the Son of God, in Jesus Christ." For Christians, Christ is "the object of faith, of hope, of love, of devotion, of self-sacrifice, of veneration, of worship.[...] The entire life of Christ is truth; [...] Nothing external clings to Him and His life, no formalism, no ritualism; [...] He restricted himself to the Old Testament in His teaching, avoided all artifice, rhetoric, and unnecessary erudition, but nevertheless instilled a new life into His whole system. [...] Christianity created a new moral world by the sanctification of the relation of man to God [...] Christianity became the true teaching for life; the Gospels teach the love of life not of death. [...] Christianity nipped

in the spirit of the Sturm und Drang ideology (in the dramatic poem *Nathan the Wise*).

in the bud the morbid suicide tendency of ancient polytheism and returned life to people."[82]

Masaryk expanded on Judaism in his review of Ernest Renan *Le judaisme comme race et religion* (1883), which was initially published that same year in the *Sborník historický I*.[83]

Masaryk differentiated between universal and national religion. The universal religions were Buddhism, Hinduism, Christianity and Islam. National religions, in his view, included the religion of the Greeks and other ancient nations, which were now extinct except for two: Zoroastrianism and Judaism. Masaryk considered beyond doubt that Judaism was a national religion. The fact that it later became "the universal religion of the enlightened world" was thanks to the Jewish prophets of the 8th century B.C.: "they created a pure religion, making it moral and universal: and they were all the more rigorous in that non-believers found immortal comfort by living lives of stringent justice on earth."[84]

"This expression of pure religion is a unique phenomenon in the history of mankind. There is nothing national about that religion: whoever calls on God the creator of heaven and earth, who loves good and punishes evil [...] has abandoned national boundaries in favour of a broad, universal awareness. The Jewish prophets were well aware of what they were doing and consistently suppressed animal sacrifice and temple worship."[85]

Masaryk wrote that Isaiah was the founder of Christianity. The destruction of the Temple [in 70 A.D., M.P.] was very fortunate, because had it still been standing one could not be sure that Christianity would have entirely renounced it. The prophets proclaimed the coming of a golden age, when justice would reign and idolatry would disappear (Isaiah). The ideas of progress are an expression of that universality that gave rise to dissemination and preaching.

Renan declared that the Jews were no less mixed than other nations; they intermixed during captivity, such as in Assyria, and later in Greek and Roman times. Renan inferred from the history

---

82) Ibid, pp. 153–155 (with minor amendments by the present translator).
83) T. G. Masaryk. "Ernst Renan o židovství jako plamenu a náboženství." In *Masarykův sborník*. Vol. 1. 2nd ed. Praha, 1934, pp. 66–73.
84) Ibid., p. 67.
85) Ibid.

of the Jews after Christ in Palestine, Gaul, Italy, Arabia, and in Ethiopia and Russia, that Judaism was originally national "of Palestinian, Semite stock", whereas Jews were no longer of pure race, but were mixed with other nations.

It cannot be claimed, Masaryk, says, that there is a fixed "Jewish type". Renan does not accept this, for him there is no single Jewish type "...the specific customs and mores of the Jews were a result not of a different race but of a different manner of living."[86]

Masaryk goes on to criticise Renan on the grounds that his work was unsatisfactory. Renan lacks clarity when speaking about the Jewish religion. Masaryk: "I do not believe that Jewish monotheism became a world religion; it is not true that Christianity is exclusively or even to a great degree based on Judaism."[87]

Masaryk maintained that although the prophets had laid the basis for a new and pure religion, and Jesus was a Jew, Christianity emerged much more from the European and Graeco-Roman spirit and that of other Indo-European nations. The Greek and Roman churches and the Protestant churches are more European than Semitic. While Jewish monotheism was transformed into Christianity, Graeco-Roman culture developed from polytheism to monotheism.

Masaryk also disagreed with Renan's view that the Jews were as mixed a nation as other European nations: they were chiefly mixed with Semitic or related nations. After presenting other arguments (the Khazars) Masaryk deduced that "Jews are indeed a nation that is less mixed than the European nations. There was marked aversion on both sides – from Jews and Christians alike, which is why the kind of intermixing that occurred between Romans, Gauls, Germans and Slavs did not take place. [...] The Christians did not hate the Jews so much as despise them, which is why they never wiped them out anywhere: hatred destroys, whereas contempt only oppresses and drives out."[88]

Masaryk concludes his review by stating that Renan only dealt with the Jewish question and anti-Semitism indirectly, and

---

86) Ibid., p. 70.
87) Ibid.
88) Ibid., p. 72.

that he proved that "Jews are a mixed nation like other nations in order to protect them in a way."[89]

Masaryk returns to Jesus in his *Fundamentals of Concrete Logic* of 1885, and Jesus features in all his subsequent works, while Judaism is only referred to marginally.

"I cannot highlight the magnificent scope of medicine better than by recalling Christ: He whose kingdom was not of this world cures the sick and heals, being a physician, body and soul."[90]

Reflection on the relationship between theology and philosophy leads the philosopher to understand: "Because he is instructed by the great educator of mankind – Christ – that one must love one's neighbour as oneself and not resist evil if he is to attain the highest level of exalted gospel morality."[91]

Masaryk states, regarding monotheism, that it is becoming a universal world view. Anaxagoras, Socrates, Plato, and Aristotle remained at that level of development, but after Aristotle, philosophy started to return to myth more often than to polytheism. "In that state of decline, Graeco-Roman philosophy received support from the Jewish nation and monotheism became a world view."[92]

"Understandably, Catholic monotheism often made concessions to polytheistic and even fetishistic views at various times and in different places, and for a long time it prevailed in name only. For that reason it accommodated with inferior views and came down to their level such as in the case of its teaching about Christ's God-manhood, the doctrine of the Trinity, the veneration of Saints, and later of the Virgin Mary, etc."[93]

Thus Masaryk understood Judaism logically as the foundation on which Christianity arose. In the person of Christ, however, a fundamental turning-point was reached. In the unpublished addenda to *Fundamentals of Concrete Logic* in 1931 in wrote: "...Jesus was a religiously outstanding man, the greatest of the prophets... He differs from the Old Testament prophets, however, who were angry, whereas the character of Jesus was

---

89) Ibid., p. 73.
90) T. G. Masaryk. *Základové konkrétné logiky*. Praha, 2001, p. 82.
91) Ibid., p. 170.
92) Ibid., p. 173.
93) Ibid., pp. 173–174.

intrinsically calm and had a quiet certainty. He was truly the embodiment of love."[94]

In sections 24 and 25 of his *Slavonic Studies* of 1889 Masaryk dealt inter alia with the views of Russian philosopher and critic Kireyevsky about the influence of Arabic culture and opined that his characterization of it was "very good overall." Nonetheless Masaryk was surprised that Kireyevsky made no mention at all of Jewish influence, which had a much greater impact on the West (and the East) than Arabic philosophy. He also corrected a number of Kireyevsky's other assertions, stating inter alia: "mediaeval Arabic scholarship is proof that not only the West but also the East developed scholasticism –the work of Jewish Old Testament scholars".[95]

In Section 45, in the part dealing with absolutism in philosophy as advocated by Kireyevsky, Masaryk states that he confuses the concept of absolute religion philosophy with the concept of nationality. "Thus the Jews considered themselves to be the only chosen ones..."[96]

A further book by Masaryk, *Jan Hus. Naše obrození a naše reformace* [Jan Hus. Our Revival and Our Reformation], published in 1896, includes an exposition of Palacký's religious philosophy, but there are no references to Jews.

Masaryk fundamental work on religion, *Moderní člověk a náboženství* [Modern Man and Religion] was published between 1896 and 1898 in volumes IV and V of *Naše doba*. In it Masaryk says the following about the Jews: "...the Greeks by their love to their beautiful fatherland formed a free community. But it was the Romans who first formed a really free community. Roman freedom was developed from monarchical despotism more deliberately than in the case of the Greeks. That is why the Romans were the real representatives of law – they were for law what the Jews were for religion: but just as the Jewish religion was egoistic so Roman law was egoistic; it was recognised as applying only to the Roman people themselves."[97]

---

94) As quoted by J. Olšovský. "Ježíš v Masarykově pojetí", *Masarykův lid*, 14, 2008, No. 1, pp. 1–2.
95) T. G. Masaryk. *Slovanské studie. Slavjanofilství Ivana Vasiljeviče Kirejevského*. Praha, 2007, pp. 44–45, note 46.
96) Ibid., p. 64.
97) T. G. Masaryk. *Modern Man and Religion*. London, 1938, p. 181.

"As soon as man noticed the conflict in the world and the disparity between the divine and the temporal, he presumed that the divine had deserted him; and he felt his weakness and dependence on the divine, which he now imagined to be outside of and beyond himself. This was an illusion – for the divine was not beyond man; but by means of the temporal, of matter, nature caused a conflict within him and overpowered him just because he sought the divine in it.

[...] Religion became even more important, and it was especially the Jewish people who, throughout their history, lived through that religious conflict the most painfully and the most fervently.

But the desire for salvation was satisfied – Jesus of Nazareth in His person combined the divine with the human [...] Christ, after all, did not altogether reconcile the divine and the human – the Christians began again to yearn and be sad [...] Catholicism did not appease the desire for salvation, and out of religion it made yet again the Old Testament struggle between the worldly and the divine."[98]

In 1899 the journal *Čas* published Masaryk's lecture entitled "Polygamy and Monogamy", in which Masaryk declared categorically that a man should have only one wife and a woman should have only one husband in a marriage.

Monandry and monogamy are the objective of sexual development, Masaryk states, and proceeds to outline that development. In Old Testament times polygamy was permitted. David had an entire harem; the woman was subordinate to the man and had no place in the temple, but divorce was permitted. The man was to observe higher decrees: he was not to marry an unchaste woman or a widow. Man and wife were to be Adam and Eve "one body". The New Testament is more advanced. To a significant degree Christ accepts the point of view of the Old Testament, permitting divorce and having no objection to successive marriages, but his own idea is ascetic. Celibacy is valued more highly than marriage. The apostles adhere to Christ and the Old Testament – and would seem to have been closer to the Old Testament than to Christ. According to the Old Testament the woman should be subordinate to the man; the man is not accountable to

---

98) Ibid., pp. 172–173.

the woman, the woman is accountable to the man. The woman must not speak in assemblies, and celibacy is superior to marriage. The mediaeval church, both Roman and Greek, was established according to those regulations. Then came the Reformation, Humanism, and Socialism; man and woman were now on a totally equal footing, equality at work and in care for society. In marriage there was a need for "unity of spirit". Virginity and celibacy are not superior to or purer than pure marriage. Christianity regards matter and the body as something unclean, but this is not so. There is no harm in moderation, however. Masaryk proclaims in conclusion: "unsentimental, unromantic love; love of a man and a woman who are absolutely equal".[99]

Elsewhere Masaryk pronounces on the mutual relationships of Christian and non-Christian churches. The Jews are oppressed by the Christian churches. In American synagogues "Christ and Christianity are mentioned with love." Masaryk cites a rabbi of New York's Beth El Temple: "Modern Judaism joyfully acknowledges Christian humanitarianism and claims Christ as one of its greatest sons."[100] (Which does not apply nowadays by any means.)

Masaryk's *Handbook of Sociology* contains this very characteristic sentences: "The essence of religion can apparently be discovered from study of ancient Indian writings (Max Müller). Others recommend study of the Old Testament. In reality those who are incapable of reading their own inner selves or understanding the religious life of their own times will be incapable of understanding those sources."[101]

In 1904 Masaryk gave several lectures on the topics of religious freedom, what constitutes religion, and religious crises, and these were published the same years in the booklet *V boji o náboženství* [The Battle over Religion], which was republished in 1932 and 1947.

The lectures include some of Masaryk's key ideas about religion, such as: "We are able to value the Bible and similar books as the product of religious endeavours of ages past, but by now

---

99) T. G. Masaryk. "Mnohoženství a jednoženství", Čas, 13, 1898–1899, 18. 3. 1899, pp. 183–185; 25. 3. 1899, pp. 199–202.
100) T. G. Masaryk. "Rozhled v církevním životě v roce 1901", Čas, 16, 1902, No. 112, 24. 4., pp. 1–2.
101) T. G. Masaryk. "Rukověť sociologie. Podstata a metoda sociologie", *Naše doba*, 8, 1901, pp. 739, 824.

our knowledge and practice are largely based on other theoretical foundations. And we also base our religion on the same theory – there are not two truths, there is just one truth. There is just scientific truth, verified and well-founded; that is also why modern man must be grounded in scientific truth, and his religion will be grounded in conviction, not faith. Believing means believing something and someone – there is no other authority than science and enlightened man. We discovered this and therefore demand freedom for the further religious evolution."[102]

Later in the same booklet Masaryk enumerates everything that religion is not: it is not philosophy or science, it is not theology, the catechism, morality, ceremonial, art, or even mysticism. Masaryk is convinced that it is "...pure religion free of all mysticism, or the [...] legacy of the mystic period of Antiquity."[103]

"The greatest example of pure religion is Jesus: Jesus was exceedingly clearheaded; at least his religion was free of the exclusive character of mysticism or ecstasy; mysticism is evident, on the other hand, in pathological Paul, hence the great difference between the religion of Jesus and that of Paul. And Luther, for instance, who was a follower of Paul, is also no exemplar for us. He was hot-headed like Paul, and hot-headed people, such as prophets and reformers, represent religious anger; Jesus presented a pure, peaceful religion – calm and clear. We too want a clear, pure and unnebulous."[104]

He gives another example of Jesus: we want a spiritual and non-material religion. "We want a higher morality! Our religion must manifest itself in higher and nobler moral opinions; morality must be above ceremonial. Jesus provided us with a good example of this. Jesus did not follow the Pharisees and did not require verbosity – he would pray in silence, where no one could see him; religion for us is not showing oneself in public places, even a temple. Jesus teaches us to focus our love of God on our neighbours."[105]

And further: "And I have said repeatedly: I still regard Jesus as our supreme teacher of religion: the historical Jesus, not the

102) T. G. Masaryk. *V boji o náboženství*. Praha, 1947, pp. 11–12.
103) Ibid., p. 23.
104) Ibid., pp. 23–24.
105) Ibid., p. 27.

dogmatic Christ, not God, but man, and precisely as a man are we able to love, honour and follow him as our teacher, example and ideal."[106]

The booklet also has several references to the Old Testament, which forbade pictorial representation of God; the Old Testament was superseded by the New, and we are now surpassing the New Testament – from the revealed to the unrevealed God, from revealed to unrevealed religion.[107]

The final section is devoted to the religious crisis of Christianity, which originally surpassed Judaism and its theology within the context of Jewish culture – and therein lies the importance of Jesus.

In 1904 Masaryk dealt with religious life in Europe. In the closing chapter of his article (VI) he also focusses on the religious movement in Judaism and the Russian religious thinker Ahad Ha'am and his religious significance. He states that the religious crisis does not only involve the Christian churches, but also the Jews, with several movements contending with each other: Orthodox, Liberal, Zionist and Reform. The problem of the Austrian Jews is that in the face of anti-Semitism they have to ally themselves with the liberalism, but to what extent, Masaryk asks. Regarding anti-Semitism, Masaryk writes: "...I have long thought that Jews in our country have not adopted a correct approach to it – they are not sufficiently open, frank and resolute. In my opinion anti-Semitism is our wound, and only ours; it damages us, saps us morally, and coarsens us. It does no material damage to the Jews, and it only causes moral damage if the Jews try to overcome it negatively, by guile, whereas it must be overcome positively, morally and religiously.

I have not got involved in Jewish religious issues, having enough work with our own, but it is impossible not to be aware of the problem and reflect on it. I am grateful to a number of Jews who have understood my approach to their religious issues; they drew my attention to a thinker who can provide some very positive lessons. I refer to Ahad Ha'am (Ahad Ha'am is a pseudonym meaning "one of the people", his real name is Asher Ginsberg). Ahad Ha'am writes in Hebrew and has addressed all the

---

106) Ibid., p. 29.
107) Ibid., pp. 32, 35.

problems of Judaism in many works and articles; he made an outstanding contribution to the foundation a large-scale Hebrew publishing house, and took over the editing of the major Jewish encyclopaedia.

Ahad Ha'am is a man with a modern education who writes in Hebrew about all sorts of issues such as those formulated by Nietzsche and other contemporary thinkers; we can understand why Ahad Ha'am writes in Hebrew if we bear in mind there are 5½ million Jews in Russia! And if we add that there are today 11 million Jews all in all, its significance is all the greater.

Ahad Ha'am is above all an opponent of liberalism and hence of Jewish westernism; he is not at all impressed by the freedom of western Jews and their liberal mixture of chauvinism and cosmopolitanism 'Can I envy the rights our brothers enjoy? No, and again no! It is true that I have no rights, but I don't have to give my soul for them...' Ahad Ha'am is a Jew, simply a Jew; the question, why has he remained a Jew, is one he does not understand at all.

Ahad Ha'am presents the entire philosophy of history from this standpoint. The evolution of nations is governed by the law of imitation; Jews have also imitated surrounding nations at various epochs and due to various factors, but that imitation must not be an effort at total assimilation. 'The advancement of national autonomy by imitation in the form of emulation.' For that reason Ahad Ha'am does not preach rejection of European culture; on the contrary he wants Jews to fully embrace that culture; but he does not want them to abandon their national character. When several New-Hebrew writers declared the whole of Judaism as worthless under the influence of Nietzsche and his watchwords about the reappraisal of values, Ahad Ha'am took a stand against them. He preaches the renaissance of the Hebrew language and New-Hebrew literature, and he himself has made an excellent contribution towards enhancing the Hebrew language with modern terminology. Ahad Ha'am struggles against Nietzsche and individualism, showing that the Old Testament is entirely social and requires devotion to the whole.

Ahad Ha'am demands from the Jews 'a revival of the heart', an inner revival. For that reason he his assessment of anti-Semitism is quite different from that of most Jews: anti-Semitism must not be the reason or motivation for efforts at revival; such efforts must spring from Jews' own, deepest awareness. For the same reason Ahad Ha'am is also no Zionist, insofar as Zionism is a reaction against anti-Semitism; he himself was already in Palestine in 1891 and 1893, and his implacable criticism exposed the lack of success of Zionist colonisation.

In a word, Ahad Ha'am seeks the redemption of Judaism via a spiritual and religious revival, rejecting means that are totally alien and even mechanical; for that reason he does not criticise anti-Semitism and opponents from outside, but instead he searches the hearts and minds of his own nation. It is quite evident that influences of Russian thinking, and anti-European Slavophile thinking can be heard in Ahad Ha'am however, the New-Hebrew writer (or prophet?) has a more friendly attitude to the achievements of culture, as far as I can see, than some of his Russian exemplars."

Masaryk also commented on Montefiore's essay on Liberal Judaism: "The Englishman C. G. Montefiore, editor of the Jewish Quarterly Review, published an essay on Liberal Judaism in 1904. Montefiore accepts the results of modern criticism of the Old Testament, but he defends the religious particularities of Judaism both against Jewish orthodoxy and against Christian liberal theologians who deny its right to exist. Montefiore considers the essence of Judaism to be found in the prophets and strivings for pure monotheism, and that foundation is so valuable that it deserves to be preserved as the basis for an independent Jewish religion. Montefiore assesses the Law and rabbinical literature solely in literary terms. According to Montefiore the Jewish religion was not indissociable from Unitarianism and was essentially autonomous. The Jews' religious mission is not yet finished. Montefiore is therefore opposed to assimilation by blood, but purely for religious reasons; he resolutely denies the anti-Semitic theory of pure blood. The orthodox religion is of worth because of historical value and could be reformed in liberal sense. In the view of Montefiore, parts of the New Testament surpass the Old Testament in terms of their spirituality and inwardness, although some parts are inferior to the understanding in the Old Testament; the view that the Old Testament has only a god of justice, whereas the New Testament has a god of love is not justified; Jesus was a great and deeply spiritual teacher, but has no absolute metaphysical value for Judaism.

I do not find these conclusions sufficiently substantiated. I believe the difficulties of liberal Judaism arc greater than Montefiore states; however, he could be an instructive example for our Czech liberal Jews as regards a *religious* understanding of the Jewish question."[108]

In a later essay *The Intelligentsia and Religion* from 1906, Masaryk declares: "Catholicism took over Judaism and paganism and cultivated asceticism – that odd religious and moral athleticism, consummating the energy of the will in a one-sided, unnatural and mutilating fashion. Along with asceticism it also adopted an incorrect and coarse opinion about women and marriage. Although it is possible to find here and there in the Old Testament a favourable view of woman and marriage, very soon there prevailed the unnatural and incorrect view that celibacy and virginity were superior to married life."[109]

Masaryk later added in the *Talks*: "Love – strong love, true love, the love of a man and woman who are sexually pure – is, as it says in The Song of Songs, as strong as death, no, stronger then death, because it supports life and creates new lives."[110] And further in the above essay: "Nevertheless, inhumanity, which can result from erroneously-founded religion, manifests itself in those dreadful, mass atrocities that were committed not only against infidels, Mahomeddans and Jews, but also against heretical Christians. The vile blood libel was fabricated against the Jews and it is still maintained and nurtured by the church, as we have seen in the Hilsner case."[111]

In his *American Lectures*, Masaryk rejects revelation. "The church regards the source of religious knowledge to be a special revelation. Religious truths, it maintains, are revealed by God himself. These are God's truths that cannot be perceived by mere human reason, and therefore, it is maintained, revealed truths are superior to reason... Moses, when he allegedly received the 'Ten Commandments' from God, was the leader of those who believed him... The teaching of revelation is handed down from generation to generation. Theology therefore includes evolution;

108) Ibid., pp. 523–524.
109) T. G. Masaryk. *Inteligence a náboženství*. Praha, 1907, p. 103.
110) K. Čapek. *Talks with T. G. Masaryk*, p. 84.
111) T. G. Masaryk. *Inteligence a náboženství*, p. 115.

its truth is proclaimed to be absolute. God also reveals himself through miracles, they say... Humans cannot do miracles, and everyone is interested in a miracle, until they realise there is no such thing as miracles and direct revelation."[112] "... In religion one senses and becomes aware of one's relationship with the world and with people. Or to put it another way: in religion we confront the mystery of eternity as a whole. Eternity would be the single word to sum up our problem. The problem of eternity is what you will find in all elements of religion and what is at the very heart of religion. And the manner in which human beings answer that question determines how their religion is formulated."[113] "Religion is what we call the inner life, but not science or philosophy. I concede that there is also practical philosophy...; practical philosophy is quite simply morality and ethics. But not even morality can replace religion. I can replace philosophy and scientific morality with theology, but religious, inner life is something other than theology. For that reason, it is my scientific conviction that science and philosophy will never replace religion."[114]

On 9 December 1910 Masaryk gave a lecture in the Women's Club on the topic "Women in the Teachings of Jesus and Paul": "I am in a somewhat delicate situation having to expound to you the teachings of Jesus and Paul regarding marriage, women, the family and love, because I must speak about the religion in which the vast majority of us were raised and in which we live. What also makes the situation delicate is the effort to be strictly objective and being well informed about the matter. The matter is Scripture: the Old and New Testaments. And of course my task would be easier if I could assume a knowledge of Scripture. In fact I intend to read it to you in order to present word for word what is written there. However, I must also give some interpretation.

I said we must calmly, objectively and factually understand and judge what we were raised in, and in which we live, namely Christian teaching, the teaching of the church, particularly that of the Catholic church, which is common to the majority of our nation. Most theologians, and particularly Jesus and Paul, who

---

112) T. G. Masaryk. *Americké přednášky*, pp. 47–49.
113) Ibid., p. 40.
114) Ibid., p. 62.

are our chief concern here, constantly refer to the Old Testament, and Old Testament opinions continue to be quite natural for the great mass of the people, just as they were back in Antiquity. From the Old Testament I would recall these verses from the very beginning where it speaks of the creation of man and woman (Genesis 2.22–24): "And the rib, which the Lord God had taken from man, made a woman, and brought her unto the man. And Adam said: This is now bone of my bones, and flesh of my flesh: she shall be called Woman, because she was taken out of Man. Therefore shall a man leave his father and his mother, and shall cleave unto his wife: and they shall be one flesh." Hence the main sense of this Old Testament teaching is that they are one. But in the Old Testament there is polygamy and patriarchy. The holy ones, the patriarchs, did not have just one wife, they had two or more. So the family was polygamous, but in most polygamy was replaced by monogamy for economic reasons. The same applies today in the Middle East for the same reasons. So in the Old Testament monogamy became the rule, but everywhere marriage assessed chiefly from an economic standpoint: for practical reasons the family became an economic unit in which the woman and the man were equally dominant. All their work, including war and trade, took place in primitive conditions and we must imagine those people in those conditions, quite different from today's, if we are to understand the opinions in the Old Testament. Old Testament marriage was also judged from the standpoint of *population*. In ancient times the populations were small and there was constant warring, which reduced the size of populations even more. And because people wanted to have lots of children – like the sand in the sea, as it says in one Old Testament image – the Jews multiplied and spread as much as they could.

There is no mention in the Old Testament of what we now call *love*, the love of a man and woman. I am not saying that there were no instances of pure, ideal, splendid love, such as we today would like to see, *but by and large that concept was unfamiliar to the thinking of that time.* And you would also search in vain for that concept in the New Testament, where love of one's neighbour is spoken of, but not love as we now understand it, namely, love of a man and a woman. For instance, when love is spoken about in Old Testament such as in the Song of Songs, which is interpreted figuratively in the church as the relation of Jesus to the church, it is a sensual love song of a Middle Eastern type, glowing with colour. It is altogether probable that there were fine relationships here and there, and nature itself prompted two people, a man and a woman, to truly love each other. And to show how the relationship between a man and a woman – for which we now use the one word 'love' – appears in the Old Testament, I will read from Proverbs chapter 31 (verses 10–31), because it sums up the best teachings of the Old Testament about the matter. That teaching was also taken into the New Testament and still forms part of the church's official position on family life. The chapter praises a noble-minded wife in the following words: 'How hard it is to find a capable wife! She is worth far more than jewels! Her husband puts his confidence in her, and he will never be poor. As long as she lives, she does him good and never harm. She keeps herself busy making wool and linen cloth. She brings home food from out-of-the-way places, as merchant ships do. She gets up before daylight to prepare food for her family and to tell her servant women what to do. She looks at land and buys it, and with money she has earned she plants a vineyard. She is a hard worker, strong and industrious. She knows the value of everything she makes, and works late into the night. She spins her own thread and weaves her own cloth. She is generous to the poor and needy. She doesn't worry when it snows, because her family has warm clothing. She makes bedspreads and wears clothes of fine purple linen. Her husband is well known, one of the leading citizens. She makes clothes and belts, and sells them to merchants. She is strong and respected and not afraid of the future. She speaks with a gentle wisdom. She is always busy and looks after her family's needs. Her children show their appreciation, and her husband praises her. He says, "Many women are good wives, but you are the best of them all." Charm is deceptive and beauty disappears, but a woman who honours the Lord should be praised. Give her credit for all she does. She deserves the respect of everyone.'

As I said, it is one of the best passages on my topic in the Old Testament. And when we analyse this fine conceptualization, which is the essence of the most advanced views of the Old Testament, the patriarchal attitude is still evident. The patriarch: literally the father who rules, in this case, over the family; you can see that family, in which the woman is the chief homemaker, the one entirely in charge of running the home. The man is less concerned about the home, so he searches for a prudent house-wife. When you realise this, you cannot say it is quite the ideal relationship between a man and a woman. It is still the cruel pa-triarchal domination such as one could find among the Romans, the Greeks and other nations of the world of that time. This is not to say that the man, the ruler of the family, always adopted a cruel attitude to the family; of course, there were also instances of tenderness. Nonetheless we still see before us the image of the woman running the household, established as the head of home and the family. The patriarch lives and works outside the home and the family. These Old Testament views are the basis for those of the New Testament. I am to present you Jesus's teaching. But there is one comment I must make first: I told you I am in a deli-cate situation if I am to arbitrate about Christian opinions. I cor-rect myself. The opinions of Christians are based on the teach-ings of Jesus and Paul, and on other apostles, should anyone wish to follow it up in more detail. We will consider first whether there is a difference between Jesus and Paul, and if so, what is it? We will then reflect on the leaven of Jesus and Paul – Jesus himself used to term leaven – with reference to the formation of mediaeval Catholicism and later developments in the church. I won't speak about Christianity at all, but about its main found-er, in terms of the theology, namely, Jesus. There is one partic-ularly important passage for us, one which continues to cause exegetes a lot of difficulties, in which it speaks of eunuchs for the sake of the kingdom of heaven. It is usually interpreted to mean that a man has achieved the summit of perfection if he decides not to enter into marriage and devote himself totally to religious life, and therefore the celibacy of man or woman is bet-ter than marriage. Let us examine this passage more closely. It says that the Pharisees came to him and asked him if a man can divorce his wife for any reason at all. It is evident from this that in those days conditions were fairly lax and divorce for banal reasons was commonplace. Jesus quotes the Old Testament and says that Moses permitted a man to divorce his wife. But he goes on to say that it was not like in the beginning, but the practice developed only when morals declined. Moses permitted it 'for the hardness of your hearts'. The passage I refer to then follows

(Matt. 19.9–12): And I say unto you, Whosoever shall put away his wife, except it be for fornication, and shall marry another, committeth adultery: and whoso marrieth her which is put away doth commit adultery. His disciples say unto him, If the case of the man be so with his wife, it is not good to marry. But he said unto them, All men cannot receive this saying, save they to whom it is given. For there are some eunuchs, which were so born from their mother's womb: and there are some eunuchs, which were made eunuchs of men: and there be eunuchs, which have made themselves eunuchs for the kingdom of heaven's sake. He that is able to receive it, let him receive it.' I have said that this passage is generally interpreted to mean that it is better not to marry and it is necessary not to do so for those who devote themselves totally to the kingdom of heaven and want to live a fully religious life and work for religion and the church. Were I to present all the various opinions expressed in interpreting this passage there would be more than enough for a separate lecture. I'll tell you what is my own opinion. My view of it is that Jesus is not speaking here about asceticism, but speaking here about being a eunuch for the sake of the kingdom of heaven as a great sacrifice. He is also not giving advice as Paul later does. It strikes me as quite natural that he is confronting people with religion as an ideal which obviously requires sacrifice. Whether it be an artist, a scientist or a soldier, who is fully devoted to an idea, they can all find themselves in a situation in which they must break all ties and remain alone. That is my understanding of this passage, and I fail to see in it what Paul subsequently make of it. On the contrary Jesus seems to feel the pain that he brings to the sacrifice with his life. If reference is made to the fact that Jesus had no wife, we must conclude that he was not married before he died, but we do not know if he would have married had he lived longer. Moreover we must not forget that Jesus never presented himself as a universal example. And therein can be seen what I would call that natural attribute: that one should sacrifice one's and everything for some idea. I recall, for instance, what is said in Luke 14.26: "If any man come to me, and hate not his father, and mother, and wife, and children, and brethren, and sisters, yea, and his own life also, he cannot be my disciple." And in Chapter 18.29: "Verily I say unto you, There is no man that hath left house, or parents, or brethren, or wife, or children,

(73)

for the kingdom of God's sake," etc. For those who accept Jesus naturally and not as the church teaches, that too is natural. You have to hate your life and your soul if you want to be mine. That is what must be sacrificed to the idea or the idea. And when you compare it the passage quoted earlier, lo and behold the two are naturally linked. In other words: sacrificing everything for the sake of the kingdom of heaven if need be. Jesus agreed with divorce, total separation. We can see that in Matthew in the interesting Sermon on the Mount, where Jesus starts to present his commandments and contrasts the Old Testament with himself. In the case of infidelity Jesus finds it natural that people will separate. It is clear from this that Jesus viewed the whole issue very humanely, that life together would no longer be possible where there is no fidelity. You can observe his mercy when he forgives the adulteress in opposition to those who wanted to stone her to death. So I can conclude up my views on Jesus's teaching by saying that it was not ascetic. It might be argued that there are nonetheless elements of asceticism here and there. In the light of such doubts let us consider the whole of Jesus's teaching and we will see that it is strictly humane and natural. The literature in scripture does not have the meaning that was ascribed to it in later epochs. From this we see there is a difference between Jesus and Paul. It will now be necessary to say how great is that difference. Paul's teaching became the teaching of the official church, not Jesus's. Jesus did not say much about this issue.

Paul, on the other hand, articulated very detailed precepts. From that we can see that in this respect Paul already greatly differed from Jesus. Theologians maintain that Paul actually says what Jesus intended to say. I don't believe it. It is typical of Paul that he adopts quite an ascetic stance – asceticism in the strictest sense of the word. He was living in the first century after Christ among Romans and Middle Easterners, where relations between the sexes were not the nicest, and for that reason he often proposes asceticism in opposition to sexual misconduct and perversion, and often very strictly. Indeed he is so strict that the teaching assumes quite a different sense than it does in the case of Jesus who is naturally humane. An important and almost crucial passage of Paul for us is 1 Cor. 7. Briefly, what Paul literally says there either as advice or as an addition to Jesus's teaching is: celibacy and virginity, not to be married, is superior and more moral than being married; it is better to remain a widower or widow and not remarry. It must be stressed all the time that Paul's asceticism, his 'ideal' of people not marrying, probably had a historical motivation, namely, that he believed in the imminent end of the world. This must always be borne in mind if we are to judge Paul correctly. Like many Christians who were awaiting the coming of Christ and his kingdom, Paul for his part awaited the Last Judgement, and for that reason life in 'this world' is already worthless to his mind. We have to imagine ourselves in his situation. The Day of Judgement is coming, the end of the world; Jesus will come and then will come what Paul imagines: eternal life. And so from that standpoint he supports his utterly ascetic view that celibacy and virginity are morally superior to marriage. In spite of all this we can see that Paul is inconsistent; for him man is superior to woman. The superior example is the Old Testament view. Let us take, for instance, 1 Cor. 11. Here it speaks about the value of man and woman: 'For a man indeed ought not to cover his head, forasmuch as he is the image and glory of God: but the woman is the glory of the man. For the man is not of the woman: but the woman of the man. Neither was the man created for the woman; but the woman for the man.' In other words, man is rated morally superior to woman. Or in Ephesians 5.22: 'Wives, submit yourselves unto your own husbands, as unto the Lord. For the husband is the head of the wife,' etc. We can see all the time that this in not love as we speak of it today. It is fear of the Lord and fear of the husband. This religious view assumes a different love. Paul is a Jew and a Pharisee to boot. There is a lot of the Old Testament about him, so he adheres to fear of the Lord and fear of the husband, in other words, a different moral relationship than we are familiar with nowadays. Paul excludes women from worship of God and the outcome has been the Catholic church's *mulier taceat in ecclesia*! Women are excluded from lower and higher orders of the priesthood; in short, the man is religiously superior. Although I disagree with Paul and his attitude, I readily admit that the moral earnestness with which he counters vice was correct. Paul repeatedly warns against impurity, and the Christians in particular against the lives led by the Romans, the Greeks and other nations of the time. He says he is body and soul a member of Christ and a temple of the Holy Spirit. But that exaggerated

(75)

contrast of the soul and body, of woman and man only intensi-
fies even more in his religion. Admittedly the Pharisees considered the woman to be inferior, but here it was given a religious
blessing. These are the religious elements that evolved without
understanding in the mediaeval church into the church teaching
that now prevails.

Of the other apostles, Peter actually adopts Paul's teaching:
'wives, be in subjection to your own husbands [...] Even as Sara
obeyed Abraham, calling him lord.' Indeed a century ago that is
how mothers and women in this country addressed their men.
Peter also states that women are 'weaker vessels'.

I don't need to argue further. It strikes me, to put it succinct-
ly, that between Paul and Jesus we can see a marked difference,
that different being asceticism. And even if Jesus displayed some
elements of asceticism, they were insignificant overall, whereas
with Paul we have not only asceticism but also the religious de-
valuation of women.

"On the basis of Paul's views the mediaeval church developed
its teaching in the matter briefly as follows: that the woman/
mother is weaker than the man, religiously speaking, and therefore inferior. The monk becomes the church's ideal in religious
and moral terms, not the priest! Monasticism starts to develop
in Egypt and elsewhere as early as the 2nd century A.D. Since
then it has been the ideal of Christian living: surmounting the
world by a monk who not only rejects family life but suppresses
all natural life. One spends his entire life standing on a pillar,
another in a cave, etc. In general terms: the monastic ideal and
also the highest morality is not to live in a family, for a family
or with a family. So men don't marry, and women don't marry
and become nuns. I repeat: this is Paul's view, not Jesus's. Asceticism was also in use by the Romans and so-called pagans.
Asceticism greatest achievement was the unnatural breaking of
human beings instead of their natural development. Clerical
celibacy emerged through the influence of asceticism, but only
after lengthy battles. Note that it was not all at once or immediately. It is very difficult to date it precisely. Up to the 4th century
priests married quite normally, as is still the case in the eastern
church. This is an undeniable fact. It was only at the Council of
Nicaea in 325 A.D. that a proposal for clerical celibacy was ta-
bled, but it was not accepted. Monasticism was not established

until the 6th century. The monk and the priest were two types, two different institutions of the one church. That church, which took asceticism as an ideal, was divided within itself. Even the priests did not live consistently in accordance with Jesus's ideal, or Paul's. Eventually, from the 6th century onwards the marriage of priests is increasingly prohibited in the West. It was not until the 12th century that celibacy was officially established in the sense we now know it. Just how cruelly it was imposed we can judge from the fact that authority to cleanse the church – and that included the introduction of celibacy – was given to the secular rulers. The rulers had the right to make serfs of the wives and children of priests. And so celibacy was in very many countries by violence alone. At many synods in Spain and in Rome strict orders were issued for celibacy to be introduced and cruel examples to be made of transgressors. The reasons for the introduction of celibacy are to be found in the conditions of the church at that time: as soon as the church became dominant and the priest was a soldier, whose life was constantly at risk, particularly when the church advanced eastwards and spread from Rome and Italy to the countries of the North. In the same way that a soldier nowadays is celibate for economic reasons, that was one of the reasons for the introduction of clerical celibacy. When there was a priest in almost every village, he was supposed to be someone who believed and lived the church's teaching, and being sanctified, in other words, superior, he was supposed to be aloof from everything that was permitted to ordinary people on account of their 'hardness of heart' as a greater or lesser sin. This is, please note, the prevailing teaching that is being instilled into children from their earliest years. A monk always ranks higher than a priest because the monastic ideal is superior. The natural man cannot accept something like that. It tells me how Catholicism has degraded marriage after elevating it to one of the seven sacraments. I concede it and would fully acknowledge it if, during that sacrament, it were not declared at the outset that marriage can only be lawfully conducted by a priest, whereby the church extends its social and political power. Thus marriage and its indissolubility becomes extremely powerful – while contrary to Jesus's actual teaching. The church does not permit divorce. Maybe I will hear the comment that mediaeval Catholicism created the cult of the Virgin Mary. That veneration of the

(77)

mother of God certainly has some nice aspects about it, but she was venerated as a virgin, as undefiled, and therein we can see woman as being something impure and defiled according to the Catholic church's teaching. So I would say that a fatal error of the Roman Catholic church is having confused purity and chastity with virginity. The fact that a married person can be purer and superior to a male or female virgin, because it is a question of the relationship of body and spirit – this is not considered decisive by the church. That is its chief error, I repeat, as well as the ascetic ideal that degrades woman and marriage – the entire basis of life, in short. I am trying to be just, but I must admit I find this teaching thoroughly objectionable and consider nothing baser. You can see the distasteful example of the clergy, and I don't want to guess what percentage of priests abide strictly by and live in accordance with their ideal. The lives of many priests actually do harm to society; the church remains silent about errors but the rumours circulate all the time. You must be aware of these unpleasant things all the time. I say that I cannot remain silent about it, nor can I speak calmly about it."

"... That is all I wanted to say. I would sum it up briefly as follows: Religion is love and I know the great value of Jesus's teaching, and I fully accept his religion of love. But in official religion there is neither understanding nor sympathy for the highest union of a man and woman. I think one can document what this means for people's education. I think I have fulfilled my task."[115]

In 1913 Masaryk published two volumes of his work *Russia and Europe* [published in English as *The Spirit of Russia*], which includes a chapter about Russian religious philosophy and the thinker Vladimir Solovyov. In it Masaryk has the following to say about Solovyov's attitude to the Jewish question:

"The question of the Jews was one by which Solov'ev [sic] is more disquieted than that of the Poles. In the Jews he discovers a living link between Old Testament days and the stage of religion and revelation, of which Christianity was an organic succession. The relationship between Jews and Christians is, therefore, a very special one. In Solov'ev's apocalyptic vision [...] the significance of this question is symbolically indicated when the

115) T. G. Masaryk. "Žena u Ježíše a Pavla." In *Masarykův sborník*. Vol. 2. Praha, 1927, pp. 233–241.

author makes the number of Christians exceed the number of Jews by no more than one half.

Upon his deathbed Solov'ev begged his friends to keep him awake because he had many prayers to say on behalf of the Jews. In the complex of Russian problems, the Jewish question is one of the most momentous, and Solov'ev frequently discussed it. The importance of the question for Russia depends upon the fact that there are nearly six million Jews in country, a population equal to the whole state of Belgium.

To Solov'ev the Jewish problem is a Christian problem, a religious problem. Solov'ev's treatment of the Jews as pioneers of commerce and industry recalls the manner in which Marx handles the question; it was not the Jews, but the Christians, who had created the cult of the golden calf. Cultured Europe, which had become dechristianised, and had devoted itself to the serve of mammon, was here the offender. The Jews were merely consistent in the way they followed the example thus set before them. If economic life is to be humanised it must be resubordinated to the religious and moral life. For Europe and Russia this can be effected in no other way than by the great union of the churches, in which the Jews will find their place. As a theocratic nation they will be at home in this renovate theocracy; now they are estranged from themselves just as the Christians are estranged from themselves. But true Jewish principles lead to Christianity, just as true Christian principles lead to Judaism. The union of the churches, therefore, will at the same time be a union between the renovated Christians and the renovated Jews: these latter being the better part of Jewry, namely the Russian Jews, who have maintained their religious principles in greater purity than have their western brethren. The Jews as town dwellers will retain their social and economic function, but this function will assume a different meaning, it will be guided by a loftier aim. Its aim will be to humanise nature and material life.

The utopian character of Solov'ev's ecclesiastical policy is manifest. He works with unhistorical schemata.

Solov'ev's essential error is, of course, that he assumes church doctrine to be absolutely true, and that from this outlook he touches up the whole of history; for him, not Jesus and Jesus's teaching, but church doctrine and church dogma are decisive. He fashions for himself the ideal of a Christian church and an ideal of a Christian state. If, as Solov'ev tells us in his *Ethics*, the church is to represent sympathy with the soul, and the state is to represent sympathy with the body, there will doubtless be an organic harmony between church and state; but these as we know them are something altogether different. As a matter of historic fact we recognise different types of theocracy, and Solov'ev is right when he rejects extant theocracies as false, as coercive..."[...]

"From this outlook we must consider and appraise Solov'ev's own views concerning the Poles and Jews. He gave due recognition to the valuable religious inheritance of these two peoples, who were, when he wrote, more hostile to the Russians than any others. The Poles and the Jews, he declared, must lend aid to the Russians. The messianism of the 'theocratic nation' was not a source of privilege, but involved duty and service; it did not give any right to dominance or hegemony. True patriotism, said Solov'ev was to be found in national self-knowledge, not in national self-complacency; whereas the nationalists had reduced the Slavophile idea of messianism to the level of zoomorphic, zoological patriotism. True patriotism involved conviction of sin and confession."[116]

Concerning Jesus, Masaryk repeats: "Jesus showed long ago that all thought and all action centres round the problem, how man conceives his relationship with his fellow-men and to God; and while Jesus tells us to love God and to love our neighbour, John amplifies the command in the words, 'If a man say, I love God, and hateth his brother he is a liar: for he that loveth not his brother whom he hath seen, how can he love God that he hath not seen?'"[117]

Masaryk's views on religion (which he was reluctant to speak about, because "religion should be lived and should be the most intimate thing that one has and is in a spiritual sense") include his speech on receiving his doctorate at the protestant theological faculty on 24 May 1923. Masaryk said inter alia:

"Whenever I have thought about Christianity and its essence I find myself confronted by three religious figures: Paul, Plato and Jesus.

116) T. G. Masaryk. *The Spirit of Russia*. Vol. 2, pp. 239–244.
117) Ibid., p. 473.

Paul, the theologian and founder of the church – the Old Testament and the Jewish people in its unique mission! He just immersed himself in the literary, philosophical and scholarly works of other peoples and by comparing them with the Old Testament tried to discover its significance and the meaning of that people's mission because of that Law. The prophets, Jesus and then Paul.

Alongside Paul, Plato, the artist and philosopher: the Greek nation and its unique status in history; its philosophy, science, art and literature, culture in general: and how our spiritual life has been conditioned ever since by that Jewish and Greek legacy!

And lastly, Jesus. I have already admitted that he is the one I value the most, and I believe absolutely that he is the best teacher of religion and morality. And Jesus lived his religion and wrote nothing. Others wrote about him, and the Christian nations all processed Jesus's leaven into an amazing synthesis.

What those religious figures expressed, each in his own way, Paul said in his hymn to love. Faith, hope and love! Faith, opinion – from these science and philosophy, as well as theology; Paul himself. Hope, something derived from art and artistic creation – Plato. Love – Jesus and his religious and moral teaching. People's attitude to God and each other.

Christianity has been transformed and formulated in diverse ways in the churches of different countries. The main issue is understanding the difference between Catholicism and the Reformation. Catholicism lays greater stress on the celestial element and the church, the Reformation was more concerned about doctrine and morality, and about the human being. Jesus's two commandments: love God, and love your neighbour – these are the two main aspects of religion: piety and morality – and these are expressed in separate ways in Catholicism and Protestantism. Nowadays, after studying and analysing these two forms of Christianity, we are coming round to the precept that one should not get bogged down in mysticism, nor become fossilised in intellectualism.

The synthesis of these three elements – because Paul doesn't say love alone, only that love is the greatest of them – is the task of spiritual life; faith, hope, and love – science and philosophy, art, religion, and morality – these are the elements of each person's spiritual integrity.

Psychological reason, feeling, and volition are the main forces of spiritual life. Properly analysing and determining their relationship with each other, that is the supreme task of philosophical and theological analysis. Stress is frequently laid on the contrasts between intellect, feeling and volition, not only in religion but also in other spiritual fields – synthesis, harmony and unity is a requirement.

Every person has a religion. Those who believe they don't have are wrong. Sometimes atheists display more religion than theists. Every nation and every age has its religion.

It is question of analysing through sensitive psychology the variety of different religious figures. This is now being done; we must not define the essence of religion deductively, by means of deduction from some narrow formula. When I recall my mother teaching me to pray, when she would kneel and I would kneel with her – at that moment we knew nothing about formulas.

Religion also has a national attribute that derives from the character of different nations; it is the task of our theology and science in general, to analyse that specific national attribute.

And lastly we come to politics, which we touched on: Caesar or Jesus? This is how I would put it; it follows on from my earlier speeches. I have often complained that we expect everything from the state. This is an Austrian and German idea: venerating the state. This is the old era, the era of dynastic absolutism: the new era favours democracy and a republic, not only as a form of government but as a universal attitude. True democracy is based on morality; not on church doctrine, not on theology, and not on religion."[118]

In 1925 Masaryk returned to the topic of the Old Testament in a speech to children: "There's a psalm in the Old Testament, I think it's number 90, a prayer of Moses, in which the length of human life is given as seventy years, or perhaps eighty if the person is strong. Our new hygienists and doctors tell us that if each of us lived as we should, sensibly and properly, we could each live at least one hundred years."[119]

118) T. G. Masaryk. "Speech on being awarded a doctorate at the Hus Protestant Theological Faculty, 24 May 1923." In *Masarykův sborník*. Vol. 2, pp. 90–92.
119) "Děti u pana prezidenta." In T. G. Masaryk. *Cesta demokracie*. Vol. 3, p. 97

A summary of Masaryk's views on religion is contained in *The Making of a State*.[120]

The third part of Čapek's conversations with Masaryk (1928–1935), entitled *Masaryk on Thought and Life*, includes the sections "Religion", "Christianity", "The So-called Cultural Conflict", and "Still on Religion".

Masaryk describes the influences he was exposed to during his university studies in Vienna (Brentano), and Leipzig, which "living" philosophers influenced him, and who had the greatest impact on him. Plato, from him he came to Socrates, whom he compared with Jesus; for him Jesus was a religious prophet, while Socrates was a philosophical apostle. He then names Comte, Hume, and Mill. In that connection he says:

"Similarly, Greek philosophy, science, poetry, and art sprang up in the midst of nature and primitive life – a revelation, as much as the Old and New Testament are a revelation of the Palestine desert and primitive Judaism.

"While we are on the subject of Greeks and Jews, think of the influence these two small nations have had on the whole of civilised humanity. The Greeks gave us art, science, and politics, the Jews theology and religion. [...] All Europe is still living off the legacy of the Greeks and the Jews..."[121]

"In the older religions, even in the Old Testament, religion is fear, terror before the deity; God, Jehovah, is terrible; in Jesus' teaching there is no longer any fear.

The prophets form a class by themselves – the religious geniuses, more like zealots than prophets; authority that is quite unique is exercised by the founders of religion, like Moses, Jesus, Mohammed, and the reformers."[122]

Čapek: "I have noticed one thing: whenever you mention your own faith you quote Christ and the Apostles."

Masaryk: "Yes. Jesus – I usually do not say Christ – for me he is the example and teacher of religiousness; he teaches that love towards a kind God, love of one's neighbour and even of one's enemy, and thus pure, unstained humanity, is the substance of reli-

120) T. G. Masaryk. *The Making of a State*, pp. 437–438.
121) K. Čapek. *Talks with Masaryk*, p. 107.
122) *Masaryk on Thought and Life. Conversations with Karel* Čapek. London, 1938, pp. 88 and 89.

gion. Religiousness and morality for Jesus are the chief elements of religion. Notice that in the Gospels – in comparison with the Old Testament, or with Greek mythology – there is almost no mythology, almost no cosmology, and eschatology, almost no history; ...Jesus gives almost nothing but moral instructions..."[123]

Čapek: "This love, of course, also existed before Jesus."

Masaryk: "But it was Jesus who consummated it; he came 'to fulfil the law,' also that universal and eternal law of love. The historical act of Jesus consisted in the fact that he was the first clearly, and by his own example, to define religiousness not only as a relation towards God, but also to one's neighbour. Before Jesus religion used to be – and after him it is often enough – unkind, inhuman, harsh; take the cruelties that the Jews of the Old Testament committed in the name of what, according to them, was the true God! Similarly the Mohammedans. But the Christians as well, although they had the gospel of love, they spread their faith with fire and sword; they devised the Inquisition, and taught people to hate those who held other beliefs..."[124]

In the chapter entitled Christianity:

Čapek: "You said Jesusdom. By that are you suggesting that the teaching of Jesus did not full materialize in the Christian churches?"

Masaryk: "Yes. After all, from its very beginning Christianity does not contain Jesus' teaching alone; it also comprised the Old Testament, and plenty of religious syncretism that was oriental, Greco-Roman, and Hellenistic. It originated among the Jews, but it grew and spread among the Greeks and Romans..."[125]

In 1926, Anna Gašparíková recorded how Masaryk spoke about religion: "The preacher mentioned that the expression of monotheism was not as obvious in the case of the Greeks as it was with the Jews. 'Plato and Aristotle were monotheists,' the President said, 'but, look at it this way: people retain the religious notions about the church they were born into even when they are above all of that. I find it is true about me. Those Greeks also expressed themselves in their own way. Then there is the basic difference between the Jews and the Greeks: the Jews were

---

123) Ibid., p. 94.
124) Ibid., p. 101.
125) Ibid., p. 103.

a religious people, the Greeks were thinkers. On the one hand the prophets and Jesus, and on the other, Plato and Aristotle."[126] Masaryk was unable to avoid religious issues even in his interview with the Austrian writer Emil Ludwig:

"'For me,' he began, 'Jesus is religion. I have formed a very definite idea of Him from the gospels and ancient writings and I have adopted His supreme commandment as my rule of life. It has two poles: Love God and love the neighbour. Theoretical theology and ethics, practical worship and morality. [...] Theism first becomes religion when I feel myself as a part of the world whole in personal relation with God; when I feel that there is Someone who cares for the Whole. Therefore what is essentially religious is in the experience of this relation, in this feeling of security. [...] Jesus was a man, a prophet, and therefore I can love Him. Towards God, however, I have reverence. I always have that feeling terribly strong. But to love? That sounds too anthropomorphical to me. [...] I doubt whether man can love God. [...] (A)nd when I take the command to love God as the highest command of Jesus, this love must mean something different from the love of one's neighbour. Love of one's neighbour – that is for me the naturally given sympathy with the men who stand beside me, my fellow-men; therefore it does not need to be proved.'"[127]

When, in the interview, Ludwig returned to the concept of revealed truth, Masaryk replied: "I take account of two revelations: the old Jewish revelation, which was a formulation of theism — monotheism, of course, the law and the prophets. But I also take the Greek revelation into account, Homer, Phidias, Praxiteles, Plato, etc. From these two sources of the spiritual life of Europe we must nourish our own, not choosing between the one and the other. The task is to arrive at a conclusion that is above both."[128] Before World War II the influence of Judaism on Masaryk's opinions was addressed by Professor Friedrich Thieberger. He noted that Masaryk believed in a personal God and was never for one moment in his life an atheist. He believed in individual Providence, a higher plan and purpose

---

126) A. Gašparíková-Horáková. *Z lánského deníku 1929–1937*. Praha, 1997.
127) E. Ludwig. *Defender of Democracy. Masaryk Speaks*. London, 1936, pp. 17–20.
128) Ibid., p. 21.

of life, and in life after death. He concluded that the "religious Judaism" and the Old Testament played only a small role in Masaryk's religious awareness. Thus Thieberger declared that: "To him religious Judaism was not a reality which concerned him personally as a religious person or which appeared to him as an important problem of mankind in the future. [...] Jews were to him a sociological factor, an historically separately formed community, much more interesting than a religious community [...] anti-Semitism as a social phenomenon concerned him much more than the question of the Jewish religion." Judaism, did stand at the cradle of Christianity, and Masaryk discovered the Jewish origin consciously and unconsciously. However, the lack of knowledge about Judaism was confirmed by the fact that "a man of Masaryk's spiritual breadth and mental alertness was so little touched by it."[129]

Eduard Lederer thought that Masaryk believed nascent Christianity would have dissipated into Hellenistic pantheism, naturalism and mysticism without the Old Testament, and that without a knowledge of the Old Testament and Judaism it is not possible to understand the foundations of European thought.[130]

Anna Horáková-Gašparíková recorded a conversation at Topoľčianky on 7 September 1932: "Even in the next talk, she [Alice Masaryková – M.P.] did not entirely agree with her father, the President, when he said he preferred reading Plato to the New Testament, although he accepted Jesus and liked him. He valued the scientific method of the Greeks: they believed there was grandeur in everything, he stressed. He said that the primitive Jewish way of thinking in the Bible was often an obstacle to him. The prophets were a way of preaching, while Aeschylus was drama."[131]

129) F. Thieberger. "Masaryk's Credo and the Jewish Religion." In *Thomas G. Masaryk and the Jews, a collection of essays*, pp. 49–50.
130) E. Lederer. "Hledání boha." In *Ročenka akademického spolku Kapper 1930/31*. Praha, s. d.
131) A. Gašparíková-Horáková. *Z lánského deníku 1929–1937*, pp. 104–105.

5. Masaryk and Anti-Semitism; the Hilsner Affair

...I am convinced that he who has Jesus for his guide cannot be an anti-Semite. That is clear to me because Jesus was a Jew, because the apostles were Jews, because ancient Christianity, particularly Catholicism, has much in itself that is essentially Jewish. If I accept Jesus, I cannot be an anti-Semite. I can only be one or the other, Christian or anti-Semite!

T.G.Masaryk speaking in the Reichsrat in Vienna, 1907

ANTI-SEMITISM IN AUSTRIA AND THE CZECH LANDS IN THE SECOND HALF OF THE 19TH CENTURY

The second half of the 19th century in the Austrian monarchy saw the defeat of the 1848/49 revolution, the era of Bach absolutism, the "October Diploma" of December 1860 that liberalised social conditions and ushered in a period of liberalism prior to the Austro-Hungarian Compromise of 1867 and the subsequent December Constitution, which enshrined dualism – transforming the Austrian monarchy into a dualist Austrian and Hungarian state, and whose provisions accorded the Jews civil rights. Nevertheless, the Slav nations, particularly the Czechs, who were striving for "Bohemian state rights", felt a sense of frustration. Unsuccessful attempts at Czech-German reconciliation and Badeni's unsuccessful reforms, against the background of rising German and Czech nationalism, and anti-Semitism, kindled anti-Jewish feeling.

Anti-Semitism rapidly proliferated in the Austrian monarchy in the 1870s and 1880s, and fell into two main types.

Pan-German nationalist anti-Semitism was represented in Vienna by Georg von Schönerer, a member of the Reichsrat (Imperial Council), who proclaimed the need for the removal of Jewish influence in all areas of public life. After its return to parliament in 1897 his party won 21 seats.

Far more influential, however, was Christian-Catholic anti-Semitism represented in Austria by the Christian-Social Party, founded in 1893 and led by Karl Lueger. Also a member of the Reichsrat (from 1885), he collaborated with Schönerer. His was a vulgar anti-Semitism, reflecting the sentiments of the lower middle class, who felt themselves threatened by Jewish competition. Capitalism and Marxism were both depicted as Jewish inventions. It derived from the anti-Jewish traditional Christian doctrine that the Jews murdered Jesus, etc. Lueger eventually became mayor of Vienna.

In the Czech lands modern anti-Semitism began to take shape from the 1880s. It was rooted in two different ideological currents.

The first, which had its origins in the nationalist milieu of the Old Czech and Young Czech parties, many of whom were members, at the time of the crisis of prevailing liberalism (which sought to assimilate the Jews), shifted to radical anti-Semitic positions and a chauvinist platform actually founded on racist ideas.

The second current was represented by clericalists, whose ideas derived from the traditional anti-Judaism of the church. They blamed liberalism, the Jews, and the Freemasons for the decline of existing social order, and regarded them as revolutionaries. They also included a national platform of anti-Jewish positions.

The only opponents of anti-Semitism were members of Masaryk's Realists' Party (later renamed the Czech People's Party), and the Social-Democratic Party, who were attacked by their opponents as part of a worldwide Jewish conspiracy.[132]

132) Regarding Czech anti-Semitism see primarily the detailed study by M. Frankl. *"Emancipace od Židů"*. Český anti-Semitismus *na konci 19. století*. Praha – Litomyšl, 2007; idem. "Can We, the Czech Catholics, be Anti-Semites?", *Judaica Bohemiae*, 33, 1998, pp. 47–71; idem. "The Background of the Hilsner Case. Political Anti-Semitism and Allegations of Ritual Murder 1896–1900", *Judaica Bohemiae*, 36, 2001, pp. 34–118. Further: E. Goldstücker. "K dějinám českého anti-Semitismu." In *Hilsnerova aféra a česká společnost 1899–1999*. Praha, 1999, pp. 142–147; J. Kuděla. "Antijudaismus, anti-Semitismus a anti 'politika'", *Dějiny a současnost*, 15, 1993, No. 2, pp. 2–5; B. Soukupová. "Česko slovanská stra-

At the time of Masaryk's arrival in Prague at the Czech university in 1882 the situation on the Czech political scene was as follows: The most influential party was still the National Party (Old Czechs), whose origins dated back to 1848 and became politically active after 1859. Its main leaders were František Palacký (who was no longer alive in 1882), F.L. Rieger, F.A. Brauner, and Albín Bráf, together with representatives of the nobility. Its press organs were *Pokrok* (to 1886), *Hlas národa,* the German-language *Politik,* and from 1871, the daily newspaper *Čech.*

In 1874, the National Liberal Party (Young Czechs) split from the Old Czech party. Its leadership included Karel Sladkovský, Eduard and Julius Grégr, and A.P. Trojan. Future leaders included Josef Kaizl and Karel Kramář. Their press organ was *Národní listy.* In 1891 the party was victorious in the Reichsrat elections, and their new parliamentarians included T.G.Masaryk. However, in 1893 Masaryk left the party after disagreements with Kramář and Kaizl, and resigned his seat in parliament. The party lost its leading position in the 1907 elections.

Other active political parties included The Czechoslavonic Social-Democratic Party (from 1878), whose leaders included Ladislav Zápotocký, J.B. Pecka and Bohumír Šmeral (press organ: *Právo lidu*), the Independent People's Party in Moravia (from 1891) of Adolf Stránský, the Christian-Social Party for Bohemia and Moravia (from 1894), led by Jan Šrámek, the Catholic National Party in Moravia (from 1896) headed by Mořic Hruban, the Radical Progressive Party (from 1897) represented by Antonín Hajn and Antonín Čížek (press organ: *Samostatnost*), which brought together part of the progressive youth that that left the Young Czechs, The National Social Party (from 1898) led by V.J. Klofáč, The State Rights Party (from 1899), headed by Alois Rašín, and K.S. Sokol, which published *Radikální listy*, The Agrarian Party (also 1899), and Masaryk's Czech People's Party (from 1900).

The Czech People's Party was founded in 1900 by the so-called "Realists", who supported T.G.Masaryk. In 1906 the party merged with the Progressive Czech Club founded in 1904 by the editor of the magazine *Osvěta lidu* Alois Hajn, to form the Czech

na sociálnědemokratická a anti-Semitismus (1889–1899)", *Lidé města*, 2, 2000, No. 3, pp. 48–72.

Progressive Party, with Masaryk as political leader. In terms of election results it was one of the least influential parties; in 1907 it won two seats in Bohemia and Moravia, and in 1911, only one.

Masaryk sought to influence Czech public opinion through his articles for three journals: *Athenaeum, Naše doba* and *Čas.*

Athenaeum, a journal devoted to literature and scholarly criticism, was published between the years 1883 and 1893, and sought to promote original Czech scholarly works. Volumes 1–5 were edited by T.G. Masaryk, volumes 6–10 by J. Kaizl. The journal played a key role in the controversy over the authenticity of the Manuscripts of Dvůr Králové and of Zelená Hora[133], publishing articles by Masaryk, the philologist J. Gebauer and others. It was published monthly, except in two summer months. It ceased publication in 1893 and was succeeded from 1894 by the journal *Naše doba* (Our Times), edited until 1914 by Masaryk.

Čas (Time) was a journal of current affairs, founded by Jan Herben. It was published in Prague between 1886 and 1915, initially as a fortnightly, from 1888 as a weekly and from September 1900 as a daily. It came under the influence of T.G. Masaryk in 1893, and from 1900 it became the press organ of his Czech People's Party. It ceased publication in 1915. Influential figures connected with *Čas* included T.G. Masaryk, Cyril Dušek, Josef Svatopluk Machar, Jindřich Vodák, and Gustav Jaroš.

Jan Herben (1857–1936), was a devoted student and supporter of Masaryk. As a journalist and publicist, initially editing *Národní listy*, and then editor-in-chief of *Čas* (1886–1915), he played a crucial role as an opinion former. From 1918 he was a member of the National Assembly of the Czechoslovak Republic, a senator from 1920 to 1925, representing the National Democratic Party, and from 1925 to 1927 he was editor of the daily *Lidové noviny.*

After his arrival in Prague, Masaryk did not pay systematic attention to Jewish issues, let alone the question of anti-Semitism in particular.

Leaving aside the autobiographical fragment "Náš pan Fixl" (Our Mr Fixl), Masaryk made – mostly marginal – reference to

---

133) "Manuscripts of Dvůr Králové and Zelená Hora." In *Wikipedia: the free encyclopedia* (online), https://en.wikipedia.org/wiki/Manuscripts_of_Dvůr_Králové _and_of_Zelená_Hora.

the Jewish question in *Suicide and the Meaning of Civilization,* in his review of Renan's *Jewishness,* and in *Karel Havlíček.* Masaryk regarded the Jews as a nation, and any sort of anti-Semitism was unacceptable to him. This was related to his religious conviction and his profound attachment to Jesus – a Christian cannot be an anti-Semite.

Nevertheless, before the Hilsner affair erupted, and also after it, Masaryk did write a number of articles that were directly concerned with anti-Semitism. One of them was an unsigned paper in the journal *Čas* about Drumont's tract *La France Juive.*[134]

Václav Tille summed up Masaryk's critique of Drumont as follows: "Masaryk begins by declaring that there is no anti-Semitism in our country, but only because of our cowardice and thoughtlessness. Masaryk believes the Jewish question concerns the whole of Europe and is related to the social question. Drumont has in mind forcible measures, such as confiscation and expulsion. Masaryk is of the opinion that it is above all necessary to consider whether the Jews will coalesce with the European nations in the foreseeable future or not. If we are compelled to answer that question negatively, then Jews must be accorded the civic status they rightly deserve. Masaryk does not ignore the reproach that Drumont addresses to the French Jews, when he points out how they benefitted from the Revolution, which, on 27 September 1791 abolished all exceptional legislation against them, and how they enriched themselves in a short space of time, and the influence they exert on the nobility, artists, newspapers, and the entire nation. He perceives that if a small minority is victorious in a battle against an overwhelming majority, then it is probably resorting to unequal weaponry, and that inequality must be balanced in a lawful way, so certain restrictions, appropriate to Jewish characteristic and customs would be necessary as a just defence of an Asian tribe. He adds, however, that at the present time this seemingly impossible requirement would depend on the progress of intelligence and

---

134) (T. G. Masaryk.) "Časová otázka ve Francii. E. Drumont, La France juive", Čas, 20. 3. 1888, pp. 7–14. A brief summary of Masaryk's article was given by V. Tille. "Masaryk a francouzská literatura." In *Masarykův sborník.* Vol. 5. Vůdce generací. I. Praha, 1930–1931, pp. 330–345. For more recent edition see T. G. Masaryk. *Z bojů o rukopisy 1886–1888.* Praha, 2004, pp. 429–453.

morality in ourselves."[135] The views expressed by Masaryk in the article are extraordinary.

A further text by Masaryk on the topic of anti-Semitism is an article in *Naše doba* from 1899 entitled "Anti-Semitism in Antiquity".[136] The text starts with a report by the Egyptian priest Manetho in the 3rd century BC about the history of Egypt and the origin of the Jews. The most rabid anti-Semite of antiquity was Apion of Alexandria who authored anti-Jewish pamphlets and spread rumour and fabrications about the Jews. Josephus responded in a polemic entitled *Contra Apionem*. In Rome, Cicero was a proponent of anti-Semitism, having studied with Apollonius Molon, who wrote anti-Jewish pamphlets. The Roman poets proved to be anti-Semitic: Horace spoke with contempt of the Jews, Martial mocked Jews, and in Juvenal's works Jews are portrayed as beggars; Tibullus, Ovid and Pompeius Trogus wrote about them as proselytes. The principal literary anti-Semite was Tacitus. The exception was Terentius Varro, who praised the way Jews worshipped God.

Masaryk also reviewed three anti-Semitic booklets by Father František Vrba.

Regarding the booklet *Národní sebeobrana* (National Self-Defence) Masaryk wrote:

"National Self-Defence is not just a crude broadside against the Jews. While this is true, taken as a whole, and this applies above all to the atmosphere of the entire book, it is unpleasant and actually harmful. This is not Christianity, but the slops of vinegar and gall that Christ was given to drink. 'And when he had tasted thereof, he would not drink,' it is written. In this book Fr. Vrba perceives Jews at the main evil, and of course he describes anyone as a Jew, such as deputy Daszyński. It's a minor detail, but it only goes to show what zealotry leads to."[137]

135) V. Tille. "Masaryk a francouzská literatura", p. 334.
136) T. G. Masaryk. "Anti-Semitism ve věku starém", *Naše doba*, 6, 1899, pp. 310–318, 399–400.
137) "Budoucnost národa, Národní sebeobrana, Rolnický program české strany křesťansko-sociální, 1896", *Naše doba*, 6, 1899, p. 315.

A key text is an article by Masaryk in *Die Zeit* from 4 November 1899, which analysed in detail the causes of anti-Semitism in the Czech lands.[138]

On 26 January 1900 Masaryk attended a meeting of the *Slavie* student association on the topic of anti-Semitism. After the opening address, Masaryk took the floor, declaring that anti-Semitism was an accumulation of many issues. There was clerical anti-Semitism; there was no conflict between Christianity and Judaism, although the Christianity of the New Testament was morally superior to the Old Testament. In addition, there was nationalist German anti-Semitism (Paul de Lagarde), and racial anti-Semitism, which was part of popular anti-Semitism. The Czech and Moravian Jews were the most intelligent of all European Jews, Masaryk, continued. Czech anti-Semitism, proclaimed by the clerical and radical parties, was a disgrace to Czech studenthood.[139]

On 5 November 1901 Masaryk attended a debate of the Union of Czech-Jewish Academics on the topic: "Are the Jews a destructive element?" Masaryk took the floor and said inter alia "antipathy towards Jews is the result of clerical education and superstition. [...] Clericalism, certain customs, non-recognition, a taste for not working, and physiognomic history implant anti-Semitism in us – and it is greater than Christians are willing to admit and Jews are willing to see." Masaryk declared that he was no anti-Semite and was not prejudiced, but he could not be a philo-Semite in the liberal sense. Some kind of residue from his upbringing prevented him from observing Jews impartially.[140]

In 1901 Masaryk was involved in a controversy with the leader of the Old Czechs, F.L.Rieger, over an interview which the latter gave to the Catholic journal *Rozkvět*. Among other things he stated: "By its hatred of Catholicism the People's Party introduces disintegration into the nation, which is a Jewish charac-

---

138) *Die Zeit*, 4. 11. 1899. "Jan Patočka also writes about this in detail in his study Masaryk v boji proti anti-Semitismu (Masaryk in the struggle against anti-Semitism)." In J. Patočka. *Masaryk. (Soubor statí, přednášek a poznámek).* Praha, 1979, pp. 15–16 (samizdat).
139) See "Studentstvo o anti-Semitismu. 'Slavie' a prof. Masaryk", *Českožidovské listy*, 6, 1900, No. 3, pp. 1–2.
140) Cf. "Jsou-li židé element rozkladný", *Českožidovské listy*, 7, 1901, No. 22, p. 3.

teristic. History shows us that Jewry never had a unifying effect, but caused disintegration. That is why I never want the Jewish element to coalesce with our national entity... As far as Professor Masaryk is concerned, I observe that he is an out-and-out personal enemy of the Catholic God and Catholic clergy..."[141]

Masaryk reacted with uncustomary trenchancy in an open letter to Rieger, in which he stated that Rieger was "now hounding the Jews in a spirit of popular anti-Semitism."

THE HILSNER AFFAIR

In 1899 Masaryk was drawn into further conflicts within Czech and Austrian society around the so-called Hilsner Affair, which spilled over from central Europe, and became a European affair, and in fact an international one, in view of the reaction in the USA.

"The campaign surrounding the Hilsner affair was a bad business: it meant doing battle with superstition about ritual murder. I took little interest in the trial until a former student of mine, a Moravian by the name of Sigmund Münz, came from Vienna and prevailed upon me to make a statement. I knew the books by the Berlin theologian Starck dealing with the origins and history of ritual superstition and gave my opinion on the matter to Münz. He made it public in the *Neue Freie Presse* and suddenly I landed in the middle of a melee. Vienna's anti-Semites set the Czech nationalist and clerical press on me, and when they attacked, well, I was forced to defend myself, wasn't I? And having taken the first step, I had to go on. That meant studying criminology and physiology, all of which I wrote about in great detail. When I travelled to Polná to inspect the scene of the crime and its surroundings, they said I'd been bribed by the Jews. A group of non-students came to my lectures to shout me down. While they shouted, I wrote a protest against their stupid calumnies on the blackboard, calling upon them to give me the reasons for their demonstration. (Only one of them did so; he came to see me that afternoon, a slender, decent young man who later became the poet Otakar Theer.) To make certain the

---

141) Quoted from S. Polák. *T. G. Masaryk. Za ideálem a pravdou.* Vol. 4. Praha, 2005, p. 78.

demonstrators did not think I was afraid of them, I walked all around the lecture hall, challenging them to argue their points; no one dared. And how did the University react? Instead of taking a strong stand and restoring order, it suspended my lectures for a fortnight. That evening the demonstrators came to my house. I was in bed with a chill, so my wife went down to them and told them I was ill but if they wanted to speak to me they could send up a delegation. No one came. I felt very bad about the affair not so much for myself as for the low level of it all. Yet during the war I came to realize how useful it had been. The world press is partly managed or financed by Jews; they knew me from the Hilsner case and repaid me by writing sympathetically about our cause – or fairly at least. That helped us a great deal politically."[142]

The accusation of ritual murder, in addition to the accusation of desecration of the communion host and the poisoning of wells, was one of the most frequent allegations against Jews in the Middle Ages. The consequences were pogroms against the Jews, burning alive or drowning, and individual murders. The absurd superstition that Jews needed Christian blood, either for "curing" themselves, or to mix into matzos before Passover, first appeared in 1144 in the English city of Norwich, and spread throughout Christian Europe, including the Czech lands until the 19th century.[143]

It was not even eliminated later in the period of Jewish emancipation, when anti-Judaism was transformed into anti-Semitism, whether economically or nationally motivated anti-Semitism, or racially-motivated anti-Semitism, which is the worst of all.[144]

The first accusation of ritual murder in the 19th century occurred in 1882 in the Hungarian town of Tiszaeszlár and exacerbated the growing atmosphere of anti-Semitism in central Europe. That was followed by similar incidents on the Greek island of Corfu in 1891, and the German town of Xanten during the years 1891–1892. In 1893 a Viennese priest, Josef Deckert pub-

142) K. Čapek. *Talks with Masaryk*, pp. 167–168.
143) For details see A. Pařík. "Obvinění z rituální vraždy a Hilsnerova aféra I", *Střední Evropa*, 16, 2000, No 101, pp. 105–111.
144) See A. Pařík. "Obvinění z rituální vraždy a Hilsnerova aféra II", *Střední Evropa*, 16, 2000, No. 102, pp. 105–114.

lished a pamphlet about the case of Simon of Trent from 1475 claiming to have "documentary evidence" of ritual murder.[145]

Accusations of ritual murder also surfaced in the Czech lands in the eighteen-eighties and nineties. They were provided with a "modern" ideological basis by August Rohling, a professor of the Prague theological faculty of the then German university, in his book *Der Talmudjude* (1871). By 1876, it had already run to three editions in Czech translation. In it – and in a later book, in which he replied to criticism on the part of rabbis – Rohling defended and expanded on the theory of ritual murder. His book was widely read throughout the Czech lands and gave rise to a number of anti-Jewish incidents, until its further publication was eventually banned.

When girls went missing in Falknov and Kojetín in 1887, links were made with the Tiszaeszlár incident, and it led to anti-Jewish violence in Kojetín. Similar incidents occurred in Nové Benátky in 1892 and in Kolín in 1893. In Kolín, when a missing girl was found dead, the case was publicised in the public press as ritual murder, which led to anti-Jewish demonstrations on such a scale that troops had to be called in to suppress them. There were instances of blood libel even after the Hilsner affair, the last being in January 1900. They all resulted in anti-Jewish riots, the looting of Jewish shops, attacks on Jewish schools, etc. Reports of ritual murder allegations and the stealing of blood were zealously circulated by the Catholic and anti-Semitic press.[146]

On 1 April 1899 a young girl, Anežka Hrůzová, was found dead in a wood not far from Polná, on the borders of Bohemia and Moravia. It was just before Passover and the rumour started to circulate that she had been ritually murdered by Jews to take her blood. A young Jew from Polná, Leopold Hilsner, was accused of the murder. In September he was found guilty by a jury

---

145) See previous footnote.
146) See in particular: M. Frankl. "Obvinění z rituální vraždy v Kolíně", *Dějiny a současnost*, 20, 1998, No. 6, pp. 14–18; idem. "Obvinění z rituální vraždy v českém anti-Semitismu na konci 19. století." In *Hilsnerova aféra a česká společnost 1899–1999*. Praha, 1999, pp. 152–159; H. J. Kieval. "Death and the Nation: Ritual Murder as Political Discourse in the Czech Lands", *Jewish History*, 10, 1996, No. 1, pp. 77–91; A. Pařík. "Obvinění z rituální vraždy a Hilsnerova aféra III", *Střední Evropa*, 16, 2000, No. 103, pp. 110–118.

at Kutná Hora, on the basis of evidence from so-called eyewitnesses, and sentenced to death. Masaryk intervened on behalf of Hilsner (see below). As a result, a retrial was held about a year later (in October 1900) at Písek, and in spite of expert testimony Hilsner was once more sentenced to death – only the references to ritual murder were withdrawn. After the Emperor commuted the sentence to life imprisonment, Hilsner spent the next eighteen years in prison before being amnestied in 1918. He lived another ten years under a different name, receiving occasion financial assistance from Masaryk via the Czechoslovak Embassy in Vienna. His conviction was never annulled.[147]

The death sentence on Hilsner was passed on 16 September 1899, shortly before the fall of Count Thun's government in Vienna, caused by the opposition of German deputies to attempts

---

147) In Communist Czechoslovakia it was not possible to write about the Hilsner case and Masaryk's role in it. The only available literature, although difficult to access, was E. Rychnovsky. "The struggle against the ritual murder superstition." In *Thomas G. Masaryk and the Jews, a collection of essays*, or historical documentation in libraries, where these had not been discarded. The exception was 1968 which saw the publication of an article by Z. Solle. "Malá česká dreyfusiáda", *Dějiny a současnost*, 10, 1968, No. 5, pp. 20–22, and a slim volume by B. Černý. *Vražda v Polné*. Praha, 1968. During the period of harsh neo-Stalinist normalisation Patočka's study "Masaryk v boji proti anti-Semitismu" was published in samizdat, in: J. Patočka. *Masaryk. (Soubor statí, přednášek a poznámek)*. Praha, 1979, pp. 1–92, which described the events of the entire Hilsner affair in detail. After freedom was restored in 1989 Bohumil Černý's book was re-published under the title. *Justiční omyl – Hilsneriáda*. Praha, 1990, and other works were published, including: H. Krejčová. "Hilsneriáda", *Dějiny a současnost*, 14, 1992, No. 3, pp. 20–24, and a seminal work by J. Kovtun. *Tajuplná vražda*. Případ Leopolda Hilsnera. Praha, 1994. The hundredth anniversary of the Hilsner affair saw the publication of several works, such as the collection *Hilsnerova aféra a česká společnost 1899–1999*. Praha, 1999; B. Adler. *Boj o Polnou*. Polná, 1999; the collection *Hilsneriáda (k 100. výročí 1899–1999)*. Polná, 1999; the above cited work by Pařík; *Modernizace, identita, stereotyp, konflikt. Společnost po Hilsneriádě*, ed. B. Soukupová, and P. Salner. Bratislava, 2004. A number of studies on the issue of anti-Semitism in the Czech lands were published in specialist journals. Finally in 2006 there was published the originally samizdat study by Jan Patočka: "Masaryk v boji proti anti-Semitismu." In J. Patočka. Češi. Vol. 2. Praha, 2006 (= Collected writings of Jan Patočka, 13), pp. 33–112. A summary of literature on the Hilsner affair is provided by J. Prchal. *Hilsneriáda. Výběrová bibliografie*. Polná, 2000, p. 20.

to change the relative status of the Czech and German languages in the Czech lands.

The repeal of the language ordinances in October sparked anti-government unrest among the Czech populace, and demonstrations were suppressed by detachments of the army and police. In many cases the riots were directed against the Jewish population. In Prague and in several other Czech and Moravian towns it led to bloody conflicts. The protests against the Jews and the Germans spread to other towns and resulted in deaths, and dozens were wounded.[148]

There was also an anti-Semitic demonstration in Polná on 29 October, where the gendarmerie were obliged to intervene.[149]

The anti-Semitic agitation spilled over into the Vienna parliament and the nationalist and clerical press. Long-established Austrian anti-Semitism had put forth its fruit.

At the time of the trial at Kutná Hora in September 1899, at which Hilsner was sentenced to death, Masaryk had spent the entire summer at Bystřice pod Hostýnem and took no interest at all in the proceedings. Before he returned to Prague he received a letter from one of his students, the future writer, historian and sociologist Sigmund Münz. Münz wrote to him of his astonishment at the anti-Semitic reporting of the second trial of Dreyfus and the Polná case in Czech newspapers, including the "liberal" and progressive press.[150]

Masaryk replied to Münz in a letter which was published by the Viennese daily *Neue Freie Presse* on 29 September. After commenting on the Dreyfus trial Masaryk writes: "Concerning the trial at Kutná Hora, I don't want to dwell on 'ritual murder'. This is a closed issue, both culturally and historically. But allow me the following comment on this case. Anti-Semites tirelessly portray Jews as the epitome of shrewdness and cunning, so how do these characteristics equate with the brutally frenzied crime in Polná? If some evidently secret society or sect wanted human blood, its insane criminal instinct would lead it to seek its unknown victims – to be abducted alive – in larger towns, not in the countryside. That is my attitude to all of the cases presented

148) J. Kovtun. *Tajuplná vražda*, pp. 243–251.
149) Ibid., p 263.
150) Ibid., p. 236.

as ritual murder in the recent period; the murder at Polná goes against all the assumptions that anti-Semites themselves entertain regarding a secretly conducted ritual murder. But if indeed a poor wretch would be found somewhere who would fall prey to anti-Semitic suggestions, this case would also be the fault of anti-Semitism and its vile propaganda.

The way I see it, at the present time anti-Semitic superstition about ritual murder is chiefly of economic significance. The anti-Semites pretend that they want to liberate people from economic vampires, but in fact the people, or popular classes are in fact being prepared by economic fetishism for vampires of every kind, of Jewish and Christian persuasion alike.

As one can see, this anti-Semitic superstition is widespread and international; so it is appropriate for all those opposed to it to act jointly. If the present statement can contribute in some way to achieving this, you may publish it as you see fit. Your obedient servant, T.G. Masaryk."[151]

After Masaryk had acquainted himself with the records of the Kutná Hora trial and the medical report of Dr Josef Bulova, as well as the evidence of the investigating judge Baudyš, he wrote a pamphlet *Nutnost revidovat proces polenský* (The urgent need to review the Polná trial),[152] in which he rejected the supersitition about ritual murder: "Certainly a Christian must not maintain that ritual murder results from the spirit of the Jewish religion; after all a Christian accepts the entire Old Testament, and does that have such a spirit? The Talmud doesn't preach ritual murder either. Nor is there any secret sect practising ritual murder."[153]

The *Prager Tagblatt* published an excerpt from the pamphlet on 7 November, and the entire issue and the pamphlet itself were confiscated. *Národní listy, Radikální listy* and *Katolické listy* immediately attacked Masaryk and his proposal for a trial review. Nonetheless, on 9 November Masaryk's pamphlet was the subject of an interpellation in the Vienna parliament and could thereby be published. It came out in German on 11 November in *Die Zeit*[154] and it was also published in Czech.

151) Ibid., p. 237.
152) Praha, 1899, 16 pp.
153) J. Kovtun. *Tajuplná vražda*, pp. 270–271.
154) T. G. Masaryk. "Die Notwendigkeit der Revision des Polnaer Prozesses (Interpellation Kronawetter)", *Beilage zu Nr. 267 der Zeit*, 11. 11. 1899.

Masaryk's pamphlet was not, as Masaryk said, "written for the Jews – it was written for the Czech intelligentsia, so that it might realize how much lack of judgement, lack of thinking [...] hot-headed rashness, and actual inhumanity and cruelty, exists among us, and the intelligentsia in particular. It is an amoral situation. [...] I demand from intellectual leaders the right to freedom of thought..."

Masaryk ended: "... I will not allow myself to be shouted down and denounced by anyone using baseless legal formalities and crude lies about bribery and other allegations..."[155]

Masaryk did not oppose the students' right to demonstrations. He criticised *Národní listy, Radikální listy* and *Katolické listy* for the way they wrote about his pamphlet, and how they lied and incited.

The demonstrators had no idea what his concern was regarding the Polná trial. It was not anti-Semitism, but the trial as such. Masaryk was simply investigating whether the trial was "classic evidence for ritual murder". It has proved that it wasn't and was waiting for it to be admitted soon. However, a review of the trial would not solve the issue of anti-Semitism, it would simply show that no ritual murder had taken place at Polná.

Anti-Semitism could take many forms: clerical, Zionist, socialist (Marx), etc. The opposite of anti-Semitism was not philo-Semitism.

Masaryk published his findings after studying the stenographic record, as was his right. He took no orders from anyone in the matter. He raised the issue of the official confiscation in a parliamentary interpellation.

"I won't allow anyone to crush me, and I will not give in to lies and misconstrued slogans."[156]

Masaryk published articles under the titles of "Proclamation" and "The Urgent Need to Review the Polná Trial". The former stated that Masaryk had written his study of the Polná trial independently, without speaking to or consulting anyone about it. He had simply received a report from Dr Bulova and studied the

---

155) T. G. Masaryk. "České veřejnosti", Čas, 13, 1898–1899, No. 46, 11. 11. 1899, pp. 728–729.
156) T. G. Masaryk. "Ještě slovo o těch demonstracích", Čas, 13, 1898–1899, No. 48, 25. 11. 1899, pp. 754–755. After the confiscation of the second edition. It contains what he wanted say on 11 November.

stenographic record. Bulova and Masaryk had come to the same conclusions – "after logical consideration, the same facts lead to the same conclusions".

In the article: "The Urgent Need to Review the Polná Trial", Masaryk set out seven reasons why the trial should be reviewed and ended by stating that his study was a "critique of various facts and ideas."[157]

In a further article: "The Urgent Need to Review the Polná Trial II", Masaryk refuted the objections of judge.[158] He proved that the corpse had been transferred to the site of the supposed murder. The wound indicated that Anežka's throat had not been cut.

In a letter to Kanner (the editor of *Die Zeit*) Masaryk set out his plan for further action, whose aim was the release of Hilsner on moral grounds, and he expressed optimism that the trial would be reviewed. On 18 November 1899, Masaryk published an article in *Die Zeit* entitled "The Myth of Ritual Murder in the Light of the Polná Trial", in which he dealt with his general conclusions from his analysis of the murder. The article was the germ of his second pamphlet about the case. It was an afterword to the first pamphlet and the starting point for the second pamphlet, in which it was included as the sixth chapter.[159]

Masaryk's articles and the two pamphlets about the Hilsner case were written and published at the time of Masaryk's sharpest arguments with students at the university during November and December 1899. Masaryk's lectures suffered interruptions until the end of the winter semester of 1900. Masaryk was also the target of a campaigns of slander, both from the German nationalists and anti-Semites in the Vienna parliament and from their press, and also from the Czech anti-Semitic radicals, clericals and nationalists, published in *Radikální listy, Katolické listy, Národní politika, Národní listy,* and *Šípy* among others. Masaryk

---

157) Prof. Masaryk. "Prohlášení", *Čas*, 13, 1898–1899, No. 48, 25. 11. 1899, pp. 760; Nutnost revidovati proces polenský, ibid., pp. 760–761.
158) T. G. M. "Nutnost revidovati proces polenský II", *Čas*, 13, 1898–1899, No. 49, 2. 12. 1899, pp. 779–780.
159) T. G. Masaryk. "Der Aberglaube des Ritualmordes im Lichte des Polnauer Prozesses", *Die Zeit*, 21, 1899, No. 268, 18. 11., pp. 97–99; J. Patočka. "Masaryk v boji proti anti-Semitismu." In J. Patočka. Češi. Vol. 2. Praha, 2006 (= Collected writings of Jan Patočka, 13), p. 69.

received support only from his own papers: *Čas* and *Naše doba,* as well as from the social-democratic *Právo lidu* and *Studentské směry*, and also *Studentský sborník*.[160]

In late 1899, and early 1900, there were signs of a favourable reaction from Austrian and international public opinion to Masaryk's actions over the Hilsner case. The Austrian press noted that the first person to have taken an open stand against anti-Semitism in Austria was a Czech. Masaryk's name became familiar to a wider European public, and he emerged as a significant world figure. He had undergone a telling and challenging trial and stood the test. He had matured in that hard political battle and proved capable of heading a struggle in support of his own political programme.[161]

Masaryk tried to have the confiscation of the first pamphlet cancelled. He failed in his attempt during the first trial, but the trial received a lot of publicity in the foreign press and was a moral victory for Masaryk, demonstrating his energy and courage.[162]

Masaryk's reasons for intervening in the Polná affair were summarized as follows by Jiří Kovtun: "He was not concerned about one man. He was concerned about principles, and launched a major offensive in their support. He became convinced that the blood libel was as dangerous in the moral world as dangerous epidemics are in the physical world. He felt he had a mission to halt this infection and heal the patient. And he started to work tirelessly at that task."[163]

Masaryk himself subsequently explained the reasons for his involvement in the Hilsner case when replying to Karl Lueger in the Vienna parliament on 5 December 1907: "I then wrote a pamphlet, not in order to defend Hilsner, but in order to protect Christians from superstition. It distressed me that such a sinister superstition could be based – I must admit –on opinions put about by doctors and other authorities... As I said, I was not defending Hilsner; it is a matter for the police and justice to

---

160) For details see J. Patočka. *Masaryk. (Soubor statí, přednášek a poznámek).* Praha, 1979, and J. Kovtun. *Tajuplná vražda*, pp. 275–308.

161) J. Patočka. "Masaryk v boji proti anti-Semitismu." In J. Patočka. *Masaryk*, pp. 41–43.

162) Ibid., pp. 44–46.

163) J. Kovtun. *Tajuplná vražda*, pp. 267. See also J. Kovtun. "Proč Masaryk zasáhl do Hilsnerova případu", *Polensko*, 8, 1999, No. 1, pp. 1–2.

ascertain whether or not he is guilty. I stepped in not to defend the Jews, that is their affair, but in order to sweep away our people's superstition, because in my view every superstition is harmful, and this one in particular..."[164]

In his foreword to the second pamphlet on the affair Masaryk stated inter alia: "A nation that so unthinkingly succumbs to a clerical superstition about ritual murder will naturally succumb to all superstitions. But I repeat: in the Polná case it is not the nation, the people who should be blamed, but its leaders, doctors, lawyer, clergy and journalists. In particular, therefore, the clerical anti-Semitic misuse of the Polná trial is – for all those who have not yet lost their reason – a warning!"

The pamphlet consisted of the following sections: I. The self-indictment of the sworn Polná experts; II. A demonstration of anatomical philology; III. Alleged exsanguination; IV. The time and place of the Polná crime; V. Regarding the psychological motivation of the Polná crime; VI. The logical construction of the accused's guilt. Masaryk concluded the last section with the words: "The entire Polná trial and its anti-Semitic exploitation is an assault on common sense and humanity." The original record of the trial and the autopsy report were included as an appendix.

In a brief afterword, Masaryk wrote (how timely!) inter alia: "...my critique of the Polná trial has taught me that the state of politics corresponds to wider social conditions. *Our politics reflect our conditions in general...*" [Emphasis M.P.] Masaryk concluded the afterword by saying: "I would now like to bring this study of the Polná case to a close by expressing the wish that it should help eradicate the ritual murder myth. It became clearer and clearer to me as I worked on it that the ritual murder myth is a terrible indictment of the Czech nation. Czech Jews and the Jews of the Czech lands in general (as confirmed by many educated and highly critical experts on Judaism) are among the elite not only of Austrian Jewry, but of Jewry in general. How it is possible to impute to them a barbaric ritual murder?! And if among these educated Jews of high moral standing there was a ritual sect – how barbaric would the general cultural condi-

---

164) J. Kovtun. *Slovo má poslanec Masaryk*. Praha, 1991, pp. 213–214; also T. G. Masaryk. *Parlamentní projevy 1907–1914*. Praha, 2002, pp. 75–80.

tions of us Christians have to be for such a sect to evolve and maintain itself?! The more one reflects on the ritual murder myth the more absurd it appears, and more dangerous for our people. It is a myth that blinds people and coarsens them – this is graphically evident in the Polná trial, on a large and small scale... Only an honourable, energetic and factually conducted review can end the cultural, religious, legal and medical disgrace of the Kutná Hora trial."[165]

In February 1900 Masaryk published the first of a series of articles in *Naše doba*.

Masaryk opened his article with the words: "...the reader will soon realize that belief in ritual murder is unjustified, that it truly is a myth; this realization will also reveal the social and political destructiveness of clerical anti-Semitism which is the main problem in our country. Only this realization and conviction that the ritual murder myth is dangerous for us as a nation and it opens the gates to superstition and violence [...] prompted me to put this article together."

In his introduction, Masaryk described the course of the anti-Semitic debates in the Vienna parliament in November and detailed the arguments advanced by supporters of the ritual murder theory. In the next section he demonstrated convincingly what pseudo-scientific sources they based themselves on – all of them crude forgeries. He highlighted the detrimental role played by Professor Rohling, a protégé of Archbishop Schönborn of Prague. Rohling was regarded as the leading authority on the theory of ritual murder, but in the end he had to leave public life and Vienna in disgrace. In the final part he informed the reader about the main scientific works that disproved the theory of ritual murder (Starck, Delitzsch), and analysed the Trent and Damascus cases of so-called ritual murder in 1475 and 1840. He concluded his article in these words: "Anti-Semites are blind tools of a clericalism that is seeking to restore its spiritual and secular power, a clericalism that is striving for spiritual blindness, a soul-destroying clericalism. It is called the Jew, but in reality it is modern science and philosophy, modern free thinking.

---

165) T. G. Masaryk. *Význam procesu polenského pro pověru rituální*. Berlín, 1900.

And does the Czech intelligentsia want to assist this undeniable spiritual murder by means of the myth of ritual murder?"[166]

Forced to take a vacation until the end of the winter semester of 1900, Masaryk used the time to engage in an extensive programme of lectures away from the faculty, where his courses were not renewed until the beginning of the summer term on 19 April.

In 1900 the Czech People's Party (the Realists) published its outline programme, which comprised a section on the Jewish question, drafted by Masaryk (see the chapter Masaryk and the Czech-Jewish Movement).

Radikální listy continued its anti-Semitic campaign against Masaryk. They were supported by the Austrian clerical anti-Semite Schlesinger, who promoted it in parliament, and by the conservative clericalists. Masaryk was actually prevented from staying in a hotel in Písek during the second trial, when he and the editor of *Čas* tried to book rooms. Masaryk was ostracized from Czech society.

Masaryk took great efforts to prepare public opinion for the Písek trial, which took place in October 1900, publishing a number of articles in *Čas,* including on the day when the trial opened (this article was confiscated and appeared with a few minor alterations the next day), and in the course of the trial.

On 14 November 1900 a verdict was reached at Písek, whereby Hilsner was declared guilty of being an accessory to the murder of Anežka Hrůzová, and guilty of the murder of Marie Klímová[167], and he was once more sentenced to death. There was no mention of ritual murder, but the propagators of the myth triumphed in the charges, among other things in the fact that the Kutná Hora indictment was used as the basis for the trial in Písek.

In the subsequent three trials Masaryk was sentenced to fines; the anti-Semitic press continued to slander him, claiming that he had changed his father's Czech name from Masařík to Masaryk, etc.

---

166) T. G. Masaryk. "O pověře rituelní. Antisemitská debata parlamentní", *Naše doba*, 7, 1900, pp. 321–335, 481–491, 579–589.

167) Marie Klímová, a servant, was murdered not far from Polná in 1898. She had been missing since July and her body was found in a wood at the end of October 1898. The two cases were linked in the trial of Hilsner. For details see, among others, J. Kovtun. *Tajuplná vražda*. Praha, 1994.

On 23 November 1913, the Union of Czech Progressive Jews (founded in 1907) organized a rally to protest the Beilis trial in Russia (Beilis was charged with ritual murder but acquitted by a jury). T.G.Masaryk spoke at the rally, informing his audience of the situation of five to six million Jews living in Russia, and emphasising the high level of anti-Semitism prevailing there. He stated that since 1905, 37 thousand Jews had died in pogroms on the territory of Russia. Then he drew a profile for his listeners of two "experts" who had proved the existence of ritual murder in Kiev, the psychiatrist Sikorsky and the Catholic priest by the name of Justinas Pranaitis. He declared that responsibility for the Kiev trial lay with the Russian intelligentsia. At the end of the rally a resolution was passed calling, among other things, for a review of the Polná trial.

In his *Memories of Masaryk* Edvard Lederer mentions a conversation he had with him at the time of the Hilsner affair, when Masaryk said: "I always considered the Jews of Bohemia to be the elite of all Jewry in the monarchy. Consequently I was very disappointed to hear such expressions from among them, as, 'If only this Hilsner affair was over, even if they convicted him.' Such a wish is unworthy of a person who loves justice. Even if Hilsner is a tramp, he is still an innocent man found guilty. I entered this case, not because I was a philo-Semite, but because of a deeply felt humanity and because the disgrace of the belief in the ritual murder would fall upon the Czechish [sic] people. If a group of people could live among the Czechs for centuries and use human blood for ritual purposes, it would show what little culture the Czech nation has, since it has failed to educate this primitive people to true humanity over a period of centuries."[168]

Masaryk spoke about the Hilsner affair with hindsight in 1914 in an article for *Čas* entitled "Ty židovské peníze" [That Jewish money].[169]

Although there was a certain ambivalence in Masaryk's views on anti-Semitism – perhaps as a result of his need to overcome the anti-Judaism of his childhood years, or of its residue – when

---

168) E. Lederer. "Memories of Masaryk." In *Thomas G. Masaryk and the Jews.*
169) T. G. M. "Ty židovské peníze", *Čas*, 28, 1914, No. 62, 4. 3., pp. 2–3. More recently in T. G. Masaryk. *Politika vědou a uměním. Texty z let 1911–1914*. Praha, 2011, pp. 387–389.

the time came to act, when Hilsner was accused of ritual murder – that quintessence of anti-Semitic prejudice – Masaryk did not hesitate and took up the fight, and his opponents were legion: Austrian and German anti-Semites, Czech anti-Semites, whether nationalist, radical or clerical, as well as the students who had been turned against him. He experienced an enormous media campaign targeted against him, and was called a traitor to his people and ostracised from it. He was accused of accepting Jewish bribes, publicly upbraided, and personally attacked. Although Masaryk failed to achieve Hilsner's release – which was not, in fact, his intention – he emerged from the Hilsner affair as the moral victor, fortified for the battles that still awaited him. Masaryk helped rid the Czech nation of absurd myths about ritual murder. News of his involvement in the affair spread round the world and gained him sympathizers from Europe to the United States.

6. Masaryk and the Czech Jewish movement

I don't believe in the Czechization of the Jews as it was carried out in the previous generation – from both sides. Jewish and Christian. I don't believe in merely mechanical means; I do not value Czechization in name only; I don't believe in that electoral or other deviousness.

T.G.Masaryk in *Čas*, March 1914

THE STATUS OF JEWS IN THE CZECH LANDS POST-1650

After 1650 the situation of Jews in the Bohemian kingdom started to change for the worse. That year the Bohemian parliament rescinded the imperial charter of Ferdinand II (1619–1637) and introduced a number of restrictions related to Jewish economic activity. Jews were no longer allowed to impose tolls or duties, employ Christian servants, or to trade on Sundays and holy days, and they were obliged to leave localities where they had not resided before 1618.

Emperor Leopold I (King of Bohemia 1657–1705), ratified the decision of the Bohemian parliament of 1650, but he shifted the date of their expulsion to 1657 (the year he came to power), thereby preserving the existing extent of Jewish settlement. During his reign Jews had to leave a number of towns, including Kadaň, Tábor, Pardubice, Teplice, Týn and Planá. In 1670, Jews were also expelled from Vienna, and some of them settled in rural communities in Bohemia and Moravia. In 1679, a so-called "reduction commission" was set up to draw up proposals for reducing the number of Jews in Prague. From the mid-17th century to the reign of Joseph II (1780), "official anti-Semitism" was the policy of the state authorities. Although it slowed down after the plague in Prague in 1680 and the fire in the Prague Ghetto in 1689, it reached its peak during the reigns of Charles VI (1711–1740) and Maria Theresa (1740–1780). In 1724, the authorities carried out a detailed census of the Jewish population in the Czech lands (except Prague); according to its results there were 30,000 Jews in Bohemia and 20,000 in Moravia. (According to a later census in 1729 there were 10,207 Jews in Prague.) On the basis of the census a so-called "*familianten Gesetz*" was promulgated, a law fixing the number of Jewish families in Bohemia at 8,451 and in Moravia at 5,106 (*numerus clausus*). This law, which remained in force until the revolutions of 1848/49, meant that only married (or widowed) Jews and their offspring had the right to reside in the country; after the death of the father, that right passed to the eldest son, who alone had the right to marry and start a family. If the other sons wanted to marry, they had to leave the country; most of them went to Hungary or Poland. Families with only daughters were considered "extinct", and the daughters could only marry abroad.

That same year, 1726, a so-called Translocation Rescript was enacted which prescribed the places to which Jews could move (rural Jews were not allowed to move to Prague). Jews were required to move to restricted areas, and if they were in villages and smaller towns and mixed with the Christian population, they had to move to places reserved for them. The worst measures, however, were taken during the reign of Maria Teresa – the last monarch in Europe to expel Jews – who, between 1744 and 1745, expelled the Jews from the Bohemian Kingdom, on the pretext that they were collaborating with the Prussians. Under pressure from the estates and after protests from abroad, they were allowed to return to their original places of domicile (including Prague) for a period of ten years. In 1758 they were permitted to remain there on condition of paying an annual "tolerance tax" that was introduced in 1748. The *familianten Gesetz* and the *numerus clausus* were confirmed. In 1762 the authorities issued a further discriminatory regulation ordering Jews to wear yellow markings on their clothes. Toward the end of her reign (in 1777) Maria Teresa expelled the Jews from her domain at Hodonín.[170]

---

170) See T. Pěkný. *Historie Židův Čechách a na Moravě*, pp. 90–106.

LAWS CONCERNING JEWS IN THE REIGN
OF JOSEPH II

A major change came about in the status of Jews came about during the reign of Joseph II (1780–1790), who, in accordance with his policy of enlightened absolutism, decided to make the Jews useful subjects of his modern, reformed, centralized state. He issued as number of tolerance edicts and decrees concerning the Jews, which initiated a process that led to the granting of further freedoms to Jews in the years 1848/49 and their eventual civic emancipation in 1867. "Tolerance patents" were issued in 1781 for Bohemia and Silesia, in 1782 for Moravia and Lower Austria, in 1783 for Hungary, and in 1789 for Galicia.

First and foremost Jews were no longer required to wear yellow markings, and in the economic sphere they were permitted to engage in all crafts and trades (with several restrictions, such as milling of grain), as well as to establish guilds and factories, rent farms (but they were not allowed to buy or own land), engage in commerce, visit royal boroughs, and, on market days, to lodge with Christians under the same roof.

In the sphere of schooling and education, larger Jewish communities had to set up their own German-Jewish primary schools, where the subjects taught included German (i.e. it was the introduction of secular schooling.) Jewish children in smaller communities could attend the state-run Christian schools. In further education, Jews could attend the normal secondary school, where the language of instruction was German, as well as university (except for the theological faculty).

Jews started to be liable to compulsory military service; in commercial, official and public correspondence they had to abandon Hebrew or Yiddish in favour of German; they had to adopt German names, and in accordance with the legal reforms they were subject to the same jurisdiction as Christians in civil and criminal matters. The rabbinical court was abolished, and Jewish courts could only deal with marital disputes and religious matters.

Jews were no longer obliged to live in ghettoes, but this ordinance was implemented in a dilatory fashion and only fully came into force in 1848.

All these regulations in the fields of education and the courts, such as the use of German as a teaching and official language, and then as the language of communication, as well as the adoption of German names, coupled with the spread of Jewish Enlightenment (*Haskalah*) from Germany to the Czech lands, resulted in a marked Germanization of the Jewish population. However, this subsequently started to change during the second half of the 19th century after the 1848–49 revolution, as the Czech culture and language gained ascendance over German. As a result, after leaving the ghettoes, many Jews found themselves in predominantly Czech towns, and above all in Czech-speaking villages, and they started to use Czech and attend Czech schools, etc.

Nevertheless, the Josephinian reforms did not yet accord Jews equal status with the newly-tolerated adherents of non-Catholic religions. The tolerance tax and *familianten Gesetz* remained in force until 1848, along with a number of other special taxes.

All the Josephian reforms relating to the Jews were summarised in the so-called *Systemalpatent* of 1797, which remained in force until the revolution of 1848. This slightly increased the number of Jewish families permitted to reside in Bohemia and Moravia, fixed the level of tolerance tax, and laid down conditions for eldest sons to marry: they had to submit a certificate of knowledge of German, a certificate of Jewish religious knowledge attested by a rabbi, also in German, and they also had to submit a declaration of assets. Jews were still prohibited from changing their residence without permission. If they moved somewhere else within the Austrian empire they had to pay a charge equivalent to 10% of their assets; a charge of 20% applied if they moved abroad.

The *Systemalpatent* prohibited Jews from having Christian apprentices or employing farm workers, as well as buying real estate outside the ghetto, being employed as civil servants, or becoming members of the bourgeoisie. Jews were also subjected to other commercial restrictions. Only Jews baptised into the Christian religion could own land or enter the civil service.

Rabbis had to have a German education and pass examinations in German. From 1800 even Jewish cantors and teachers of religion had to have a command of German.[171]

---

171) Ibid., pp. 107–120.

JEWISH EMANCIPATION

Thanks to his reforms, the reign of Joseph II (1780–1790) opened the way to Jewish emancipation. The process was accelerated thanks chiefly to the secular education of Jewish children in German-language Jewish schools, where they were taught the German language, arithmetic, geography and ethics. This undermined traditional religious schooling in the cheder or yeshiva (the lower and higher levels of Jewish education). Coupled with this were religious reforms (the rise of reform Judaism), and administrative reform of Jewish communities. The traditional Jewish world was disrupted in favour of the modern world ushered in by the Enlightenment.

(In this respect the Austrian monarchy was the first European country to initiate the process of Jewish emancipation. It was followed by France: after the revolution Jews were accorded equal rights with all other citizens in 1791. The French revolutionary and Napoleonic armies then extended the equality of Jews to Holland, Italy and the German states, including the Rhineland and the Hanseatic towns. After the fall of Napoleon in 1815, there was a partial regression to pre-revolutionary conditions in some countries.)

In Bohemia and Moravia the process of Jewish emancipation was by no means straightforward. The *Systemalpatent* of 1797 determined the legal status of Jews until the revolution of 1848. Nevertheless there were attempts to revise it, which eventually succeeded in 1841, during the reign of Ferdinand V (1825–1848), when the *familianten Gesetz* was relaxed, and provisions regarding expulsion of Jews were rescinded. Deportation was abolished as a punishment, and the purchase and renting of demesne and municipal land, but not other types of land, was permitted. The tolerance tax and the numerus clausus remained in force

In the revolutionary year of 1848 there were 75,000 Jews living in Bohemia and 38,000 in Moravia. The Jewish intelligentsia, which had grown meanwhile in the Austrian monarchy (including Bohemia and Moravia), thanks to the Josephinian reforms, took an active part in the pre-revolutionary ferment, as well as in the actual revolutionary events in Vienna, Prague, Budapest and other cities. The 1848 revolution was another important milestone on the path to Jewish emancipation; it brought about the abolition of the *familianten Gesetz* and the numerus clausus for rural Jews; also abolished were the institution of the inkolat (feudal residential rights), the tolerance tax and ghettoes. Jews were accorded freedom of movement and settlement, and access to public employment, such as teachers in state schools. (Although the freedoms gained by the Jews were called into question and restricted after the revolution there was no return to pre-revolutionary conditions.)

Following the abolition of the ghettoes, thousands of Jews moved from the overcrowded cities to mostly Czech small towns and villages in the period 1848–1870. When the period of neo-absolutism came to an end, Jews were given unrestricted rights to own land, which enabled them to settle en masse in the Czech countryside. However, from the end of the 1860s, some Jews started to abandon poorer rural areas and return to the industrial and commercial centres of Bohemia and Moravia (though no longer to ghettoes), where they engaged in business, trade and academic life. Thus a population of poor Jews prior to 1848 was gradually transformed into well-off members of the rural and urban middle class, and by the end of the 19th century there emerged a Jewish bourgeoisie.

The process of Jewish emancipation culminated in 1867, in the transformed dualist monarchy of Austria-Hungary, when Jews achieved political and civic equality before the law, as well as passive and active electoral rights, the right to acquire assets of all kinds and engage in any business, etc. This brought about a positive change in their legal, economic and social standing.

However, in the period between the 1848 revolution and the completion of the emancipation process, other problems arose for the Jews, namely, how to maintain their specific Jewish identity in the face of the process of assimilation, first with the German and then with the Czech nation, both of which had inhabited the Czech lands for centuries.

ASSIMILATION

One result of Jewish emancipation was the decline of traditional values and ties among the Jews. In their efforts to be assimilated into the nations amongst which they lived, emancipated Jews discarded their national and cultural traditions, adopted that nation's language and many of them converted to Christianity.

In the bi-national Bohemian kingdom, however, they faced the choice of which ethnic group they were to favour – the Germans or the Czechs. At first it was not a real choice, because the Josephinian reforms had steered them clearly along the path of German culture and the German language, which had been introduced as compulsory in German Jewish primary schools. The first generations of the Jewish intelligentsia that emerged prior to the revolution of 1848 asserted themselves chiefly in literature and journalism, since they still had no access to the civil service. Jewish authors from Bohemia and Moravia in the first half of the 19th century wrote in German, although they often opted for Czech and Jewish themes. The best known of them were Moritz Hartmann, L.A.Frankl, Salomon Kohn and Leopold Kompert. Many Jews were confirmed in their pro-German orientation when Siegfried Kapper's efforts in favour of Jewish assimilation with the Czech nation were rebuffed by Karel Havliček Borovský in 1846. Those efforts were premature – the revived Czech nation was seeking its own identity at the time and was obliged to differentiate itself vis-à-vis the German nation and was unable to absorb another ethnic group. By contrast, the Jewish population's drift toward Germanness was supported by the Austrian government, which started to introduce liberal reforms after 1860. Moreover, Jews had the Austrian government to thank for the constitution of 1867, which completed their emancipation process. So it seemed that the assimilation process of the Jewish population in Bohemia and Moravia was resolved in favour of Germanic identity, language and culture. Against the background of the Czech-German conflict at the end of the second half of the 19th century, when the Czech nation was gradually gaining the upper hand, a process was taking place in which a significant section of the Jewish population was inclining towards assimilation with the Czech nation, language and culture. (This process continued practically to the end of the first Czechoslovak Republic, confirmed by census results in 1921 and 1930.)

The opening of the ghettoes after the 1848 revolution, the opportunity for Jews to settle anywhere in Bohemia and Moravia, and above all, in the countryside, the opportunity to buy land and obtain an education in Czech schools, from which the first generation of the Czech Jewish intelligentsia emerged in the 1870s – these were the main factors of Czech-Jewish assimilation.

1876 is regarded as the beginning of an organised Czech Jewish movement, when the Association of Czech Academic Jews was founded as a totally non-political organisation. The members of the movement favoured the nation into which they were born and lived, and they supported the Czech ethnic group and its endeavours in confrontation with Germanness. Its founders included Leopold Katz (1854–1927), Adolf Stránský, the founder of *Lidové noviny* (1855–1931), Jakub Scharf (1857–1922), and Augustin Stein (1854–1927), who became the first Czech president of the Jewish Religious Community in Prague and first editor of the *Czech Jewish Almanac*, an annual that was published from 1881 to 1938. In the 1880s and 1890s, Jews began to have a growing influence on the development of Czech industry and trade (Bohumil Bondy, Jaromír Prager, Leopold Pollak).

Czech Jewish associations and press organs continued to be established until World War I, including, in 1883, Or Tomid, an association for promoting worship in the Czech language, in 1893, the National Czech Jewish Union (which had started to publish *Českožidovské listy* [Czech Jewish Press] in 1894), in 1897, the Czech Jewish Political Union, in 1904, the weekly *Rozvoj* [Development] (Viktor Vohryzek), and in 1907, the Union of Czech Progressive Jews. They were supporters of Masaryk, and foremost among them were Viktor Vohryzek (1864–1918), Edvard Lederer-Leda (1859–1944), Bohdan Klineberger, Viktor Teytz and Max Lederer. The group left the Young Czechs and largely inclined towards Masaryk's Czech People's Party (Realists), founded by Masaryk in 1900, which set out its attitude to the Jews in the fifth chapter of the party's programme. Some of them, including Viktor Vohryzek and Edvard Lederer, became activists in the party; Jindřich Kohn and Lederer were members of its wider executive committee. Czech Jewish assimilation was propagated and defended by Jindřich Kohn (1874–1935), who took over from Vohryzek as the intellectual leader of the Czech Jewish movement, which was the wellspring of many Czech Jewish writers from Vojtěch Rakous to Viktor Fischl and Arnošt Lustig.[172]

---

172) For more detail see H. Krejčová. "Kalendář českožidovský 1881-1938." In *Židovská ročenka, 5750/1989-1990*. Praha, *1990*, pp. 127-132.

As mentioned earlier, one of the first to suggest the integration of Jews into the Czech nation was Siegfried Kapper (1821–1879),[173] a writer and poet writing in Czech and German, who was born into a Jewish family in Prague. In the years prior to 1848 he championed the emancipation of Czechs and Jews. He drew his literary inspiration from the Czech and southern Slav milieu; in his writing on Jewish themes he stressed the patriotism of Czech Jews. In his poetry collection České listy [Czech pages] (1846) he identified with the Czech cause and urged Jews assimilate and work for emancipation. His ideas were strongly rebuffed by the leading Czech journalist Karel Havlíček Borovský in České včela [The Czech Bee] in its issue of November 6, 1846.

However, another Czech revivalist involved in the discussion about integrating Jews into Czech life, Václav B. Nebeský, took the part of the Jews and endeavoured to win them for the Czech cause.[174]

In his review of Kapper's collection Havlíček recommended the Jews to assimilate with the Germans:

"It is well known that in our columns Nebeský once powerfully and gallantly wielded a sword in defence of Jewry, albeit needlessly, since none of us who read Czech literature oppress the Jews. However, as regards the other aspect of the ideas of Mr Nebeský and now Mr Kapper also, namely that Jews living in the Czech lands should regard themselves as Czechs, we can only regard this idea as false and very mistaken. For the Israelites cannot be considered solely in terms of faith and religion, in the sense that Czechs can be Catholic, Protestant, Mosaic, or possibly Mohammedan, but also in terms of origin and nationality. And how can Israelites belong to the Czech nation, when they are by origin Semitic? It would be easier to consider Germans, Frenchmen, Spaniards, Englishmen, and so on, to be part our nation than Jews, since these nations all have more in common with us than Jews do. Thus it cannot be said that Jewish inhabitants of Bohemia or Moravia are Czechs practising the Mosaic religion. We must consider them to be a special Semitic nation

---

173) About Kapper see H. Krejčová. "Siegfried Kapper, symbol českožidovského hnutí." In Židovská ročenka, 5751/1990–1991. Praha, 1991, pp. 86–87.
174) See V. B. Nebeský. "Židovské vzpomínky", Česká včela, 1. IV. and subs., 1845.

that happens to live among us and sometimes understands our language or can speak it. And experience shows that the attitude from which we perceive the Jews is correct. Because, clearly, all Jews – regardless of the country or the part of the world they inhabit – perceive themselves to be one nation, to be brothers, and not merely to be fellow believers. And the bond that binds them one to another is much stronger than the one that binds them to the country they inhabit. There is surely no need to prove that one cannot have two homelands, two nationalities, or serve two masters. Therefore, anyone who wishes to be a Czech must cease to be a Jew."[175]

Havlíček later moderated his position: "...When we consider the condition of the Jew without any prejudice and with a rather more seasoned eye, i.e. with knowledge of the history of humankind, we immediately observe that their former subjection and their lack of equal rights with us brought them to the present level of their customs and manners, and that they themselves bear only little or no blame for their present debasement. Previous regimes generally exploited the Jews, demanding such high taxes that it was impossible for them to make a living by honest means, because those regimes regarded Jews as some kind of living silver or gold mines, which can be mined incessantly; moreover the Jew was excluded from the most important human rights on the basis of unchristian prejudice, contrary to the true spirit of Christ, and was not allowed to buy property and land, was not allowed to engage in certain trades, and even had to buy the right to marry for an extortionate sum, and meanwhile endure enormous ignominy and ostracism in his life. Is it any wonder that in these circumstances the Jew had no love of Christians who treated him in such an unchristian fashion? Is it any wonder that, being weak and oppressed, he used all sorts of covert ways to harm his enemies and considered that anything, even the worst kind of behaviour was permitted against them? Is it any wonder that, having no rights, no honour in public life, he just piled up money in every legal and illicit way, in order to use it at least underhandedly, by bribery, to better himself? – No

---

175) K. Havlíček Borovský. "České listy od Sigfrída Kappera", *Česká včela*, 6, 20. 11. 1846. English translation in: *The Jews of Bohemia and Moravia: A Historical Reader*, ed. W. Iggers. Detroit, 1992.

it's no wonder whatsoever, and one can rightly say in respect of Jews: As you made them, so you have them..."[176]

T.G.Masaryk said the following regarding the Jewish question at the time of Havlíček: "In the days of Havlíček the Jewish question in our country became more pressing.

In 1848 anti-Jewish riots and what caused them were commonplace: the Jews sided with the German nation and regime against us; by and large the Jews were pioneers of capitalist entrepreneurship, and the mass of our people still held to the views of an agricultural population in feudal bondage. And so the Jews put themselves on the same footing as foreigners. Havlíček himself [...] says that it goes without saying that our working people suffer neglect 'in factories belonging by and large to foreigners or Jews'.

When Siegfried Kapper's České listy appeared in 1846, Havlíček reviewed it in the Česká včela (November 6), and criticised it from a literary angle; he made efforts to make justify his criticism as convincingly as possible, because he didn't want the Jews to join us.

This was because in Česká včela the previous year (April 1, 1845 and subsequent issues, under title of 'Jewish Reminiscences') Nebeský had warmly defended the Jews, quoting inter alia Hamann's statement that they are 'a wonder' and Molitor's that they are the 'crown of humanity', who were forced nonetheless to wear yellow patches on their coats because of ignorance and intolerance.[177] At that time (in Vienna) Nebeský made efforts to win over Jews – including Kapper – for our literature. Havlíček called it an eccentric whim and attributed the genesis of Czech Pages to it, and not to the author's own compulsion. For those reasons Havlíček did not want Jews to be regarded as Czechs." At this point Masaryk cites essentially the same passage of Havlíček from Česká včela as above. Masaryk then continues: "Havlíček concedes that the Jews are in an invidious position at a time when a powerful idea of nationhood prevails, because it would not be practical to have hope in the renewed national independence of the Jews and seek to promote

176) K. Havlíček Borovský. "Emancipace Židů", Slovan, 12. 10. 1850.
177) Johann Georg Hamann (1730–1788), German philosopher and writer; Wilhelm Molitor (1819–1880), German poet and Roman Catholic priest.

the Hebrew language – Havlíček believes they should accept the modern idea of nationhood, but should join the Germans, since they have already adopted their language de facto, as can be best observed in the case of the Polish and Hungarian Jews.

That rejection of the Jews goes against Havlíček's theory of what constitutes the basis of nationhood. The fact is that he himself conceives nationhood mainly in terms of language; his position was impossible to maintain, and so Havlíček modified his views into a much more moderate anti-Semitism.

When the constitution gave the Jews equality, many people opposed their emancipation. In *Slovan* (I/1850) [...] Havlíček has an article entitled 'The Emancipation of the Jews'. [...] He had received a letter from the town of Soutice in which the correspondent fulminates against an anti-Semitic sermon by the local priest; Havlíček prints the letter and sets out his own opinion on the matter.

There is now doubt, however, that having achieved equal rights with us the Jews will discard most of their character defects, since such defects are unlikely to be a characteristic of the Israelite tribe (every nation is bound to be equally virtuous and wicked), but only a matter of circumstances. It is obvious to anyone who has some experience of the world that the behaviour of the Jews in our country is similar to that of the Armenians and Greeks in Turkey, and is more or less common to all oppressed nations who live among their oppressors.

However, one cannot expect that the mere proclamation of equal rights to mean an overnight change, with all the Jews divesting themselves of their old Adam, and starting to shine with all the virtues of free citizens with equal rights: what has been engendered in that tribe down the ages will take more than a year or a day to alter; but what time has ruined, time will repair. Let us also contribute to this reform of Jewry, let us also treat our Israelite fellow citizens as people with equal rights; let us not humiliate or denigrate them; let us not annoy them in any way; and if they still adhere to many well-known past customs, let us tolerate them for the time being, being aware of their causes. Besides Christians have it in their power to defend themselves from all reprehensible behaviour generally ascribed to the Jews. Don't let yourself be cheated, don't recklessly make debts, be careful: these are practically all the rules we need to defend ourselves. So

I regard all talk of Jewish emancipation causing us great harm as pointless and exaggerated. If we are truly such a wretched and villainous nation that a few thousand Jews outstrip and surpass us in all trade, etc., then truly we are not even worth the pity!

But this is not the case, and soon we will find out that the emancipation of the Jews has not harmed us at all by and large, but has actually been of benefit, just as any just cause must be of benefit. And I don't care what anyone says: all political oppression is unjust.

And it goes without saying that for their part the Jews ought to behave like citizens with equal rights, using those newly-acquired rights with care and not provoking people against them; in particular they should show greater favour to the country that is their homeland, and not treat it like mere foreigners. This would certainly hasten their recognition by their other fellow citizens."[178]

In 1890, under the title "K židovské otázce" [Regarding the Jewish question] the journal Čas had published a response to an article in its issues 18 and 19; the response was received from "an anonymous reader" who was "an authority on the Czech Jews". The author was Masaryk.

It is a critique of the Czech Jews for having so far shown preference for the Germans and the German language.

Masaryk declared that the Jews were a nationality. Jews had a different attitude to the Czech nation than a Protestant or Orthodox Czech to Catholics, for instance. It was possible to accept the negative stance of the Jews who had no understanding for the "childish displays" of menacing Czechness and regarded it as unprofitable. It was different in Hungary, where the Hungarians had been victorious and the Jews quickly realized it. "The Czechs failed, so the Czech Jews stuck to their German."

"And so we observe the actions of the Jews calmly and dispassionately." If the Jews wanted to live among the Czech like the Germans, the Czechs would defend themselves against them, as a nation, as they did against the Germans. Every Jew was bound to know how to rid himself of the choice between two nations,

---

178) T. G. Masaryk. *Karel Havlíček. Snahy a tužby politického probuzení.* The quotation is from the 1920 edition, pp. 445–451.

neither of which wants him: it was to be found in the Old Testament Book of Ruth.[179]

Masaryk had drafted Point 9 of the Programme of the Czech People's [Realist] Party (founded in the spring of 1900, and renamed the Czech Progressive Party in 1906), which dealt with the Jewish question. The Programme stated inter alia that the Jews display "duplicity and incoherence". The foundation of their morality and world view was the Old Testament, which expressed their religion and older philosophy. In addition to the Old Testament, Jews adopted the general culture and are "frequently at the forefront of that culture". Jewish philosophy and the Jewish attitude to the world in general was strangely incoherent. It was both "too negative towards progress" and "outdatedly clerical", and "of course, Jewish clericalism is scholastic Talmudism, and again strange. [...] Having been cruelly suppressed and persecuted for so long, they could not yet fully forgive their Christian oppressors; it is a well-known fact that the oppressed take revenge, and precisely because they are oppressed, they take revenge as stealthily as possible, indirectly." Noting that the Jews were emancipated in 1848, it stated: "this freedom went to their heads." This could also be observed among the Czech population, but the rising generation is shedding this parvenu characteristic, and that was visible among the Jewish generation that has already grown up outside the ghetto. Jews were "socially one-sided" and "make use of their freedom in economic ways". When comparing impartially Jews and Christians, the programme continued, "it would be very unlikely to find precise evidence for the widespread assertion that Jews are worse than us Christians." The Czechs spoke highly of the Jews' level of education, entrepreneurship, "moderation and sense of family." Anti-Semitism would be unable to take root among the Czechs but for "the unchristian use of the pulpit, and the pandering to the worst instincts of the masses by part of the press."

---

179) "K židovské otázce", *Čas,* 4, 1890, No. 32, 9. 8., pp. 497–500. Also S. Polák. *T. G. Masaryk. Za ideálem a pravdou.* Vol. 2, p. 252 and footnote 66 on page 420, in which the author compares the text of "K židovské otázce" with a text by Charlotte Masaryk, "The Persecution of the Jews", and expresses the view that the texts are very similar and that Masaryk's authorship of the first text is indisputable.

The programme addressed the issues of anti-Semitism, assimilation, and Zionism.

"We distinguish between several types of anti-Semitism. In this country there is clerical anti-Semitism, which is specifically Catholic (or Orthodox), and propagates the blood libel; and there is Protestant anti-Semitism, which is more philosophical; in addition, there is nationalist (racist) anti-Semitism, and economic anti-Semitism. [...] Because it is superstitious and uneducated, clerical anti-Semitism is violent." Anti-Semitism did not analyse social evil, but sought it where it did not exist. It exaggerated and overestimated the Jews' significance and influence. "In our view the Jewish question can only be solved by a truly new cultural and philosophical synthesis, and by a genuine reform of moral and religious life – both Jewish and Christian."

Assimilation tended not to be precisely defined. Currently it was racial, which should precede cultural assimilation. Both the Czechs and the Jews had to reform.

The party was sympathetic towards Zionism, which was not ashamed of its Jewishness, while recognising the moral defects of Jewry. It was not the job of the Realists to discourage the Jews from colonising Palestine, "but we believe that the main and higher task of the present time is reform everywhere, and particularly at home. [...] We demand tolerance vis-à-vis the Jews in every case and in every way, and we roundly condemn all violence, and, in particular, we absolutely reject the myth of ritual murder propagated by clericalism and used to further its ends, and now by the radicals, also."[180]

Masaryk's students included Czech Jews and Jews supported his publications (Čas, *Naše doba, Athenaeum*) and his Realists party, whose progressive and liberal programme was more acceptable to Jews, in terms of its social and economic policies, than the programme of the Young Czechs. When Masaryk left the Young Czechs in 1893 and returned to parliament in 1907 for the Realist Party – thanks to the support of the Social-Democratic Party – the Czech Jews remained loyal to him.

Disillusioned with the Young Czechs, the Czech Jews switched their support to the Masaryk's Realists party, the Radical Progressive Party and the Social-Democratic Party. It was

---

180) See *Rámcový program české strany lidové (realistické)*. Praha, *1900*.

above all the younger generation of Czech Jews, such as the aforementioned Viktor Vohryzek, Bohdan Klineberger, Jindřich Kohn, Viktor Teytz, Edvard Lederer-Leda, and Max Lederer, who abandoned the Young Czechs for Masaryk's party.

Viktor Vohryzek was a prominent figure of the Czech Jewish movement. He was a convinced supporter of Masaryk, who influenced him chiefly by his arguments in favour of religion without denominational boundaries, as well as his idea that there was no need for a mediator between God and man.

Vohryzek wrote a book entitled *Epištoly k českým židům* [Letters to Czech Jews]. In its first section he reflected on the reasons for a thousand years of Jewish suffering, and concluded that it was to do with human nature. He put forward several theories for this: We live in a century of social contradictions and we Jews are declared to be harmful. We cannot be a harmful race, because Christ and the apostles sprang from us. Our principles gave rise to Christianity, the Lord's Prayer and the Psalms. Jews are described with every possible bad attribute, irrespective of the fact that Kollár, Zeyer and Vrchlický depicted Jews in a more favourable light. We have no Heine or Börne. We built factories, etc.

Second section: Our question is a religious question. Racial anti-Semitism is only a cover for religious anti-Semitism. "In short our conditions are the culmination of impetuousness and thoughtlessness. We lack moral support." The entire programme of modern Jewish religion was to be found in the verse of Isaiah: "nation shall not lift up sword against nation."

The third section comprises notes on the national economy and indicates the contribution of Jews to the country's industrial development in such centres as Náchod, Hronov, Úpice, Hořice, Hlinsko, Rosice, and Pardubice. Regarding the problem of alcoholism, Vohryzek conceded that there was much truth in the claim that Jews "carried and spread this plague."[181]

Vohryzek contributed an article about Masaryk and the Hilsner affair to an anthology published to mark Masaryk 60th birthday. In his introduction he reflected on how Viennese anti-Semitism was imported into the Czech lands chiefly by the clericalists, and then by the radicals. "Anti-Semitism became

---

181) V. Vohryzek. "Epištoly k českým židům", *Českožidovské listy,* 6, 1900, No. 6, 15. 3., pp. 8–9; No. 8, 14. 4., p. 1; No. 10, 15. 5., pp. 2–3; No. 12, 15. 6., pp. 2–3.

part of the national programme!" After the Young Czechs' candidate Václav Březnovský won a seat in the Vienna parliament in opposition to the Social-Democrats' candidate who had Jewish support, Eduard Grégr could declare: "As of today the whole of Prague now finds itself in the camp of anti-Semitism." The Polná affair was a radical/clerical anti-Semitic mixture that flourished in the soil prepared by Czech journalism. Throughout the Bohemian kingdom everyone apart from the Jews believed the myth of ritual murder. Czech doctors and German journalism, etc., had played a dismal role.

After the Kutná Hora trial Masaryk took a stand with his pamphlet, which was confiscated. "Although a layman, Masaryk, the philosopher and sociologist, subjected the entire affair to detailed expert scientific analysis..." and he wrote a book that threw completely new light on the entire matter. However, the verdict was a foregone conclusion and the defendant was still (in 1910) in prison. Nevertheless the myth of ritual murder had suffered a blow, but would only disappear when the church no longer had influence, "when the reign of darkness ends."

Masaryk had stirred up the Polná question in the interest of the Czech people and thereby roused many Jews from their lethargy. "Masaryk showed us how to solve the Jewish question: simply by progress, love for the truth, fortitude, integrity and consistency at all times and in all matters."[182]

An article about Masaryk by Vohryzek appeared posthumously in *Rozvoj* in 1919, which adopted a rather critical attitude towards him.

"Masaryk was too much of a Christian, and I think it was his greatest shortcoming, since he had dragged those shackles around for an age and could never be a freethinker! He almost always wanted to demonstrate what he believed, and then couldn't believe what he had demonstrated. [...] His strong point was that he had a good understanding of life, while his weak point was that by nature he was strong and tough, and he was incapable of understanding and forgiving the weak."

---

182) Dr. Vohryzek. "Prof. T. G. Masaryk v procesu polenském." In *T. G. Masarykovi k šedesátým narozeninám*. Praha, 1910, pp. 231–234, 2nd ed. Praha, 1930, pp. 315–320.

He said of Masaryk: "I could not love him and could not find it in me to hate him. I had admiration and respect for him. I held him responsible for the faults of the entire nation..."[183]

Vohryzek's *A Book of Life's Wisdom* includes several observations about Masaryk: "Masaryk deduces, in agreement with Heine, that Christianity had to reform its doctrine by accepting the Old Testament and thereby accommodating psychological conditions." According to Vohryzek, Masaryk says of Protestantism that it partially adopted the Old Testament, borrowing its sense of democracy, and its sense of worldly matters and organisation. The basis of Judaism, originating from the Old Testament, was empathy and worldly wisdom; the faith element was regulated by the practical element.[184]

Another representative of the so-called second generation of Czech Jews was Edvard Lederer-Leda, the author of several books on Jewish themes.[185] Lederer also contributed to the anthology to mark Masaryk 60th birthday.[186] In his article, he explains what he disagreed with Masaryk about: "Chiefly the fact he proclaimed a humanistic ideal in politics [...] also his views on the sexual question, which seem to me too forthright, and his perception of Havlíček as a proponent of humanism, and as having a religiously-based spirit. I tend to consider Havlíček as a liberal, albeit of the highest calibre..."[187]

Lederer explained that he came to know Masaryk personally when the Czech Progressive Party was being founded, and he quotes Masaryk's words regarding the Hilsner affair: "I decided to defend Hilsner because the man was innocent. I was also concerned about the honour of the Czechs. I'm called a traitor to the nation because I couldn't bear its disgrace. [...] What

183) "Z pozůstalosti dra Vohryzka", *Rozvoj* 2, 1919, No. 30, 26. 7., p. 1. In 1923 Vohryzek's selected essays and articles were published under the title *K židovské otázce*. They comprised articles from *Českožidovské listy* (1900), as well as "Epištoly k českým židům", articles from *Rozvoj* (1904–1908), the articles "My a sionisté", "Falešné předpoklady našich odpůrců", and "V boji za lidská práva".
184) V. Vohryzek. *Kniha životní moudrosti*. Praha, 1925.
185) E. Lederer. *Žid v dnešní společnosti*. Praha, 1902; idem. *Kapitoly o židovství a židovstvu*. Vol. 1–2. Praha, 1925.
186) E. Lederer. "Vzpomínky." In *T. G. Masarykovi k šedesátým narozeninám*. Praha, 1910, pp. 287–289.
187) Ibid.

would the world think about the culture of a nation, if the Jews, who had been living amongst us for centuries, could remain cannibals, as they allegedly were, according to those in our nation who spread the myth of ritual murder? [...] These Jews in the Czech lands are the elite of all the Jews in the empire. However, I had a better opinion of them! So many of them called on me to drop the affair, just so they could have peace and quiet. That discredited them in my eyes. After all it wasn't a matter of their reputation and their peace of mind, but of an innocent man! I don't care if he's a vagrant, or what he is – he's a man!" Lederer then praises Masaryk highly, but without any kind of sycophancy.[188]

Viktor Vohryzek's successor was the philosopher and lawyer Jindřich Kohn, who was closest to Masaryk and was involved with him. He was a political activist in Masaryk's Realists party and contributed to *Čas*. Kohn devoted a number of articles to Masaryk, which were published as a collection with the title *Asimilace a věky* [Assimilation and ages].[189] In one of them, under the title "Masaryk (A Political Profile)", he outlined Masaryk's main contribution to Czech national life: principles and their impact, concreteness and certainty were Masaryk's constant concern. He was a political realist, who emphasised right living and social self-discipline. Masaryk believed that Czech radicalism "should be derived from personal courage" and it must never lose sight of "personal responsibility." Throughout his life Masaryk had swum against the tide "calmly and without agitation or playing the martyr." He had disproved Marxism, wanting the individual to improve society. He hadn't underestimated the political significance of historical awareness. He wanted to continue "the spiritual emancipation from German influence", and relied on German scholarship least of all; "he was most prolific in promoting cultural relations with the Slavonic world." His political goal was Czech national independence and the independence of Czech politics. His political activity had been universal, "pointing Czech politics towards a distant future." He had worked for a programme of "internal political improvement" – i.e. autono-

188) Ibid.
189) *J. Kohn. Asimilace a věky*. Vol. 1–3. Praha, 1936.

my. Masaryk's humanism was the "goal and natural justification of all Czech national demands."[190]

In the introductory article in the publication *Masaryk a židovství* [Masaryk and Judaism] Kohn declares that it was natural for the Jewish diaspora to turn its attention to Masaryk's school of thought because "...Masaryk unites in unique fashion the logic of a highly developed, scientifically-trained brain and the wisdom of a heart which had experienced the drama of imperfect humanity."[191] The Jewish diaspora was particularly well-fitted to evaluate for itself and the world specific wisdom of Masaryk, irrespective of the fact that Masaryk made a contribution to human rights "...in the anti-Semitic zone of contagious irritation" and he gave "a part of the Czech-Jewish assimilationist movement an opportunity to lead a meaningful life on a personal basis ..." It was necessary to distinguish between two Jewish questions, one positive, the other concrete. This could be done by studying the wisdom expressed in Masaryk's works. Masaryk's humanistic wisdom developed from seeing the Czech question in the light of the question of humanity and vice versa. Masaryk created a people's school of thought that assisted "a new style of historical self-development." The same was needed by the Jewish diaspora, which was aware that liberation from the Jewish ghetto of modern anti-Semitism would be in vain without the liberating efforts of the people of the ghetto.[192]

The personality and work of Jindřich Kohn were studied in the 1960s by Josef Vyskočil (1922–1992) who published a number of essays about him as the basis of a major study.[193]

---

190) Ibid., pp. 1–5.
191) J. Kohn. "Masaryk's School of Thought and its Relation to Judaism." In *Thomas G. Masaryk and the Jews*, pp. 25–47.
192) Ibid., pp. 25–30.
193) J. Vyskočil. "Filosof dějinně ontologického pojetí humanity", *Filosofický časopis*, 13, 1965, No. 4, pp. 615–629; "K humanologickému systému Jindřicha Kohna", *Filosofický časopis*, 14, 1966, No. 5, pp. 629–642; "Českožidovské hnutí. K 90. výročí založení Spolku českých akademiků židů", *Dějiny a současnost*, 8, 1966, No. 4 a 5, pp. 18–20, 26–28; "Die tschechisch-jüdische Bewegung", *Judaica Bohemiae*, 3, 1, 1967, pp. 36–56; "Asimilace a věky. K základním myšlenkám humanologie Jindřicha Kohna," *Plamen*, 9, 1967, No. 12, pp. 79–81; "Perspektivy člověka ve světle humanitní ideologie." In *Židovská ročenka 1967–1968*. Praha, 1967, pp. 47–50; "Jindřich Kohn o židovství a lidství." In *Židovská*

Most recent studies of Jindřich Kohn include those of Jiří Franěk,[194] who has lectured about him, and of Kateřina Čapková, who gave prominence to Kohn in her work on the national identity of Jews in the Czech lands from 1918 to 1938.[195]

It is necessary to stress that although Jindřich Kohn was the ideologist of the Czech-Jewish movement, he regarded Zionism, alongside assimilation, as an equally valid solution to the situation of the Jews.[196] "Let those who have a Jewish sense of their Czech identity call themselves Jews. Those who have a Czech sense of their Czech identity are Czechs. Let us preserve both currents, and the sincerity of our final intentions," Kohn declared in 1918.[197]

In a letter to the editors of *Rozvoj*, published in its issue of 1st January 1904, Masaryk commented favourably on the decision to publish the journal weekly from 1904, as well as on the editors' intention to cover the religious movement and campaign for a broadening of the reform movement. He recommended them to take note of the influence of non-Czech Jews and of Jews outside the country.

In 1904 Masaryk said the following about the Jewish question: "It always seemed to me that the way the so-called Jewish question had been tackled so far was a tangle of insincerity, cunning and timidity on both sides."

According to Viktor Teytz, it was a rebuke that must have made every Jew's blood boil. Maybe external pressure compelled many Jews into Czechness, "for which they were not yet ripe – but we cannot be accused of cunning and insincerity, and certainly not with such a sweeping generalisation that is surprising coming from a scientist."[198]

---

ročenka 1971–1972. Praha, 1971, pp. 49-52; "Sté výročí narození Jindřicha Kohna (1874-1974)." In *Židovská ročenka 1974–1975*. Praha, 1974, pp. 21-28.

194) J. Franěk. "Jindřich Kohn." In *Masarykův sborník, Vol. 11–12*. Praha, 2004, pp. 254-265.

195) K. Čapková. Češi, Němci, Židé? *Národní identita Židů v Čechách 1918–1938*. Praha, *2005*.

196) See K. Čapková. Češi, Němci, Židé?, p. 152.

197) J. Kohn. "My a sionisté, *Rozhled*, 44, 1918, p. 3, cited in K. Čapková. *Češi, Němci, Židé?*, p. 152 and footnote 184 on p. 299.

198) V. Teytz. "Česká veřejnost", *Českožidovské listy*, 10, 1904, No. 2, 15. 1., p. 4.

During his sojourn in America in 1907, Masaryk gave an interview to the *Hebrew Standard,* in which he spoke about the Hilsner affair and expressed sympathy for Zionism, while he spoke guardedly about assimilation. When the content of the interview came to the attention of the Czecho-Jews, their reaction was one of disappointment, "furore and painful indignation", as Vohryzek and Pleschner wrote to Masaryk on behalf of the assimilationists. In 1909 the weekly *Wschod*, published in Lemberg, carried an interview given by Masaryk to its Vienna correspondent Dr Löwenherz. Soon afterwards the Zionist *Selbstwehr* weekly reprinted some parts of it, including: "The future and revival of the Jews depends on them alone. I am therefore overjoyed to hear of every movement that seeks to organise the Jews and bring about their revival.

"I regard Zionism as just such a movement. What I like most about the Zionist movement in terms of a popular movement is the openness with which it approaches all Jewish issues. I was impressed by the manfulness with which the Zionist leaders demand the implementation of their demands. I have respect for a social Zionist movement that is totally democratic... I accept that assimilation as a popular movement is impractical and laughable; besides, recent decades have proved definitively that for all its efforts assimilation has not achieved any real successes."[199]

This upset the Czecho-Jews and they demanded an explanation from Masaryk, who reacted in an interview in *Rozvoj* of 9 April 1909, conducted by its editor Viktor Teytz. Masaryk said he was misquoted in the interview in *Selbstwehr*. Regarding Zionism, Masaryk stated that he had had in mind only the general idea of Zionism as a way of awakening the self-consciousness of the Jewish masses in Poland and Russia. He declared the notion of colonising Palestine to be utopian and cited the example of New York, from which the hundreds of thousands of Jewish immigrants had no intention of emigrating to Palestine. "An emigration policy will not solve the Jewish question. [...] I didn't speak about assimilation in the way it was reproduced. [...]

---

199) J. Patočka." Masaryk v boji proti anti-Semitismu." In J. Patočka. *Masaryk,* p. 85.

I had in mind assimilation by blood, and I said that it was not possible for the time being, being prevented both by law and by Jewish prejudice. Cultural assimilation is, naturally, justifiable and natural [...] Of course Jews can become Czech in a cultural sense, but there still remains a difference; the different origin and race that cannot be precisely determined, religion, tradition. The traditions will disappear, of course, and there is no doubt that Jews who are indifferent to religion are much closer to us...

"It goes without saying that *Jews ought to take part in Czech political life*. Besides, this has already happened in our Progressive Party: Jews occupy leading posts in it and there are a number of them in our Executive Committee, and they all consider it something quite normal. The Jews must also win their rights politically: they must try to change not only the law but also society's attitude to them. Anti-Semitism need not be viewed tragically: there was and still is greater hatred of us and the social democrats, than there is of Jews."[200]

Several days later Masaryk gave a lecture about the programme of the Progressive Party and its attitude to Zionism and assimilation.

Nevertheless Masaryk repeated his reservations about assimilation later, such as in an interview in *Čas* on 4 March 1914, "...I do not believe in the Czechization of the Jews as it was conducted in the previous generation – on both sides, Jewish and Czech. I don't believe in purely mechanical means and have no regard for Czechization in name only, or achieving it by ballot or other sophistry."[201]

200) Dr. Teytz. "Rozmluva s prof. Masarykem", *Rozvoj*, 3, 1909, No.15, 9. 4., pp. 4–5.
201) T. G. M. "Ty židovské peníze", *Čas,* 28, 1914, No. 62, 4. 3., p. 3.

7. Masaryk and Zionism to 1918

As far as Zionism is concerned, I consider it the Jewish nation's hope of the future, and no one must give up such hope. In every way I like Zionism for its characterfulness. It has within it a potency of will and lends a certain character to Jewish life.
T.G.Masaryk for the Jewish daily *Haint*, 1924

At the end of the 19th century Zionism also established itself in the Czech lands as a national movement aimed at setting up a Jewish homeland in Palestine. Its founder, Theodor Herzl, the author of *The Jewish State* (1896), organiser of the 1st Zionist Congress in Basel (1897) and founder of the World Zionist Organisation, urged Czech and Moravian Jews not to assimilate with either the Czechs or Germans, and instead opt for a Jewish national orientation. However most of those Jewish Zionists were German-speaking and had a German cultural orientation. In 1899, those Jews set up the first Zionist association *Zion* and the same year two other associations merged to form the *Bar Kochba association*, headed by Hugo Bergmann, a librarian at the university library (and later rector of the Hebrew University in Jerusalem). Martin Buber, one of the pioneers of so-called cultural Zionism, gave a talk on Judaism the association, which influenced a considerable section of Prague's Jews. The weekly *Selbstwehr* was founded in 1907, and was an important exponent of Zionism until its demise at the end of the first Czechoslovak Republic. During the first republic Zionism did not represent a numerically strong component of Jewry (unlike in Poland, for instance). Nonetheless its significance grew in the nineteen-thirties with the rise of Nazism in Germany, and it helped to save the lives of at least the small section of Jewish youth that emigrated to Palestine in time. Sadly a tragic fate awaited the assimilated

Jews who were prepared to stand up for the republic.[202]

T.G.Masaryk dealt with the issue of the *nation* in detail shortly after he took up his appointment at the newly created Czech university in Prague in 1882. In 1883 he published three reviews of books by Ernest Renan ("Ernest Renan on Nationality"; "Ernest Renan on Jewry as a Race and Religion"; "Ernest Renan on Science and Islamism"). [203] In the second of these he clearly regards the Jews as a nation, long before the "father" of political Zionism Theodor Herzl, and indeed, as a nation mixed with other nations to only a relatively small extent, and then with Semitic rather than Indo-Aryan nations – a matter on which he disagreed with Renan.

Masaryk dealt with the same issue in his practical philosophy lectures in the years 1884–1885, entitled *Practical Philosophy on the Basis of Sociology.*[204] At the conclusion of those lectures, in the section on human races and nationalities, he is already talking about the Jews as a considerably mixed nation. It was precisely the factual mixing of nations and races that Masaryk used as grounds for dismissing Gobineau's racial theory of pure blood and race. Countering it, Masaryk raised the issue of a nation's character, its historical development, struggle for national ideals, the awareness of a nation's historicity, and even the question of being a chosen nation, which does not mean elevating it above other nations, or disdaining them.

The Jewish question (and not just Zionism) occupied Masaryk's attention throughout his life. In *The Social Question* of 1898–1899, in which he dealt with Marx and his perception of the Jewish question, he writes inter alia: "Marx ignores the national, tribal aspect of the Jewish question – and yet it exists. The Jews are a nation of their own, even if they have lost touch with their spoken language. But language is not the only or most important mark of nationality."[205] Regarding Zionism, Masaryk actually states, when writing about the need for a revival of the Jewish

202) For a detailed recent account see K. Čapková. Češi, Němci, Židé?, pp. 178–195.
203) *Sborník historický, Vol. 1*. Praha, 1883. (ed. A. Rezek).
204) For more detail see J. Opat. *Filozof a politik T. G. Masaryk 1882–1893*, pp. 75–99.
205) T. G. Masaryk. *Otázka sociální*. Vol. 2. Praha, 1936, p. 180.

nation: "I consider Zionism to be part of this revivalist activity. I don't mean emigration to Palestine – Jews can happily remain where they are; but they must understand that their moral character and their entire attitude to the world need to be remedied."[206]

Masaryk spoke about Zionism at greater length in Kronberger's book *Zionists and Christians*[207,] published in Leipzig in 1900 and dedicated to him:

"I very much like the Zionist movement. Trying to understand it in terms of the present, I value its nationalism, and I particularly esteem the fact that oppressed Jews (and to be honest Jews are oppressed everywhere, including in the West) are not ashamed of their nationality.

As to the economic issues surrounding the colonisation of Palestine, I regard the emigration of many Jews there simply as a particular case of the generalised migration of nations in the 19th century; the idea of colonising their original homeland is certainly attractive to Jews and very justifiable. Even though certain critics maintain that certain aspects of the colonisation of Palestine are misguided, this does not disqualify the idea or the goal.

I perceive Zionism above all in moral terms; thinking progressive Jews are aware of the defects in their character and world view, and I see in Zionism, 'a drop of prophetic oil', as the saying goes.

Thinking Jews recognise their complicity in the shortcomings of cultural work heretofore; thinking Jews want regeneration and therefore must go forward in spite of all the general defects of our civilisation. For that a change of locality is not enough. What is required is regeneration from within, regeneration with which Christians also must cooperate as being equally complicit. Unless I am mistaken, the Zionists themselves declare that the colonisation of Palestine is intended only for a certain section of Jews, as a means of assistance; for those who do not emigrate there indeed remains a difficult task.

However, clerical anti-Semitism and chauvinistic nationalism are sociologically and politically blind and because of their narrow-minded naivety are incapable of understanding that the

---

206) Ibid., p. 182.
207) E. Kronberger. *Zionisten und Christen,* Leipzig 1900, pp. 84–85.

growing complexity of social organisation does not rule out an independent, conscious Judaism, but on the contrary, advocates it."

Selbstwehr printed an excerpt from Masaryk's contribution to the collection.[208]

In his *Národnostní filosofie doby novější* [National philosophy of the recent period] of 1905 Masaryk does not directly refer to the Jewish question.

In answer to the question whether in nature there are higher and lower races, he says that there are no aristocratic races. "...there is no inferior race, in the sense of culturally inferior, destined to be slaves..."[209]

Masaryk then turns to the evolution of the national self-consciousness of different European nations and the national philosophies – the Germans, the French, the English, the Russians, the Poles, and the Czechs. He mentions Schopenhauer's anti-Semitism ("he regards Old Testament religion as the cruellest"), and describes Paul Lagarde as the "profoundest philosopher of German nationalism" and a "consistent anti-Semite."[210]

With his favourable views of Zionism Masaryk naturally came into conflict with other significant Jewish movement of the 19th century: the assimilationists. The Czech Jewish assimilationist movement had a long tradition in the Czech lands, dating back to the revolution of 1848/49. Its first organisation was founded in 1876: *Spolek českých akademiků židů* [The Association of Czech Jewish Academics]. Jews rallied to the cause of the Czech nation, which was still oppressed, adopting its language and supporting its emancipatory efforts. (This did not apply to all Jews, of course; a minority aligned itself with German liberalism, retained German as a language and continued to support the Austrian monarchy. The smallest section of Jews started to support the Jewish national movement: Zionism.) In 1907 Czech Jews founded the *Svaz českých pokrokových Židů* [The Association of Czech Progressive Jews], which brought together supporters

208) *Selbstwehr,* 3. 1. 1919.
209) T. G. Masaryk. *Národnostní filosofie doby novější.* 2nd ed. Praha, 1919, pp. 17, 18.
210) Ibid., pp. 25–26

of Masaryk's Realists Party and of the Social Democrats. The Czech Jewish weekly *Rozvoj* was founded in the same year.

One can imagine the disapproval aroused by Masaryk's views on assimilation, when in 1909 he declared: "I accept that assimilation as a popular movement is impractical and laughable; besides, recent decades have proved definitively that for all its efforts assimilation has not achieved any real successes."[211]

Masaryk was obliged to clarify his position, which he did in *Rozvoj*, where his answer was interpreted by the journal's editor (see previous chapter).

Masaryk said the following on the issue of the nation and Zionism: "... There is no one definition of nation, but there are a number of features: language, origin, religion, tradition; but language is the most important. Of course Jews can become Czech in a cultural sense, but there still remains a difference; a different origin, a race that cannot be precisely determined, religion, tradition. The traditions will disappear, of course, and there is no doubt that Jews who are indifferent to religion are much closer to us as regards mentality.

"The importance of religion must not be underestimated, because is isolates culturally and socially. After all is not a misfortune, even though Jews constitute a distinct element in the nation for the time being."[212]

Felix Weltsch writes that Masaryk wanted a more detailed discussion with his Czech Jewish supporters, to inform himself about many things that were not clear to him.

He also did not concern himself with the practical policies of Zionism and was not at all informed about the basis of Zionism in the Czech lands. He said he had not seen any Czech Zionists yet. Zionism, as he repeated on several occasions, interested him solely because it accentuated Jewish self-consciousness.[213]

Felix Weltsch added the comment that Masaryk did not believe that the settlement of Palestine could be a solution to the Jewish question. Masaryk went on to admit that a Jew could be-

211) E. Weltsch. *Masaryk a sionismus*, p. 69. Masaryk's interview for the weekly *Wschod* published in Lemberg (Lwow) was reprinted in the Zionist weekly *Selbstwehr,* founded in 1907.
212) E. Weltsch. *Masaryk a sionismus*, pp. 69–70; also Dr. Teytz. "Rozmluva s profesorem Masarykem o asimilaci", *Rozvoj,* 3, 1909, No. 15, 9. 4., pp. 4–5.
213) E. Weltsch. *Masaryk a sionismus*, p. 70.

come Czech in a cultural sense. Individual cultural assimilation was possible, but not assimilation by blood.

Masaryk's concept was always something profounder, more intrinsic. For that reason, what attracted him most in the Zionist movement was so-called cultural Zionism, represented by the philosopher and man of letters Ahad Ha'am (1856–1927), who demanded the creation in Palestine of a spiritual centre of Judaism, with a view to moral, spiritual and religious regeneration.

Masaryk wrote in 1905 about the issue of liberalism, revivalist currents in Judaism and the influence of Ahad Ha'am: "The crisis of religion is not limited to the Christian church. It is more generalised: it exists in all churches and religions; the religious problem is worldwide and concerns the whole of humanity. In particular the religious crisis also manifests itself among Jews.

As we can see from *Rozvoj* (in Pardubice), the weekly of Czech progressive Jews, there are several contending currents in our country's Jewry: orthodoxy, liberalism (old school), Zionism, and reform Jews (of various shades). *Rozvoj* itself came up with the slogan 'free Jews from the snares of liberalism'; but the reformists also had to take a stand against orthodox Judaism on specific issues, such as the Congress of National Unity of Czech Jews during the discussion on whether to maintain the teaching of Hebrew; the progressive minority (see the speech of Dr Kraus in *Rozvoj* No. 50) is opposed to this because this instruction does not actually teach religion but, some sort of knowledge of Hebrew script. Dr Thein outlines some other proposed reforms (No. 52).

Our Jews will have lots of difficulties with liberalist negation, their task is very onerous. In opposing Austrian clericalism, the church's exclusivity, and the brutishness of anti-Semitism they are obliged to go along with liberalism, like the rest of us; but the question is: how and to what degree?

Concerning anti-Semitism in particular, it occurred to me long ago that our Jews do not go about opposing it the right way; they are not open, direct and energetic enough. In my view anti-Semitism is an injury to us and to us alone, in fact; it harms us, it corrupts and coarsens us; it does not harm the Jews in a material sense, and at the most morally, so long as they try to overcome it negatively, by guile, whereas they ought to overcome it positively, morally and religiously.

I have not got involved in Jewish religious issues, having enough work with our own, but it is impossible not to be aware of the problem and reflect on it. I am indebted to several Jews who understood my interest in their religious question, and who brought to my attention to a thinker from whom one can draw very positive instruction. I refer to Ahad Ha'am."[214]

He returned to the subject of Ahad Ha'am in 1913 in *The Spirit of Russia* in the chapter about the Russian philosopher, mystic and religious thinker Solovyov: "...Solov'ev [sic] did not consider the possibility that the Jews, starting from their own religious foundations, might effect a religious reformation in the modern sense; though availing themselves of the general acquirements of civilisation. This possibility, however, is the leading idea of the Russian Jew Achad-ha-am [sic] (Asher Ginsberg), whose writings on the philosophy of history and the philosophy of religion recall in many respects those of Solov'ev, Dostoevsky, and the Slavophiles. For the consideration of the Jewish question in Russia, and for the understanding of the different parties among the Russian Jews, Achad-ha-am, in so far as he has been translated, is indispensable. I should add that Achad-ha-am's views are rooted in religious mysticism (that of the Chasidim), but that he has attained rank as a modern thinker."[215]

It was not by chance that Masaryk visited the grave of Ahad Ha'am (and the grave of another leading Zionist Max Nordau) in Tel Aviv, during his trip to Palestine in 1927. (Also buried in the cemetery is Max Brod, who died in 1968.)

In 1907 *Rozvoj* featured a news item about an interview Masaryk gave to for the *Jewish Daily News* (Masaryk was then in America), in which he said about Zionism:

"Zionism aroused courage and self-consciousness, which are the essence of the Jewish nation [...] The Jew should be proud of his race and nationality."[216]

In August 1914, during the first days of mobilisation, the German Jewish writers Max Brod and Franz Werfel, together with the philosopher Max Wertheimer, came to the editorial office of

---

214) T. G. Masaryk. "Život církevní a náboženský roku 1904", *Naše doba,* 12, 1905, pp. 522–523.
215) T. G. Masaryk. *The Spirit of Russia. Vol. 2*, p. 240, note I.
216) "Prof. Masaryk a sionismus", *Rozvoj,* 1 (4), 1907, No. 10 (22), 6. 9., p. 4.

Čas to discuss with Masaryk the possibility of publishing a sort of peace proposal in the newspaper. Masaryk was not particularly welcoming and expressed no interest in their proposal, and instead spoke of "entirely different things than those which were closest to our hearts, and dismissed us with comparatively blunt, but not rebuking, words."[217]

Max Brod described the visit as a great disappointment,[218] but he was to write later: "I subsequently admired Masaryk in particulars as a philosopher and ethicist, and as a practical politician; however, I had to reject his basic concept of small states in central Europe."[219]

Seton-Watson's memorandum of a conversation with Masaryk contains the following remarks directed to Prince Thun, Governor of Bohemia, from October 1914: "The Germans of Prague are very aggressive and excited, and as they are mainly Jews, the anti-Semite feeling is growing more acute. It is essential that you (Thun) should hold back the Jews and render them less aggressive ('herausfordend'); otherwise there might be a Jewish Pogrom, and that would only be the beginning, and would be infinitely regrettable."[220]

T.G. Masaryk made a total of four visits to the United States – in 1878, 1902, 1907 and 1918. The reason for his first trip was clear, it was to marry Charlotte Garrigue, whom he had met previously in Leipzig. Masaryk had good English and an extensive knowledge of American history and literature in particular.

In 1902 Masaryk travelled to the USA chiefly to lecture at the University of Chicago. He was then a professor at the Czech University, a member of the Vienna parliament, a successful author, and magazine publisher. For this trip he was assisted by several Americans, chiefly Charles Crane, a Chicago industrialist, who would play an important role in his 1918 trip, and also in Czechoslovak-American relations. Another important figure was Leo Wiener, a Polish Jew and one of the founders of Slavonic studies in the USA, who lectured at Harvard. Ma-

217) See M. Brod. "A Conversation with Professor Masaryk", *Thomas G. Masaryk and the Jews*, p. 282.
218) M. Brod. *Streitbares Leben, 1884–1968*. München, 1969.
219) Ibid.
220) R. W. Seton-Watson. *Masaryk in England*. Cambridge – New York, 1943, p. 41.

saryk knew Wiener from the latter's visit to Prague in 1901, and their acquaintanceship would also continue later. In an article for the weekly *Nation* about the situation in the Czech lands, Wiener also introduced Masaryk to American readers, stressing that Masaryk's political programme envisaged competition between Czech and Germans, and also Jews. He highlighted Masaryk's knowledge of English and his invitation to Chicago. In his lectures and speeches Masaryk focussed on Czech history and literature, Slavonic issues, Austria, and political life in that country. On that occasion he already declared that the Czech lands had been independent in the past and would be independent once more.[221]

In 1907 Masaryk arrived in the United States as a well-known politician, both in Vienna and in the Czech context, whose record included his personal involvement in the scientific and political battles over the Dvůr Králové and Zelená Hora manuscripts, and the Hilsner affair. In Boston he attended a congress of religious liberals and lectured widely. His visit was covered by the Jewish press in articles from August to October. In one article in the *Jewish Exponent* Masaryk was featured as a champion of his Jewish neighbours. In New York, Galician and Bukovina Jews organised a rally in his honour. Masaryk spoke at it at length about the Hilsner affair and his part in it.[222]

Masaryk's last visit to the United States in 1918 was the most important of all. The outcome of Masaryk's strenuous political, diplomatic and organisational efforts was the proclamation of an independent Czechoslovak Republic and its recognition by the United States. He was assisted in that activity by many Zionist Jews, and above all L.D. Brandeis (1856–1941), a member of the Supreme Court and Honorary President of the World Zionist Organisation, which had an influence on President Wilson, as well as by Judge J.W. Mack (1866–1943), first President of the American Jewish Congress, and the important Zionist leader Nahum Sokolow (1861–1937), to whom Masaryk apologised in 1921 for being unable to attend a meeting of the World Zionist Congress in Karlovy Vary.

---

221) J. Kovtun. *Masarykův triumf. Příběh konce velké války.* Praha, 1991, pp. 56–61.
222) Ibid., pp. 61–65.

Later, in *Světová revoluce* [World Revolution, published in English as The Making of a State] Masaryk stated: "In America, as elsewhere, the Jews stood by me; and particularly in America, my former defence of Hilsner [...] did me a good turn. As early as 1907 the New York Jews had given me a gigantic reception. Now I had many personal meetings with representative of Orthodox Jewry as well as with Zionists. Among the latter I must mention Mr. Brandeis, a Judge of the Supreme Court, who came originally from Bohemia and enjoyed President Wilson's confidence and enjoyed his trust. In New York Mr. Mack was a leading Zionist and I met Nahum Sokoloff (sic), the influential Zionist leader. In America, as in Europe, Jewish influence is strong in the press, and it was good that it was not against us. Even those who did not agree with my policy were reserved and impartial."[223] Masaryk was in verbal and written contact with Louis Brandeis. Brandeis reacted to Masaryk's military concept of resistance with his own notions about the future of Europe, and expressed his fears about the news of Polish anti-Semitism.[224]

On 10 September 1918 the Executive Committee of the Zionist Organisation of America sent a message to the Czechoslovak National Council with the following wording:

"Together with all other Americans, we rejoice greatly at President Wilson's declaration that Czechoslovakia is to build an independent national life for itself and will be freed from the Central Powers. We particularly want to note the satisfying relations that have always existed between the Czechs and Slovaks and the Jews of these countries which are now to be united into one State. We trust that the free State of the Czechoslovaks will recognize the rights of all minorities, and we hereby express our gratification at being able to send this declaration to Masaryk, who is one of the noblest statesmen of the Allied Powers." (Zionist archives, File L 6/10/1.)[225]

On 18 and 24 September 1918 the Zionist Organization of America sent Masaryk letters of support signed by its President, J.W. Mack, and in the case of the second letter, also by its Exec-

---

223) T. G. Masaryk. *The Making of a State*. London, 1927, p. 222.

224) *S. Polák. T. G. Masaryk. Za ideálem a pravdou.* Vol. 5, p. *305 and footnote 34* on p. 509.

225) A. M. Rabinowicz. "The Jewish Minority." In *The Jews of Czechoslovakia*. Vol. 1. Philadelphia – New York, 1968, p. 244, note 35.

utive Secretary Jacob de Haas. Masaryk was informed that the organisation's Executive Committee had passed a resolution rejoicing at the establishment of a Czech-Slovak nation, and its accession to the peace association. The organisation stressed the friendly relations between the Czecho-Slovak and Jewish nations and voiced its conviction that the Czechoslovak state that will be created will continue with the protection of rights of all minorities. It also expression satisfaction at the recognition by the American government that was conveyed to T.G.Masaryk as chairman of the Czechoslovak National Council.[226]

After 3 September 1918 (the recognition of the Czechoslovak National Council as the de facto government), Masaryk replied to the American Zionists on behalf of the National Council expressing appreciation for recognition of the Republic. He also expressed his sympathy with Zionism and underlined its moral significance.[227]

The Jewish National Council (JNC) in Prague said that it was greatly pleased with Masaryk's response.

On 8 November 1918 *Selbstwehr* published a message from Masaryk to American Zionists:

On its front page under the headline: "Masaryk for Zionism. Message to American Zionists about Jews in the Czechoslovak State", it stated:

"The newly-established press bureau of the Jewish National Council for the Czechoslovak State has received the following telegram: Stockholm 4 November. The Jewish press bureau in Stockholm announces from New York: Professor T.G.Masaryk, Chairman of the Czechoslovak National Council has sent a message to the Zionist Organization of America, in which he stated that Jews in the future Czechoslovak would *enjoy the same rights* as all other citizens of the state. He also expressed his full sympathy with Zionism. He expressed his conviction that the Zionist movement is *not chauvinistic in character*, but is striving for the

---

226) S. Polák. *T. G. Masaryk. Za ideálem a pravdou. Vol. 5*, pp. 305 and 306 a note 35 on p. 509, which contains the English text held in the T. G. Masaryk Archive.

227) See *Selbstwehr*, 6. 12. 1918, No. 46, taken from the *New Jewish Chronicle* of 11. 10. 1918. The English text is quoted in A. M. Rabinowicz. "*The Jewish Minority*", pp. 165–166.

regeneration of the entire Jewish nation. Masaryk's message received a powerful response around the world."

On page two: Full-page JNC memorandum to the National Committee (Singer, Fischel, Brod):1. Recognition of the Jewish nationality and freedom of individuals to profess that nationality. 2. Full civic equality for the Jewish people. 3. National minority rights for the Jewish people, and the democratization and unification of Jewish communities.[228]

The 6 December 1918 issue of *Selbstwehr* had on its front page a communique of the Jewish National Council about disorderly conduct in Prague, which National Party's newspaper Bohemia blamed on German citizens of Jewish nationality.

On page 4 it carried the authentic text of Masaryk's message and its German translation. The English text came from the *American Jewish Chronicle* of 11 October 1918, the fourth paragraph of which stated: "As far as the Zionist movement is concerned I can only express my sympathy with it and the national movement among the Jewish people in general, because it is of great moral value. I watched the Zionist and the national movement in Europe and in our country, and I learned that it is not a movement of political chauvinism, but of moral regeneration of your nation."[229]

Masaryk cooperated with the Zionists as part of the Central European Union that was set up in New York at the beginning of October 1918, with Masaryk as its elected Chairman. It was made of representatives of central European nations; at its congress in Philadelphia on 26 October, attended by representatives of twelve nations, a joint declaration was signed, and alongside Masaryk's signature is signature of the representative of Palestinian Jews, the Zionist Ben Ari from Jerusalem.

The text of the declaration is in English and Hebrew and the original is held in the Masaryk Archive.

During the last days of the monarchy, a conference of representatives of Austrian Jews was held in Vienna on 14 October 1918, at which a Jewish National Council was established and five fundamental demands were proclaimed: 1. The recognition of Jewish nationality. 2. Representation of Jews at the peace con-

---

228) *Selbstwehr*, 8. 11. 1918.
229) *Selbstwehr*, 6. 12. 1918.

ference. 3. The creation of a Jewish national homeland in Palestine. 4. The acquisition of national rights in all countries where they live. 5. Recognition as a national unit and the right to attend negotiations about the future of Austria.

A Jewish National Council was also set up in Prague on 22 October, whose members included Ludwig Singer, Max Brod, Alfred Engel, Norbert Adler, Hugo Slonitz, W. Schönfeld, Oskar Altschul, and Karel Fischel; on 28 October 1918 its leaders, Brod, Singer, and Fischel, visited the Czechoslovak National Committee and submitted a memorandum in which they demanded: 1. The recognition of Jewish nationality. 2. Equal rights for Jews. 3. All rights for the Jewish national minority and democratisation. 4. The right to unify the Jewish religious communities. Those rights were essentially adopted, and implemented in the newly created Czechoslovak Republic, where there was no anti-Semitic political party, and the strong political left condemned anti-Semitism.

It was of great advantage to the Jews who became citizens of the new state, that it was headed by T.G.Masaryk, a man who had great sympathy for the Jews, and who had already promoted their rights when he was an academic and politician under Austrian rule, the only prominent politician in central and south-eastern Europe to identify with the campaign against anti-Semitism.

In December 1918, meetings took place in Paris between Masaryk and Nahum Sokolow. On 10 December, Sokolow, as a representative of the Zionist organisation, requested a meeting with Masaryk. The meeting took place the same day in the office of the French Foreign Minister, Stephen Pichon. They met again at the hotel in Paris where Masaryk was staying. Sokolow wrote Masaryk a total of four letters, and in the final letter he requested him to show support for the Jewish refugees from Galicia. Masaryk did intervene in their favour, and the order for their deportation issued on 15 December by the government of Kramář was cancelled.[230]

---

230) According to K. Gajan. "T. G. Masaryk, idea sionismu a Nahum Sokolov." In Židovská ročenka 2002–*2003*. Praha, 2002, pp. 71–85; *Selbstwehr*, 10. 1. 1919, No. 2.

On 21 December 1918, T.G.Masaryk – elected by the Revolutionary National Assembly on 14 November President of the Czechoslovak Republic – was enthusiastically welcomed in Prague by Czech and Jewish citizens alike. The Zionist *Selbstwehr* welcomed him in its editorial as follows: "...Along with their Czech fellow citizens, Prague Jews will also pay tribute to the President. The Jews of the Czech lands were among Masaryk's most fervent devotees even before. They were obliged to him, because this great Czech always let himself be guided by justice and truth in his dealings and actions, without fearing the compact majority. Now the Czech nation's greatest thinker has assumed the post of President. [...] Jews hope that in the face of his calm and impartial judgement culturally hostile anti-Semitism will give way to more just and sober behaviour – and more honourable for the Czechs themselves – and grant the Jewish nation in the Czechoslovak state civic, national, and cultural rights, and also implement them."[231]

The World Zionist Organization also sent Masaryk a telegram welcoming him to Prague.[232]

On 22 December, Masaryk addressed the National Assembly at Prague Castle for the first time as President and reported on his activity abroad. His address was previously approved by the government, which deleted two paragraphs from the draft: those dealing with an amnesty and Masaryk's warning against anti-Semitism. "The government did not believe such a warning was necessary." [233] On 23 December 1918 T.G.Masaryk presented a provisional report on his four-year activity abroad to the Council of the Republic, a report that he subsequently reworked in 1925 and published under the title of *Světová revoluce* [World Revolution, published in English as *The Making of a State*]. In his report he also mentioned his contacts with representatives of different nations. Concerning the Jews he said: "Jews everywhere and of every persuasion are against the Poles, and this is an enormous financial and journalistic power; Dmowski is also

231) *Selbstwehr*, 20. 12. 1918, No. 48, quoted by K. Gajan. "Masaryk a Max Brod (Židovská otázka v letech 1918–1920)." In *Židovská ročenka 2000–2001*. Praha, 2000, pp. 28–50.

232) *Selbstwehr*, 3. 1. 1919, No. 1; excerpt from a telegram, see K. Gajan. "Masaryk a Max Brod", p. 32.

233) F. Peroutka. *Budování státu*. Vol. 1. Praha, 1933, p. 473.

proscribed. This is because there was an acute outbreak of anti-Semitism at that time. The Jews' attitude was that at best they would not be against the Poles, but they would not do anything for them. The influence of the Jews, even in America, is considerable and it must be taken into consideration. For instance, a member of the Supreme Court is a Jew: Brandeis, who is of Czech origin; I won him for our cause and he also has great personal influence on Wilson. Actually I tried to win over Jews for our cause everywhere and I did not have too much difficulty – the Hilsner affair was now bearing its fruits." [234] At the end of his report, among "odds and ends" Masaryk mentioned America's request for Czechoslovakia to deliver coal to Germany and Vienna: "Then there are the Polish Jews here; we have a mass request for us not to expel them. Nothing must happen to them. If we manage to maintain order until the conference, we are halfway to victory." [235]

The importance that Masaryk attached to Jewish issues, anti-Semitism, and Zionism is evidenced by the fact that on 31 December 1918 he already received leaders of the Jewish National Council for an hour-long audience at Prague Castle, namely, Ludwig Singer (Chairman) and Max Brod (Vice-Chairman), accompanied by Rudolf Kohn (Chairman of the Jewish Socialist Council). In the course of the conversation Masaryk reiterated the principles he had outlined in his reply to the American Zionist Federation on 8 November – equal rights for Jews in the new state and his entire sympathy for Zionism. Singer handed Masaryk a memorandum from the Jewish National Council which made reference to the memorandum submitted to the National Committee on 28 October. Now the JNC was applying to the National Assembly for recognition of the Jewish people's right to an independent existence. Masaryk promised to support the JNC's demands. [236]

At the beginning of 1919 Masaryk gave an interview to Jacob Landau of the newspaper *De Telegraaf* (who would later be the

234) T. G. Masaryk. *Cesta demokracie*. Vol. 1. Praha, 1933, pp. 45–46.
235) Ibid. p. 52.
236) According to K. Gajan. "Masaryk a Max Brod", pp. 33–34. The memorandum to the President is held in the Masaryk Archive, f. T. G. Masaryk, sign. R, k. 2. For the English text of the memorandum of 28 October see A. M. Rabinowicz. "The Jewish Minority." Vol. 1, Appendix A, pp. 218–221.

founder and director of the Jewish Telegraphic Agency). Asked whether the new Czechoslovak Republic would support a Jewish Palestine at the peace conference, Masaryk replied that of course he would.

Political events "at home" at the end of 1918 showed that activity on the Jewish side had been taken over by the Zionists and the organisation they created – the Jewish National Council. This became the partner in the negotiations with the National Committee and then then with the government and the National Assembly – and last but not least, with the President. The Zionists presented themselves as spokesmen for the whole of Jewry and had the support of the World Zionist Organisation, as well as benefitting from their previous relations with Masaryk, who never concealed his sympathy for Zionism, but openly admitted it.

However, the situation in the Czech lands when the war ended were not favourable to the Jews. Little was known about the fact that they had fought in the Czechoslovak legions. Jews were unjustly perceived as assistants and fellow-travellers of the now defeated Germans and Austrians, although this could scarcely concern the Czech Jews. It might appear to apply to the German-speaking Zionists and to the German-speaking higher-class Jews, particularly in Prague, Brno and several other cities. This resulted in physical attacks and threats, incited by the nationalist press. A contributory factor was the presence of 18,000 Galician Jews who had taken refuge in Bohemia and particularly in Moravia during the war, and who were a target for anti-Semitism. During the riots at the beginning of January 1919, the "wrath" of "Hussite women", for instance, was directed against the "shopkeepers" from the German Jewish centres of the ministries, etc. Masaryk vigorously denounced and rejected these outbursts.

8. Masaryk and the Jews during the First Republic

...recognising the Jewish nationality in the Czechoslovak Constitution is precisely in accord with the humanitarian traditions of the Czech people... Czechoslovakia's liberal standpoint guarantees that the recognition of your nationality in our Constitution is not a mere formality.

T.G.Masaryk, *Cesta demokracie* [The Way of Democracy], 1920

THE FIRST CZECHOSLOVAK REPUBLIC

The first Czechoslovak Republic came into existence on 28 October 1918 as one of the successor states of Austria-Hungary. In 1921 it had 13.5 million inhabitants (in 1930 14.5 million), comprising Czechoslovaks, Germans, Hungarians, Ruthenian Ukrainians, Poles and Jews; the latter had the option of registering as Jewish nationals. Jews in the Czechoslovak Republic represented 1.4% of the population. In 1921 the number of Jews was 354,203, over half of whom (196,800) opted for Jewish nationality; by 1930 the number of Jews in the republic had risen to 356,700, 57% of whom chose Jewish nationality.

The Jewish population in Czechoslovakia was by no means homogeneous. Czech Jews (in Bohemia, Moravia, and Silesia) mostly came from the middle class; they were highly assimilated and urbanised; they mostly spoke Czech, but many were bilingual Czech-German. (Only 12% of Czech Jews in 1930 opted for German nationality). A majority of Czech Jews abandoned orthodoxy in favour of reform Judaism, and overall they were among the most de-Judaised Jews of Europe. Some 50% of Czech Jews lived in Prague, and 60% worked in commerce, banking and transportation. The number of Czech Jews was decreasing as a result of emigration (albeit low), low natural population growth, and mixed marriages.

By contrast Jews in Slovakia were quite different. They formed part of Hungarian Jewry, but were much more underdeveloped. Some of them were strongly orthodox (in Bratislava and in eastern Slovakia); there was also a reform minority, and a "status quo ante" majority. They used German and Hungarian, those languages having supplanted Yiddish in the 19th century. Jews in Slovakia constituted the lower middle class, which competed with the weak Slovak bourgeoisie – one of the causes of anti-Semitism.

The Jews in Subcarpathian Ruthenia were eastern European Jews; they were underdeveloped, orthodox and influenced by Galician Hassidism; they were less Magyarised than the Slovak Jews and spoke Yiddish. They were mostly manual labourers, artisans and farmers.

In the First Republic Jews enjoyed all rights – from the right to opt for the nationality of their choice to all other benefits of a functioning democratic system. Their communities developed unmolested, and Jews had guaranteed religious freedom as a matter of course. They ran their own synagogues and their own state-supported educational system. They had their own press, publishing houses, and political parties. Jews were members of the National Assembly, senators and ministers of state. Anti-Semitism was not tolerated at state or government level – and that situation was guaranteed by both Presidents: T.G. Masaryk and Edvard Beneš. There was no numerus clausus in education for Jews, which is one of the reasons why many Jews from Poland, Hungary and other countries studied in the Czechoslovak Republic.

Jews played an important role in science, culture and the liberal professions (doctors, lawyers, etc.) They were a major presence in publishing houses, the editorial boards of influential newspapers and journals, and throughout the entire existence of the First Republic they supported Masaryk's and Beneš's so-called "Castle policy", also assisting with their bilinguality. Thus they created a bridge between Czech and German culture and interpreted the principles of Czech policies to German-speaking Europe. The most eloquent proof of the equality of Jews with other citizens of the Republic is that they represented about a quarter of the participants in weekly meetings of Czech intellectuals with Masaryk and Beneš, the so called "Friday group" – a kind of "think-tank" of the First Republic – and thereby helped influence the country's political and cultural development. Would anything of the kind have been conceivable in Poland, Hungary or Austria?

Anti-Semitism manifested itself in Czechoslovakia at the end of 1918 and beginning of 1919, chiefly as a wave of pogroms affecting Holešov, Příbram, Nymburk, Poděbrady, Klatovy, Jindřichův Hradec, Kamenice nad Lipou and Karlín. Some institutions sacked their Jewish employees.[237]

The state brought the anti-Semitic excesses under control, although the perpetrators of the pogroms received only light sentences and avoided lengthy imprisonment. The political parties that fomented anti-Semitism before World War I removed it from their programmes. None of the parties belonging to the Republic's governing coalitions had anti-Semitism in their programme. (Again it is possible to compare this with the situation in neighbouring countries). Nevertheless there were parties and associations on the political fringes that openly espoused anti-Semitism, particularly in Slovakia, or in the nineteen-thirties under the influence of Nazi Germany. They included *Vlajka* [Flag], *Slovenská strana protižidovská* [The Slovak Anti-Jewish Party], *Národní obec fašistická* [The National Fascist Community], *Národní sjednocení* [National Unification], and *Národní liga* [The National League] led by Jiří Stříbrný. These groupings constantly repeated the stereotypical image of Jews as a subversives, Bolsheviks, Marxists, Germanisers, foreigners, and cosmopolitans, attacking the policies and personalities of Masaryk and Beneš, and importing racial anti-Semitism from German.

Overall anti-Semitism during the First Republic may be described as minor, verbal and bearable, as the Jews themselves said. There were many reasons for this: the new state prospered economically, and was an island of calm and order compared to its surroundings – Austria, Bavaria, Hungary and Poland. Social tension was under control, and no powerful extremist movements emerged. Society was very developed, with a well organised working class under the influence of social democra-

---

237) See B. Soukupová. "Židovská národní identita po vzniku Československé republiky." In *Etnicita a miesto: Etnicita ako faktor polarizácie mestského spoločenstva v 20. storočí*, ed. P. Salner, and D. Leutner. Bratislava, 2001, pp. 183–204.

cy, and a strong and educated middle class. The intelligentsia was largely anti-clerical with an aversion to Catholicism – the consequence of Czech historical development (Hussitism, Reformation, the Czech Brethren, Palacký, Masaryk); insofar as anti-Semitism existed among the intelligentsia, it was among the Catholic intellectuals. Protestants did not profess anti-Semitism; their leading representatives – eminent philosophers, university professors, writers and teachers – held pro-Jewish views.

Nor was there any left-wing anti-Semitism. All the left-wing writers, poets, journalist and publicists (with very minor exceptions) were openly sympathetic to the Jews.

And over it all towered the authority of Masaryk, a resolute opponent of anti-Semitism.

(From a survey conducted among Jews in the 1990s about anti-Semitism in the First Republic it emerged that 41% of the respondents had never encountered anti-Semitism, 38% said they had encountered it only rarely or in a mild form, 12% had experienced a greater degree of anti-Semitism (verbal abuse, stone throwing, fights among children), 9% stated that they first encountered anti-Semitism in the years 1938 and 1939.)

JEWS IN THE FIRST REPUBLIC

The period of the First Republic was undoubtedly the most favourable period of mutual coexistence between Czechs and Jews. Masaryk's republic was the only country in central Europe that accorded Jews full rights and enabled them full and unimpeded development – for an entire generation.

A Jewish National Council was already established in Prague on 22 October 1918 and its leaders submitted a memorandum to the National Committee of Czechoslovakia on 28 October calling for recognition of the Jewish nationality, equal rights for Jews, and full rights for the Jewish minority, as well as the democratisation and unification of Jewish religious communities. On the same day a delegation of the Association of Progressive Czech Jews offered its assistance to the National Committee.

On 30 October, Moravian Jews joined the Jewish National Council, followed by the Silesian Jews on 10 November 1918.

At the Paris peace conference, Jewish representatives demanded the recognition of Jews as national minorities, and guarantees of their protection. The newly emerging states opposed this, however, and so, in the treaty on the protection of minorities, Jewish minorities were not specifically mentioned, with even the Czechoslovak delegation considering it groundless. (Rights of minorities were framed in general terms without mention of any specific minority.) At the same time, talks took place in Paris (and then in Prague) between Edvard Beneš, the Foreign Minister, and Dr Singer, which led to the recognition of the Jewish nationality. But Jews were also not enumerated as a national minority in the Czechoslovak Constitution of 1920, and Jews in the Czechoslovak Republic did not constitute a minority in terms of language rights (unlike the Germans, for instance), because in no local district did they constitute more than 20% of the population, but only in respect of the national census. When the first census took place in 1921, 180,855 Jews declared themselves to be Jewish (186,642 in 1930). In 1921, according to their religious affiliation (Judaism), there were 354,342 Jews living in the Czechoslovak Republic (356,830 in 1930). It emerged from the census results that in Bohemia 46.4% of Jews declared themselves of Czech nationality and 31.1% of German nationality. The Constitution gave Jews equality before the law, equal political and civic rights, and recognition of Jewish nationality, in respect of the protection of ethnic, racial and religious rights.

Jews in the First Republic did not constitute a homogeneous group in any respect. The lifestyle of Jews in Bohemia and Moravia was most similar to that of Austrian Jews, and there was a vigorous process of assimilation with the Czech nation. Silesian Jews were largely under the influence of Jews in Poland. The central role in the lives of Jews was played by the community, which performed both religious and social functions. The communities were grouped in free unions organised territorially and ethnically. The supreme umbrella organisation of the Jewish population of the Czechoslovak Republic was the Supreme Council of Jewish Communities in Bohemia, Moravia and Silesia.

On 12 October 1919, there was a General Meeting of the Association of Czech Jews, which brought together supporters of the Association of Czech Progressive Jews and the Czecho-Jewish Political Union. In December 1919, the Association of Czech Academic Jews changed its name to the Kapper Academic Association.

Jews were also organised politically. 1910 saw the foundation of the Jewish Party, which did not enter parliament until ten years later on a joint ticket with Polish parties, obtaining 1.4% of the votes and four seats. Czech-assimilated Jews naturally voted for Czech political parties. Jews who opted for German nationality voted in the majority for the Deutsche demokratische Freiheitspartei, while orthodox Jews were opposed to the Jewish Party as being too liberal in their eyes.

Four ministers of Jewish origin served in governments of the Czechoslovak Republic: Adolf Stránský, Alfred Meissner, Lev Winter and Ludwig Czech, and in the trade unions a prominent Jew was Robert Klein, who defended the rights of civil servants.

Jews were divided into two currents: assimilationist and Zionist. Assimilated Jews were integrated into their Czech (Slovak, German or Hungarian) surroundings, and viewed assimilation as the only way to resolve the Jewish question. Overall more assimilated Jews identified with the Czechs than with the Germans. The Zionists represented a political, moral and cultural movement working for the rebirth of Jewry, with the aim of establishing a Jewish state in Palestine. Their movement became stronger and more significant during the existence of the First Republic. Religiously-oriented Jews were divided into orthodox and neologs.

According to the 1921 census, Jews represented only a fraction of the population of Czechoslovakia. What distinguished them in the Czech lands was the essentially urban character of their lives – 80% of Jews lived in towns with over 5,000 inhabitants, and 60% in towns with over 60,000 inhabitants. There were various reasons for the concentration of Jews in urban areas. Jews were exposed to intense competition in the sphere of retail trade, so they shifted their activity to wholesale trade, large-scale industry and finance. Towns and cities also offered them greater scope for education, because of greater variety and higher standards. Moreover they were more exposed to manifestations of anti-Semitism in the country than in urban areas, where they could enjoy greater anonymity.

According to the Treaty on Protection of Minorities, minorities (including Jewish minorities, therefore) had the right to set up private schools at their own expense, as well as other private educational facilities, and use their own language in them.

At the same time, Jews could claim Jewish nationality without having a command of Hebrew or Yiddish, and had the right to religious observance. The law of 1919 placed private schools under state supervision, with the possibility of state subsidy. In the Czech lands the religious communities made sure that Jewish youth received appropriate instruction, which took place in private schools.[238]

In 1920, agreement was given to the establishment of Jewish national schools, and in Prague a Jewish national primary school was set up with Czech as the language of instruction. A similar school was opened in Brno (initially German-language, later Czech-language instruction). In 1920 a Jewish reformed *Realgymnasium* was established in Brno with German-language instruction. It was officially recognised in 1921, and the teaching language was changed to Czech. At that time, in Subcarpathian Ruthenia there were already nine Jewish Hebrew-language primary schools (in Berehove, Khust, Mukachevo, Uzhhorod, Vinohradov, etc.). In the 1931–1932 school year 63,987 Jewish children attended Jewish schools, 38,401 of whom were registered as of Jewish nationality.

The Jews in the republic had their own press, and in addition they held important posts in the Czech and German press. Publications included *Českožidovský kalendář* [The Czech Jewish Almanac], *Českožidovské listy* [The Czech Jewish Press], *Rozvoj* [Development], the Zionist *Selbstwehr*, *Židovské zprávy* [Jewish News], *Židovský kalendář* [The Jewish Almanac], and many others, also in German.

Jews played an important role in the Czechoslovak economy, particularly in the textile, food, wood processing, and paper industries. Jewish capital provided 30–40% of capital investments in industry. The firms Petschek and Weiman developed the mining industry in North Bohemia, while the Rothschild company developed the steel industry in the Ostrava region. Jewish banking houses and insurance companies also played an important

238) Regarding the minorities treaties: J. Kořalka. "Menšinový status jako východisko z nouze. Zásady právního postavení a ochrany menšin v českých zemích před rokem 1914 a v Československé republice po roce 1918", *Lidé města*, 12. Praha, 1998, pp. 111–133; J. Křen. *Dvě století střední Evropy*. Praha, 2005, pp. 458–459.

role. In the years of the economic crisis, many Jewish traders left Slovakia and Subcarpathian Ruthenia and settled in the Czech lands. Several thousand Jews who escaped from Germany after 1933 also came there.

Jews also played an enormous part in the cultural life of the Czechoslovak Republic, and names such as Franz Kafka, Max Brod, Franz Werfel, Ludwig Winder, Egon Erwin Kisch, Otokar Fischer, and Pavel Eisner have a permanent place in Czech, German, European and world literature.

As stated earlier, Czech anti-Semitism did not disappear with the war, and in 1918 there were anti-Jewish riots in Prague and Holešov and disturbances recurred in Slovakia in 1919. However, manifestations of anti-Semitism were minimal overall, thanks to the influence of Masaryk and Beneš, the activities of the political parties, particularly the social democrats, the activity of the churches, the influence of the democratic press, the activity of publicists, such as Josef Hromádka, Emanuel Rádl, and Milena Jesenská, as well as the overall government line. Nevertheless, manifestations of anti-Semitism emerged from the right of the political spectrum in the First Republic and grew stronger as authoritarian regimes came to power in the neighbouring countries, and then after the rise of Hitler. The fomenters of anti-Semitism were Stříbrný's *Národní sjednocení* [National Unification], Gajda's *Národní obec fašistická* [National Fascist Community], and *Vlajka* [The Flag], in the Czech lands, and in Slovakia, Hlinka's *Ľudová strana* [People's Party], as well as a number of German parties in the Sudeten areas, which rejected co-operation with the Czechoslovak Republic, above all the *Sudetendeutsche Partei* [Sudeten German Party] founded by Henlein in 1935.

After 1933, the First Republic became a refuge for Jews from Germany, and after 1938, for Austrian and Romanian Jews also, which provoked increasing attacks on the governing parties by the right-wing press, and by fascist, or fascist-leaning organisations. There was also increased anti-Semitic activity in the Sudetenland and Slovakia.

In September 1938, a further 20,000 Jews from the Sudetenland found temporary refuge in the territorially-reduced post-Munich Republic after fleeing from the border areas to the hinterland, but their fate was only briefly postponed. During the Second Republic, anti-Semitic harassment was rife in one of the worst periods of modern Czech history. On 15 March 1939, Germany occupied the Czech lands. The previous day Slovakia declared independence and the creation of the Slovak State, and Hungary occupied Subcarpathian Ruthenia. All the Jews of former Czechoslovakia now found themselves on the threshold of mortal danger.

T.G. MASARYK AND THE ZIONISTS

On its front page of 3 January 1919, *Selbstwehr* carried news of an hour-long audience of the presidium of the Jewish National Council – Dr Ludwig Singer, Rudolf Kohn and Dr Max Brod – with President Masaryk. Singer greeted the President and expressed the Jewish people's great satisfaction at his election, before setting out the programme of the Jewish National Council. He thanked the President for his message to the American Jewish Federation, and for the main idea it contained, namely, that the President recognised Jews as a national minority in the Czechoslovak state.

President Masaryk confirmed the authenticity of the English text of the message that was submitted to him, and stressed that he stood by the principles contained in the message.

Ludwig Singer submitted a memorandum, which called for recognition of the legal status of the Jewish people in the Czech (!) state, and for a certain number of seats in the National Assembly to be reserved for the Jewish people.

President Masaryk declared that he was sympathetic towards these demands and would like to support them as far as his constitutional powers permitted.

Rudolf Kohn, who also introduced himself as Chairman of the Jewish Socialist Council, set out the programme of the Jewish socialist and trade union organisations.

President Masaryk discussed with Dr Max Brod the questions of Jewish press, education and democratisation of Jewish communities, and Dr Brod stressed the importance of recognising Jewish nationality.

The JNC representatives also reported to the President the persecution suffered by the Zionist organisations and Poale Zion during the war at the hands of the Austrian government, and expressed the hope for a new era, while noting that there was considerable disquiet in the country among the Jews because of the recent anti-Semitic riots in Prague.

President Masaryk expressed his conviction that the situation in the democratic republic would become clearer, and concluded by stressing his understanding for the requests presented by the representatives of the JNC.[239]

The visit to President Masaryk was also the subject of a strictly confidential report about the activity of the JNC in Prague sent to the Zionist executive body in January 1919, which also dealt with the proceedings of the first national congress of Czechoslovak Jews held that same month. Regarding the visit to the President, the report stated that the delegation had an opportunity to mention the pogrom-style incidents on the territory of the Czechoslovak state that occurred at the end of 1918, and to draw the President's attention to anti-Jewish sentiments expressed in the Czechoslovak press, particularly the agrarian press. The delegation had also informed the President about the persecution of the Zionist movement under the old Austro-Hungarian regime. The President conceded that all this information was new to him. There was a good reason to assume that the President would support Zionist endeavours and that he would essentially respond negatively to the protests of assimilationist Jews against the Zionists' objectives. Recognition of Jewish nationality remained the Zionists' principal demand.[240]

The 1st National Congress of Czechoslovak Jews was held from 4 to 6 January 1919. The opening speech was given by Hugo Bergmann, who was followed by Ludwig Singer (on the ethical significance of the national Jewish movement), Hans Kohn (on the Jewish nation and socialism), Max Brod (on Jewish nationalism), and Salomon Lieben (on the relationship of conservative Jews to national Jewry). Other contributors to the debate included Angelo Goldstein, Alfred Engel and Markus Ungar, on the themes of Jews in Moravia and Slovakia, emigration to Palestine, Polish refugees, etc.[241]

---

239) *Selbstwehr,* 3. 1. 1919.
240) For English text see A. M. Rabinowicz. *"The Jewish Minority"*, pp. 222–223.
241) According to K. Gajan. *"Masaryk a Max Brod"*, pp. 34–35, based on *Selbstwehr,* 10. 1. 1919.

On 26 January, Masaryk gave an interview to the correspondent of the Amsterdam daily *De Telegraaf,* which was published on 4 February 1919. Subjects dealt with included the status of Germans in the so-called "German territories of the Czechoslovak Republic, the issue of Těšín Silesia, the planned "Slavonic alliance" with Poland and Yugoslavia (and also Romania, as Masaryk stressed), the economic prospects of the Czechoslovak Republic, and the Jewish question. Regarding the latter, the President said: "I am sympathetic towards both Zionism and national Jewry, and that is because I see it as a problem of moral regeneration. As far as the Jews in our country are concerned, there are so-called 'assimilationists' as well as Zionists. There are two issues here: if someone tells me they are a German, I have to accept it. If someone declares himself to be a Jew, I have to accept that too. This follows from the right to self-determination, which must also apply to Jews. Every Jew confronts these two questions: Zionism to the left, assimilation to the right. We could also say: radical or conservative, national renaissance, or maintenance of the status quo ante. It is a very interesting phenomenon. It is a problem that concerns the world as a whole. Every clear-thinking politician must deal with the issue honestly, seriously and conscientiously." In conclusion, Masaryk declared that the Czechoslovak delegation would support a Jewish Palestine at the Peace Conference.[242]

During January 1919, at talks in London, Paris and Geneva, Jewish representatives from the countries of central and eastern Europe established a Committee of Jewish Delegations to represent Jewish communities at the Peace Conference, to which Czech Jews also sent delegates. The Committee was headed by Zionist leaders Nahum Sokolow and Leo Motzkin.

On 22 March 1919, Masaryk met with JNC representatives who reported to him about the Paris talks among other things. The delegation comprised Max Brod, Emil Waldstein (Secretary) Salomon Lieben (orthodox Judaism), Karel Fischel (Poale Sion) and Alfred Engel (spokesman for Slovak questions and refugee issues).

---

242) Interview with De Telegraaf. In T. G. Masaryk. *Cesta demokracie.* Vol. 1. Praha, 1933, pp. 78–79.

Masaryk was informed about the foreign policy of the JNC in recent weeks, and he was presented with documentation about the talks of JNC representatives in Switzerland and London, which showed how the JNC delegates were acting in the interests of the Czechoslovak Republic. Masaryk expressed satisfaction with the reports, and he spoke with gratitude about the co-operation with the American Jewish peace delegation in Paris. In further discussion is was clear that there were no differences of opinion between the JNC and Masaryk about the domestic political proposals of the Jewish nation as regards the democratization of Jewish communities and the Jewish nation's right to representation in the National Assembly. The hour-long audience took place in atmosphere of sincere trust. There was ample discussion of current grievances: the situation in Slovakia, the anti-Jewish boycott, press incitement, inhuman treatment of refugees, attacks on citizens of Jewish nationality, etc. Masaryk promised to investigate the specific issues put to him. During the audience there were no verbal attacks on Czech Jews who "adopt a position without influence either in the country or in the Jewish world".[243]

On 5 April 1919 Czechoslovak Foreign Minister Edvard Beneš had talks in Paris with the JNC delegates in Paris Dr Hugo Bergmann, Norbert Adler and Oswald Freund. Beneš declared that his view on the Jewish question were identical with those repeatedly expressed verbally and in writing by President Masaryk.[244]

The Committee of the Jewish Delegations, together with the Czechoslovak delegates, Dr Singer and Dr Bergmann, drew up a memorandum that was submitted as an addendum to the Peace Conference on behalf of nationally-minded Jews on 10 May 1919. The Czechoslovak Jewish delegates made efforts to have the demands made in the memorandum included in the treaties with Czechoslovakia. At that moment they encountered resistance, chiefly from Edvard Beneš, who feared that any specific mention of Jews would mean specifying also the rights and freedoms of the German, Hungarian, Polish and Ruthenian minorities in the Czechoslovak Republic. The Czechoslovak position was not an isolated one, however, and the conference reached

---

243) *Selbstwehr,* 28. 3. 1919.
244) See F. Weltsch. *Masaryk and Zionism,* p. 79.

agreement that the Jewish demands should be framed as generally as possible.

The demands of the Czechoslovak Jews were presented by the Jewish delegates in the person of Dr Singer to Dr Beneš on 22 August 1919. The chief demand was the recognition of Jews as a national minority by the Czechoslovak government. They also demanded the incorporation of so-called Jewish clauses of the Peace Treaty (Articles 10 and 11) in the peace treaty with the Czechoslovak Republic.[245] Dr Singer therefore requested a meeting with Dr Beneš on 25 August. This did not take place, however, and Singer only received apologies and a letter from Beneš explaining that he did not agree with the inclusion of any specific clauses relating to the protection of the Jews in the Peace Treaty; the Czechoslovak delegation did not consider itself competent to include that matter in the conference agenda, and indeed could see no purpose in doing so.[246]

The JNC viewed the letter with disfavour and requested Nahum Sokolow to take up the issue.

On 28 August 1919 Sokolow met with Edvard Beneš, but the problem was not resolved. Beneš nevertheless promised to report to President Masaryk as requested by Sokolow. This also produced no result, however, and on 10 September 1919, the international Treaty on the protection of minorities was signed between the allied and associated powers and Czechoslovakia at Saint-Germain-en-Laye in the form Dr Beneš proposed.

Sections 8 and 9 of Article I of the Treaty deal with the racial, religious and linguistic rights of minorities, without their being specified.[247]

That Treaty had to be incorporated in the legislation of the successor states of the former Austria-Hungary in the form of a basic law. It was duly incorporated in the Czechoslovak Constitution of February 1920 as Section VI: Protection of National, Religious and Racial Minorities (articles 128–134). The principle of the equality of all citizens of the Czechoslovak Republic was set out in article 106.[248]

---

245) For the English text of the articles see A. M. Rabinowicz. *"The Jewish Minority"*, p. 250.
246) According to A. M. Rabinowicz. *"The Jewish Minority"*, pp. 172–173.
247) For English text see A. M. Rabinowicz. *"The Jewish Minority"*, p. 235.
248) *The Constitution of the Czechoslovak Republic 1920*. Praha, 1992.

Thus the Czechoslovak Constitution does not enumerate Jews as a national minority (nor the other minorities). However, in the reports of the Constitutional Committee and the government reports is was stated categorically that Jews could register as Jewish nationals if they so wished. This suited the Zionists, who availed themselves of that right, while the Jews in favour of assimilation were opposed. Thus the Jews in the Czechoslovak Republic did not constitute a minority according to language rights (unlike the Germans), because in no judicial district did they constitute more than 20% of the population, but only in respect of the national census. Recognition of Jewish nationality was officially announced in February 1920. It was the first time that a democratic country had recognised the rights of Jews not as individuals (as in France) but as a nation. When the first census took place in 1921, 180,855 Jews declared themselves to be Jewish (186,642 in 1930). According to their religious affiliation (Judaism), in 1921 there were 354,342 Jews living in the Czechoslovak Republic (356,830 in 1930).

On 21 June 1919, President Masaryk attended a concert by Jewish academics to celebrate the recognition of the Jewish people's national rights by the Peace Conference. The concert was preceded by speeches by the JNC Chairman, Dr Ludwig Singer, and the British envoy. Masaryk briefly responded to their speeches:

"In their speeches both gentlemen referred to my attitude to the Zionist and national Jewish movement. My greatest concern is the moral aspect of this movement. Today I can simply repeat that nothing has changed in my attitude to national Jewry. I fail to understand why Jewish nationality should be an obstacle in our country, in which there already live several nationalities. I can assure you that I will also put views into practice in the political arena insofar as the constitution allows. You can always count on me."[249] The Czecho-Jews' reaction to Masaryk's sympathy for the Zionists was expressed in an article in *Rozvoj* entitled "Foul Play by the Zionists", which stated that the Zionists' enthusiasm for the Czechoslovak Republic was insincere and that they still had a German orientation. German-speaking Jews

249) T. G. Masaryk. *Cesta demokracie.* Vol. 1, p. 151. Also *Židovské zprávy,* 2, 1919, No. 11, 24. 6., p. 2.

were deceiving the Czech public; they were pursuing sectional Jewish interests as could be seen in the recent developments in Slovakia, under threat of Hungarian invasion. The "English" envoy had been honoured by a concert consisting almost solely of works by German composers: Goldmark, Bruck, Mendelssohn, and Schönberg. Only Weinberger was Czech.[250]

Max Brod requested President Masaryk to arrange for leave of absence from his job with the postal administration in order to campaign on behalf of the Jewish national movement in Slovakia. Masaryk granted Brod's request and invited him to an audience on 19 September 1919.[251]

At the end of that year, the JNC likewise sent the orthodox Jew Markus Ungar to Slovakia to campaign in favour of Zionism among the orthodox communities.

On 28 December 1919, Max Brod sent President Masaryk a comprehensive report on his trip to Slovakia in which he described the situation of Jews in Slovakia and their problems. The President read the report and commented on it.[252] In the record it states in respect of it: "It is desirable for the government to support the conscious Jewish movement, which, in practice, means giving the Jewish nationality official recognition. However, in view of the fact that the so-called assimilationists are opposed to this movement, we recommend a degree of caution; after mature reflection and agreement with interested circles, I recommend the following procedure: Leave the enumeration of national minorities unchanged in the constitutional legislation, so that Jews need not be specifically mentioned, however, in the language law or basic rights of Jews the following provision can be given as substantiation: In the case of national census, elections and other political and official acts – and in respect of cultural and social institutions mentioned in the Treaty on Minorities (education, religious observance, social care) – the Jews of the Czechoslovak Republic are not required to declare themselves

250) "Falešná hra sionistů", *Rozvoj*, 2, 1919, No. 26, 28. 6., p. 1.
251) K. Gajan. *"Masaryk a Max Brod"*, pp. 37–38; idem. "Jen svobodní národové. Masaryk a Židé v prvních letech Československé republiky", *Roš chodeš*, 62, 2000, April, pp. 12–13.
252) K. Gajan. "Postoj T. G. Masaryka k židovství a sionismu za první republiky." In *Hilsnerova aféra a česká společnost 1899–1999*, pp. 129–137.

as members of any other ethnic (national) minority than Jewish, irrespective of what language of intercourse they employ."[253]

Masaryk already set out his position on the post-war status of the Jews while the war was in progress, when, in 1917 and 1918 he described his post-war vision in *New Europe,* part of which was published in Russia in 1918, before being published in full in Czech in 1920: "The Jews among all nations will enjoy the same right as other citizens; their national and Zionistic aims will receive after the example of England all possible support."[254]

On 7 March 1920, the Theodor Herzl Association of Jewish Academics held a dinner in Prague in honour of Masaryk's 70th birthday, at which Emil Waldstein, the editor of the Zionist weekly *Židovské zprávy* spoke on the subject of Masaryk's place in the history of the Jewish nation, and Professor Otakar Kraus on Masaryk's religious significance.[255]

The following day, 8 March, Masaryk received members of the municipal council of Hodonín, who came to express their birthday wishes. The audience lasted three quarters of an hour, during which the President asked about the situation of minorities in the town and spoke authoritatively about national Jewry and Zionism. Regarding the question about local inhabitants of Jewish nationality, Masaryk was told that about nine hundred of the one thousand Jews were in Jewish national organisations. Masaryk declared his great sympathy for the idea of Jewish nationality, and anticipated that it would lead to a healthier situation both within Jewry and outside it. Masaryk said he welcomed the recognition of Jewish nationality in constitutional legislation irrespective of language; it was imperative that German-, Czech-, or Polish-speaking Jews had the right to be recognised as being of Jewish nationality. In conclusion Masaryk mentioned the great impression that the powerful Zionist movement in America had made on him.[256]

253) *K. Gajan.* "Postoj T. G. Masaryka k židovství a sionismu za první republiky", p. *134.*

254) T. G. Masaryk. *The New Europe. The Slav Standpoint.* London, 1918, p. 73.

255) See B. Soukupová." Českožidovská a národněžidovská (sionistická) interpretace dějin. Příspěvek k tzv. vzorům myšlení a cítění národnostní menšiny", *Slezský sborník,* 100, 2002, No. 4, p. 263 and note 60 on p. 267.

256) *Selbstwehr,* 19. 3. 1920.

On 4 May 1920, President Masaryk received the JNC leaders, Singer and Brod, who raised with him the results of the elections, in which the joint list of Jewish parties had received nearly eighty thousand votes in elections to the National Assembly, and some sixty thousand in the Senate elections. Nonetheless, Singer and Brod stated, the Jewish minority remained without any representation in parliament. Masaryk said he was aware of the imperfections of the electoral system, but expressed the conviction that those votes were not wasted, but would have a positive influence on the future of Jews in the Republic. The Jewish representatives told the President about further steps they intended to take to organise Jews in the state.[257]

On 16 July 1920, the American Zionist Organization sent Masaryk a letter in which it welcomed the formal recognition of Jewish nationality in the Czechoslovak constitution.

On 5 August 1920, Masaryk replied: "...recognising the Jewish nationality in the Czechoslovak Constitution is precisely in accord with the humanitarian traditions of the Czech people... Czechoslovakia's liberal standpoint guarantees that the recognition of your nationality in our Constitution is not a mere formality."[258]

The Constitution of 29 February 1920 referred to only one constitutional law, the Act on Languages, also of 29 February 1920.

In 1920, the left-wing movements *Hapoel Hatzair* and *Tzeirei Zion* merged and formed a new united political party *Hitachdut* within the framework of the Zionist movement. This party failed to assert itself as a political force, and in 1924 ceased operating in the Czechoslovak Republic. Its supporters continued to exercise some influence in the Zionist Territorial Federation and some of its former members supported Chaim Weizmann in elections at the 15th Zionist Congress and his list of candidates: *Left Centre* (including Ludvík Singer, Hugo Herrmann, Ervín Vogl, and Angelo Goldstein).[259]

---

257) *Selbstwehr*, 7. 5. 1920.
258) T. G. Masaryk. *Cesta demokracie. Vol. 1*, p. 345.
259) K. Čapková. "Specific Features of Zionism in the Czech Lands in the Interwar Period", *Judaica Bohemiae*, 38, 2002, pp.135–136

Another group formed by former members of *Hitachdut* were the so-called "Zionist Realists", inspired by Masaryk's ideals of humanity. Its programme, which was based on the ideas of A.D. Gordon, who had influenced *Hapoel Hatzair*, and on Masaryk's philosophy, was set out in articles in *Selbstwehr* in the years 1925–1926. Their leaders included Oskar Epstein, a teacher at the Jüdisches Reform-Real-Gymnasium [Jewish Reform High School] in Brno. The group failed to make a mark at the conference of the Zionist Territorial Federation held in July 1926, and gradually withered away in the course of 1927.[260]

T.G. Masaryk was also a political exemplar of the Zionist Revisionists, who often compared him to their idol and leader Jabotinsky. They cited his emphasis on democracy, while at the same time stressing the importance of order and discipline. The Revisionists appreciated the fact that Masaryk had not hesitated to take up arms (the legions) for the purpose of the creation of a national state. They regarded the Czechoslovak Republic as an example of how they should defend themselves in the event of military attack. On his visits to the Czechoslovak Republic, Jabotinsky never failed to express his admiration of Masaryk. When Masaryk died, Jabotinsky sent a telegram to Beneš stressing Masaryk's example for all oppressed nations fighting for their independence.[261]

On 23 February 1921, the Joint Foreign Committee in the British Parliament (including Sir Stuart Samuel and Lord Rothschild) proposed Masaryk for the Nobel Peace Prize.

During his visit to Slovakia in September 1921 President Masaryk spoke about the behaviour of Jews in the Republic: "I could see that Jewry was remarkably loyal. We have been paying close attention to all Jewish matters here. We could also see that on the occasion of the Zionist Congress that was recently held in Karlovy Vary. I believe our Jewry is doing well. That is particularly evident in the way Jews are treated in localities."[262]

Masaryk made repeated references to the Jewish question during a visit to Opava in 1924: "You know very well how I and

260) Ibid., p. 137.
261) K. Čapková. "Pilsudski or Masaryk? Zionist Revisionism in Czechoslovakia 1925–1940", *Judaica Bohemiae, 35,* 1999, pp. 229–231.
262) *Bratislauer Zeitung am Abend, 20. 9. 1921.*

the government have treated the Jews. I will continue to remain true to my principles. I am for the strictest equality of rights for all nationalities and religions."[263]

In an interview with the Warsaw Jewish daily *Haint*, the President answered questions about Bolshevism, socialism and Zionism. Asked his opinion on the Jewish question, he replied: "There is no Jewish question in our country. Jews live here with total equality of rights and I think they are satisfied. I think that anti-Semitism as a political programme in our country is almost an impossibility. Some have attempted it but immediately failed. The Czech people have moved far away from racial hatred. Besides, nations don't have to love each other; it's enough if they understand each other and have mutual respect." His reply to the next question, whether he considered Jews to be a nation, was diplomatic: "This is a rather complicated question. Before the war the concept of 'nation' was linked with the concept of the state... As far as the Jews are concerned, we are willing to recognise them as a nation and give them all the national rights of minorities. But they themselves are not of one mind and there are various tendencies among them which are mutually antagonistic; only the Zionists regard themselves categorically as a nation." In response to the final question, whether he was sympathetic to Zionism and Jewish nationalism, Masaryk replied: "Of course, even if the Jews aren't a nation in the usual sense of the word, why couldn't they become a nation? ... As far as Zionism is concerned, I consider it the Jewish nation's hope of the future, and no one must give up such hope. In every way I like Zionism for its characterfulness. It has within it a potency of will and lends a certain character to Jewish life."[264]

Singer's article about Masaryk on the occasion of the President's 75th birthday expresses the feelings that the Zionists held for him: "In this sense Masaryk was and is dear to us Zionists, and in this sense he does not belong only to his nation but to the whole of humanity. His name is spoken in Zionist circles in tones of the highest respect. Not only because he condemned injustices, even when they were committed against Jews, but

263) "Moravsko-slezská cesta prezidenta Masaryka a Židé", *Židovské zprávy*, 7, 1924, No. 26, 27. 6., p. l.
264) T. G. Masaryk. *Cesta demokracie. Vol. 3*, pp. 39–40.

because at the time of moral decline in the last century, he was able to believe that Jewry also had the right to a new and full life, and to recognise that it has the strength to fulfil its duty in that respect." The article ends with the words with which the Zionists greeted Masaryk on his return to his homeland: "Blessed was the man who walked not in the counsel of the wicked and stood not in the way of sinners, nor did he make the seat of the wily his seat. For only in the teaching of Eternal Life did he take pleasure; he studied life's teaching day and night. And he stood like a tree planted by streaming water, who brings forth his fruit at the right time; he will be successful in whatever he undertakes..."[265] On 14 July 1925, Masaryk received a deputation from the presidium of the Jewish National Fund – R. Wodička, and R. Eisenstein – and the Chairman of the JNC, Ludvík Singer. Masaryk was presented with a diploma to testify that his name had been recorded in the Golden Book of the Jewish National Fund to mark his 75th birthday. They then reported on progress being made in the construction of Palestine, and on Chaim Weizmann's visit to Prague. Masaryk also asked about the forthcoming 14th Zionist Congress.[266] President Masaryk visited Palestine from 8 to 15 April 1927 (see Chapter 9 of the present book).

On 27 May 1927, T.G. Masaryk was re-elected President of the Czechoslovak Republic.

On 16 December 1927, President Masaryk received at Prague Castle the Zionist leader Nahum Sokolow (Chairman of the Executive Committee of the Zionist Congress), who would visit him for the last time in Topoľčianky in 1933.

Max Lederer, one of the representatives of the Czecho-Jews, reacted to the publication of *Talks with T.G. Masaryk* in an article in *Rozvoj*, from which the following quotations and observations are taken:

"That feeling from his youth ... is to blame for his fundamental misunderstanding of assimilation and his sympathy for Zionism." ... Masaryk displayed "an extreme intellectual fairness, not just passive but courageously active – an emotional misun-

265) L. Singer. "Masaryk." Židovské zprávy, 8, 1925, No. 10, 6. 3., p. 1.
266) "Deputace Národního Fondu židovského u pana prezidenta Masaryka", Židovské zprávy, 8, 1925, No. 29, 17. 7., p. 3.

derstanding of the essence of the Jewish problem". In the case of the Jews Masaryk thought through the problem only in religious terms, as religious questions interested him most of all..."[267]

Masaryk regards Judaism as a religion to be a live issue. Masaryk regards the Jews' theology as the source of Judaism's primitivism. Masaryk advertised Brod's book *Judentum, Christentum, Heidentum*. Masaryk has yet to pronounce on the Jewish and Czech-Jewish questions.[268]

In honour of Masaryk's 80th birthday on 7 March 1930, the Congress of Czechoslovak Zionists decided to plant a forest in Palestine. A fundraising campaign was immediately organised and raised enough money for the planting of 13,000 trees near the Sarid kibbutz in the valley of Emek Yizrael (Jezreel). The ceremonial inauguration of the forest's existence took place on 21 April 1930, and was attended by representatives of the Czechoslovak Republic and Zionist organisations. On 23 May, President Masaryk received representatives of the Jewish National Fund at Prague Castle, who informed him about the results of the project. During the 1930s, Masaryk referred to matters related to the Jewish question in several interviews he gave to foreign correspondents.

In an interview with Jacob Landau at Topoľčianky on 23 August 1933, on the occasion of the 18th Zionist Congress in Prague, the President opened his remarks by declaring that he was following the proceedings of the Congress with interest, and continued: "...the efforts to build a home for the Jewish national in Palestine has my warm support, of course."

Asked about the Jews in Germany who had been deprived of their rights, and whether the League of Nations should deal with the matter, Masaryk replied: "I presume that the League of Nations will indeed take up this matter. The Jewish problem in Germany cannot be regarded as a purely internal matter. Thousands of Jews continue to flee from Germany, having been deprived of their rights and their livelihoods. They naturally present a prob-

---

267) M. Lederer. "Staro-nový Masaryk", *Rozvoj,* 36, 1929, No. 17, 26. 4., pp. 2–3.
268) See ibid. Masaryk's attitude to Zionism during the First Republic was dealt with in detail in several articles by Professor Koloman Gajan, including: K. Gajan. "Postoj T. G. Masaryka k židovství a sionismu za první republiky", pp. 129–137; idem. "Masaryk a Max Brod", pp. 28–50; idem. "T. G. Masaryk a Židé." In *T. G. Masaryk a československá státnost.* Praha, 2001, pp. 85–103.

lem for all those countries that have offered them asylum. Those countries cannot be expected to bear the burden caused by the policies of a single country. Nevertheless I believe that the situation will improve. Anti-Semitism is nothing new."[269] In an interview with the *New York Times Magazine,* conducted with Masaryk on 28 August 1933 by Shepard Stone, reference was made to the problems of democracy in Germany, Austria and elsewhere. Concerning anti-Semitism, Masaryk stated: "anti-Semitic feeling has always existed in Germany and it exists in other countries. I do not believe, however, that it will spread in its German form beyond the borders of the Reich. Other countries know, and even Germans are beginning to realize, what this campaign against the Jews is costing Germany. [...] In my opinion these things will quieten down..."[270]

On 9 September 1933, Masaryk spoke about the issues of racism, anti-Semitism, and democracy in an interview with Vasily Suchomlin a correspondent for the *Quotidien* newspaper. He rejected the idea of "pure race" and the supremacy of higher races over others, as well as religious, racial or party fanaticism. He also said that he absolutely rejected anti-Semitism.[271]

On 26 March 1934, the English journalist and historian Elizabeth Wiskemann had a conversation with Masaryk at Lány, which she described in her book *The Europe I Saw,* published in New York in 1968. Masaryk spoke with her about Spinoza, the Jews and Nazi Germany.[272]

In an interview for the *Morgenzeitung* (Ostrava) on 9 April 1934, conducted by the publicist Schreiber, Masaryk agreed with the proposal to hold an international anthropological congress to prove that it was impossible to distinguish between different human races.[273]

On 24 May 1934, Masaryk was elected for the fourth time and shortly afterwards fell ill.

269) T. G. Masaryk. *Cesta demokracie*. Vol. 4. Praha, 1997, p. 368.
270) T. G. Masaryk. "Democracy Still Lives, Says Masaryk" (interview), *New York Times*, 12. 10. 1933.
271) T. G. Masaryk. *Cesta demokracie. Vol. 4*, pp. 374–377.
272) See J. Kovtun. *Republika v nebezpečném světě.* Éra prezidenta Masaryka 1918–*1935*. Praha, 2005, p. 760.
273) T. G. Masaryk. *Cesta demokracie. Vol. 4*, pp. 417–418.

In March 1935 Masaryk reached his 85th birthday. In honour of the occasion he was awarded honorary citizenship of Tel Aviv, and his portrait by Braun was hung in the Mayor's office at the city hall. Masaryk also gave permission for a kibbutz to bear his name: Kfar Masaryk was established by Czechoslovak Jews in 1940. (A large number of squares and streets in Israel now bear the name of Masaryk.)

To mark Masaryk's 85th birthday, the editorial in the *Selbstwehr* was based on a quotation by Masaryk from the German version of *Making of the State* about how Masaryk observed and studied people, poetry, and novels, how he assembled data and facts, how he collected biographies and reports, how he read the writings and speeches of politicians before meeting them.

To quote the editorial: "It would seem that we have much to learn from [Masaryk's] evaluation of knowledge and information, whether in respect of Zionists great and small, or English statesmen, or Arab leaders! Masaryk's life demonstrates to Zionist politicians what they need to catch up on. But his realism, as a crusade for truth and knowledge, should be heeded by every single Zionist..."[274]

T.G. MASARYK AND THE CZECHO-JEWS

The lengthy period of Masaryk's presidency provided ample opportunity for the representatives of the Czecho-Jews – Jews who chose to speak Czech and identify with the majority population – to comment on Masaryk's personality.

The Czecho-Jews celebrated Masaryk's 70th birthday with a gala evening in the Municipal House in Prague on 6 March 1920, at which Jindřich Kohn spoke on the topic of Masaryk as Educator. The evening also included recitations and musical performance.[275]

The speech by Dr A. Stein on 28 March at a meeting at the Jewish Town Hall recalled Jewry's attitude to Masaryk, and the latter's attitude to Jewry and Judaism, and drew a parallel

---

274) FW. "Masaryk – auch unser Lehrer. Zu seinem 85. Geburtstag," *Selbstwehr*, 15. 3. 1935.
275) *See B. Soukupová*. Českožidovská a národněžidovská (sionistická) interpretace dějin, p. *263 and note 60 on p. 267*.

between Moses and Masaryk: Moses had led the Jews out of slavery into freedom and the attitude of Jews to Masaryk was like their attitude to Moses. The Hilsner affair had not been an illustration of Masaryk's philosemitism; what had driven Masaryk to intervene was "the categorical imperative of his moral being, based on uncompromising truthfulness, rectitude and fairness..."[276]

On 27 May 1927, Masaryk was elected President, with German members of the National Assembly also voting for him. "The Jewish movement rejoices at the result of the election together with the entire Czech public."[277]

An article by J. Guth noted the lack of any critique of Masaryk. Kaizl, Pekař, Chalupný, and Peroutka had made some attempts, but they were only studies and not comprehensive critical works. Regarding the disagreement between Masaryk and Kramář, there was no need to refer to either of them. The article concludes with several dates from Masaryk's life.[278]

In the article in *Rozvoj* from April 1929 already mentioned, Max Lederer repeated what Masaryk had said about Jews in his conversations with Čapek. Masaryk's interpretations were not new, Lederer stated, remarking that Dr Alfred Salus told him that he had heard similar arguments from Masaryk during his lectures on practical philosophy in the years 1894–1895. Masaryk was no philosemite; whereas others like Havlíček, Svatopluk Čech and Herben may have been in their youth, Masaryk's decisions were always based on reason. He had condemned the ritual murder myth rationally. Masaryk had reflected on the Jewish question only in religious terms, as when he declared: "...the Old and the New Testaments are a revelation of the Palestine desert and primitive Judaism." Masaryk had recommended to the Austrian Chancellor Max Brod's book: *Judentum, Christentum, Heidentum.*[279] Masaryk mentioned a number of Jews that

276) *Rozvoj,* 32, 1925, No. 5, 15. 3., pp. 1–3.
277) *Rozvoj,* 34, 1927, No. 22, 3. 6., p. 1; "Masarykovo poděkování Svazu Čechů-židů za projevy blahopřání k volbě", *Rozvoj,* 34, 1927, No. 24, 17. 6., p. 6.
278) Dr. G. (Guth). "Dílo T. G. Masaryka", *Rozvoj,* 35, 1928, No. 10, 9. 3., pp. 1–2.
279) Cf. Masaryk's letter to the Austrian Federal President Michael Hainisch about Brod's book dated 1. 4. 1922 – T. G. Masaryk. *Cesta demokracie. Vol. 2.* Praha, 1934, p. 261.

fate had acquainted him with: Schlesinger when he was a student, Viktor Adler, Karel Beck, Hartmann, the widow of Moritz Hartmann. "Does he name others in the later conversations, those he associated with as a member of the Vienna parliament and in politics?" Lederer asked at the end of the article.[280]

Sometime later Viktor Teytz wrote in *Rozvoj*: "Professor Masaryk's attitude to the Czech-Jewish movement was very complex. He can't be said to have been a supporter of the assimilationist movement, and he was not a philosemite in the sense it was used in those days. He was always of the view that Zionism was closer to his opinions on nationality, but otherwise he didn't pay much attention to ideological currents in Judaism."[281]

As President Masaryk strove to adopt a balanced approach to the assimilationist movement and to Zionism. He weighed his words carefully to avoid being accused of siding with one or other of the movements.[282]

One of the last articles about Masaryk before World War II was by Zdeněk Tohn, who described him as a philosopher and politician of humanity surrounded by European and Asian nationalisms, a man with love for people and mankind, who believed in ideas and ideals and was morally genuine. Throughout, the author refers to Masaryk's conversations with Čapek, mentioning Masaryk's critique of Renan, the Hilsner affair, Masaryk's attitude to Ahad Ha'am, to monotheism, Christianity, the person of Paul of Tarsus, and how he influenced the younger generation of Jews: Vohryzek, Klineberger, Lederer-Leda and Kohn.[283]

---

280) See M. Lederer. "Staro-nový Masaryk", pp. 2–3.
281) V. Teytz. "Několik poznámek", *Rozvoj*, 37, 1930, No. 10, 7. 3., p. 4.
282) The question of the Czecho-Jews in the 1920s and their attitude to Masaryk is dealt with repeatedly and in detail by Blanka Soukupová in her studies. See B. Soukupová. "Češi-židé. K identitě českožidovského hnutí 1918–1926." In *Židovská menšina v Československu ve dvacátých letech*. Praha, 2003, pp. 51–64; and "T. G. Masaryk a židé (Židé), and T. G. Masaryk. legenda a skutečnost." In ibid., pp. 113–126. The 1930s are dealt with in: B. Soukupová. "Identita Čechů židů v nové evropské realitě." In *Židovská menšina v Československu ve třicátých letech*. Praha, 2004, pp. 36–47, and "T. G. Masaryk a židé (Židé): legenda a skutečnost." In ibid., pp. 96–111.
283) Z. Tohn. "Masaryk a židovská otázka." In *Kalendář českožidovský. 1938–1939*, pp. 44–54.

THE FRIDAY GROUP

The meetings of the so-called Friday Group (*Pátečníci*) at the home of Karel and Josef Čapek during the years 1923–1938 were also attended by T.G.Masaryk and Edvard Beneš.

A large number of the members came from a Jewish background: Julius Firt, Otokar Fischer, Alfred Fuchs, Camillo Hoffmann, Josef Kodíček, František Langer, Arne Laurin, Karel Poláček and Karel Kraus, and they accounted for about a quarter of those who attended the Čapeks' "Fridays". The members of the group belonged to the political and cultural elite of the Czech nation. After the Nazi invasion those who had not emigrated in time were subjected to harsh repression. Some were executed (V. K. Škrach and Vladislav Vančura), and several died in concentration camps, including Josef Čapek. Karel Čapek died after the Munich Agreement. The fate of those members of the group of a Jewish background, irrespective of whether they felt themselves to be Czechs, Germans, ethnic Jews, or religious Jews, or even those who had long ceased to be part of the Jewish community or were converts to Christianity, was even more tragic, as they were all destined to be murdered by the Nazis. Only Otokar Fischer, who died in 1938, and those who managed to flee the country in time – J.Firt, J.Kodíček, F.Langer and A.Laurin – escaped that fate. The rest (A. Fuchs, C. Hoffmann and K.Poláček) died in concentration camps.

The *Pátečníci* were an integral part of Masaryk's First Republic, in which Jews played a prominent role in industry and commerce. There was a high proportion of Jews in science, in the liberal professions (law, medicine), culture and art. They were an inseparable part of Czech and German literature and among the best know writers of the time, such as Franz Kafka and Franz Werfel. Many of them were translators and intermediaries between Czech and German culture, such as Otokar Fischer, Pavel Eisner, Otto Pick and Rudolf Fuchs. Through their major involvement in the press, Jews played an equally important role as consistent defenders of the country against fascism and Nazism, as mediators between Czech and German politicians, or as builders of bridges between the two cultures. Masaryk and Beneš would never have managed to create and maintain their political network (known as "the Castle" without close cooperation with the press, which promoted and publicised their policies and views.

"The Castle" influenced or controlled a large part of the press thanks to the "Castle's" publishing houses Orbis and Melantrich, and with the help of such newspapers such as *Národní osvobození* [National Liberation], *České slovo* [Czech Word], *Prager Tagblatt, Prager Presse, Tribuna, Lidové noviny* [People's News], and *Přítomnost* [Presence].

Undoubtedly one of the most important titles was Peroutka's *Přítomnost* (1924–1939), whose regular contributors included Jaroslav Stránský, Gustav Winter, Alfred Fuchs, Josef Kodíček, František Langer, Richard Weiner, Otokar Fischer, and Karel Poláček; Pavel Eisner, Otto Pick, and Jiří Weil also contributed articles occasionally; the arts section featured such names as Julius Firt, František Gel, and Egon Erwin Kisch.

Of equal importance was the daily *Lidové noviny* (1893–1945), founded by Adolf Stránský, and subsequently published by his son Jaroslav Stránský, who took over the Borový publishing house in 1925. Its editors-in-chief included Karel Poláček, and from 1936 Julius Firt was its managing director. Its Paris correspondent was Richard Weiner.

Another important periodical was *Tribuna* (1919–1938), an independent magazine whose editors included Josef Kodíček. It was founded by Czech Jews as a counterweight to the German *Tagblatt*. Its director was Ferdinand Peroutka (who subsequently moved to *Přítomnost*), and he was followed for a while by Bedřich Hlaváč, a personal friend of T.G. Masaryk.

In some newspapers "the Castle" had its confidants, such as Alfred Fuchs, who was an editor of *Lidové noviny*.

The policies of "the Castle" were supported by public figures coming from a Czech-Jewish or German-Jewish background such as Arne Laurin, the editor-in-chief of *Prager Presse,* Josef Penížek of *Národní listy* [National Newspaper], Gustav Winter a journalist on *Právo lidu* [People's Standard], Josef Kodíček at *Přítomnost* and *Tribuna,* Rudolf Heller, the publisher of *Prager Tagblatt,* and its editor Gustav Fuchs, the literary critic Pavel Fraenkl, the philosopher Oskar Kraus, the journalist and publicist Ernst Rychnovsky, the linguist Roman Jakobson, the lawyer and historian Josef Redlich, the journalist Moritz Bloch, and the poet and translator Camillo Hoffmann, not to mention Otokar Fischer, František Langer, Pavel Eisner, Otto Pick and many others.

It could be said that the only prominent journalist coming from a Jewish background who opposed the policies of "the Castle" was the editor of Kramář's *Národní politika* [National Politics] Lev Borský (real name Leo Bondy, 1883–1944), who, along with the editor-in-chief of *Fronta* Karel Horký, was one of the strongest critics of Masaryk's and Beneš's policies. He died in Auschwitz.[284]

A prominent member of the Friday Group was Otokar Fischer (1883–1938), a poet, philologist, writer, translator and literary adviser, who was born into an assimilated Jewish family in Kolín. He studied Germanistics with Professor Arnošt Kraus at Charles University in Prague, and also in Berlin. He also read Romance studies and comparative literature. He started publishing his poetry in 1911, influenced partly by the Czech poets Vrchlický, Dyk and Theer, but chiefly by Heinrich Heine, with whom he felt an ideological and aesthetic affinity, and to whom he devoted a comprehensive monograph: *Heinrich Heine,* 1923. His lyrical poetry influenced the poets František Gottlieb and Viktor Fischl. In the period 1906–1919 he was employed as a librarian at the Prague University Library, and he was literary adviser at the National Theatre in 1911–1912. In 1912 he was appointed reader in the Arts Faculty of Charles University, and professor in 1927. In 1926 he lectured in Ghent, and at various French universities in 1936. From 1935 to 1938 he was artistic director of the National Theatre, resigning from his post on the editorial board of *Lidové noviny* when he was appointed.

Fischer's output as a writer, scholar, dramatist and translator was extensive. He was about forty when he at last came to terms with what he felt to be the burden of his Jewishness, and he dealt with it in the foreword to his monograph of Heine and in his richest lyrical verse collection *Hlasy* [Voices] (1923), which is effectively an addendum to the monograph. In it he returned to his Jewish roots. He became involved in a discussion with Masaryk about Zionism and assimilationism, which was always a painful issue for Fischer. Heine was the only Jewish figure in world literature that he concentrated on; otherwise his interest was focused on Kleist and Nietzsche (devoting a monograph

284) T. G. Masaryk was dismissive of Borský, see T. G. Masaryk. *Cesta demokracie. Vol. 3,* e.g. pp. 257 and 309.

to each of them), and Geoethe (whose Faust he translated masterfully). He also translated Schiller, Hoffmanstahl, Wedekind, Corneille, Villon, and Lope de Vega, among others.

Fate was merciful to Otokar Fischer. He died of a stroke after reading the news of the Austrian Anschluss on 12 March 1938. The renowned gynaecologist and member of the Friday Group, Karel Steinbach, was summoned, but was too late to save him. (Otokar Fischer's brother Josef, a philosopher, sociologist and later member of the anti-Nazi resistance, was executed at Neu Brandenburg in 1945.)

Another of the Friday Group was Alfred Fuchs (1892–1941), who was one of those who did not escape the Holocaust. He has been described as "one of the best brains of the Republic" by the historian Antonín Klimek.[285] In his entry in the *Cultural Directory of the Czech Republic* (Prague, 1936), he labelled himself as a "Catholic convert from Judaism". Born into a Czech Jewish family, he became a writer, publicist, translator and journalist. While still a student, he published a series of articles in the literary supplement of *Čas* entitled "Ten Chapters on the Jewish Question", which was subsequently published in book form. He translated Heine above all. He studied philosophy, theology and law at Charles University. After World War I he worked as a journalist on a number of newspapers, and from 1921 to 1939, in the press department of the government presidium, becoming section head. In 1921 he converted to Catholicism. He was an editor of *Lidové listy* [People's Paper], and contributed to *Česká kultura* [Czech Culture], *Československá republika,* and *Nový národ* [New Nation], as well as *Tribuna, Přítomnost, Světozor* [World View] and other magazines. From 1921 he also lectured at the Free School of Political Sciences and the Studium Catholicum institute. He addressed the problems of Jewish assimilation and conversion, the relationship of Judaism to Christianity, and later Catholicism, the problems of modern papal policies, etc. He was an authority on ecclesiastical literature.

After the German occupation in 1939, he refused to emigrate and went into hiding among the Franciscans. He was arrested, and later tortured to death in February 1941 in Dachau concentration camp.

---

285) A. Klimek. *Boj o Hrad.* Vol. 2. Praha, 1998, p. 101.

The Čapeks' Friday events were also attended, when he was in Prague, by Kamil (Camillo) Hoffmann (1878–1944), a native of Kolín. Writer, poet, journalist, and translator (who translated Čapek conversations with Masaryk into German, as well as Masaryk's *The Making of a State* and Kamil Krofta's *A Short History of Czechoslovakia*), he was also a diplomat. He was born into a German Jewish family and was bilingual, German/Czech. After attending gymnasium in Prague and then a commercial academy, he worked in Vienna on *Die Zeit*, and in Dresden on the *Dresdener Neue Nachrichten* (1909–1919). After the war, he returned to Czechoslovakia and helped found the *Prager Presse*. In the years 1920–1938 he served as legation counsellor and press attaché in the Czechoslovak Embassy in Berlin. While there he corresponded with writers of the Prague Circle, particularly Max Brod. After 1933 he helped a number of writers emigrate to the Czechoslovak Republic (including Alfred Döblin), and saved their libraries (Heinrich Mann).

In Berlin, during the period 1932–39, he kept an extensive German-written political diary (which was published in Austria in 1995, and in Prague in 2006), although he unfortunately interrupted it between 1936 and August 1938. He was a supporter of Social Democracy. In January 1939, he was retired and returned to the second Czechoslovak Republic. After the Nazi occupation he was harshly interrogated by the Gestapo, and he and his wife were sent to Terezín, where he also kept a diary, which was probably irretrievably lost. In October 1944 he was transported to Auschwitz where he died in the gas chamber.

The writer and journalist Karel Poláček (1892–1945) was an active speaker at the Čapeks' "Fridays". As one of the other participants, František Kubka, recalled: "At the Friday evenings he spoke a great deal about assimilation, Zionism, the Wandering Jew, and Messianism. Paradoxically he came to the conclusion that none of it had anything to do with him because he was a Czech and didn't come from the River Jordan, but the Kněžna rivulet..." [286] Karel Poláček died in January 1945 during a death march.

---

286) F. Kubka. *Na vlastní oči. Pravdivé malé povídky o mých současnících*. Praha, 1959, pp. 150–151.

Several other Jewish members of the Friday Group evaded the Holocaust by emigrating. They included, in particular, Arne Laurin (1889–1945), real name Arnošt Lustig[287], a publicist and journalist. He was born into a Jewish family at Hrnčíře near Prague. As a young man he was a supporter of anarchism, and during World War I he served in the press department of the Austrian army, together with Franz Werfl and Otto Pick, forging a lifelong friendship with both of them. He contributed to the *Tribuna* and, from 1921 until it was closed down on 31 December 1938, he was editor-in-chief of the government-sponsored *Prager Presse* daily, established on the initiative of T.G. Masaryk. The editorial offices of *Prager Presse* were located in the Orbis publishing house (Firt called Laurin its "brain"). The newspaper's arts pages were edited by Otto Pick, and contributors included Otakar Fischer and Pavel Eisner.

Laurin is described by the historian Antonín Klimek as "a man from the inner circle of the Castle group"[288] and "the Castle's leading man"[289], and Klimek gives examples of his close ties to Edvard Beneš, ties which nonetheless loosened because Laurin presented his proposals to the Foreign Minister too categorically, so that in the end Beneš did not include him in the team of the government-in-exile. Laurin had anyway saved himself before 15 March 1939 by obtaining a visa and leaving for the USA, where he died in 1945 before the end of the war.

Josef Kodíček (1892–1954), theatre critic, publicist, dramaturge, screenwriter and director, also saved his life by emigrating. Born in Prague, his law studies were interrupted by World War I. During the years 1911–1913, he and Arne Laurin contributed to *Rozvoj*. Along with František Langer and Richard Weiner, he was one of contributors to the *1914 Almanac*. After the war he worked as editor of *Tribuna* and wrote for *Přítomnost*, as well as being a dramaturge at the Vinohrady Theatre in Prague, where he directed plays by Čapek and Langer. In the 1930s he directed and wrote screenplays for films based on Čapek and Langer's plays (*The Outlaw* and *Ferdyš Pištora Turns Over a New Leaf*). His translations included Feuchtwanger's *Success*.

287) Not to be confused with the Czech novelist Arnošt Lustig (1926–2011).
288) A. Klimek. *Boj o Hrad*. Vol. 1. Praha, 1996, p. 173.
289) A. Klimek. *Boj o Hrad*. Vol. 2. Praha, 1998, p. 68.

Kodíček emigrated to Great Britain, where he was an editor for the BBC's broadcasts to Czechoslovakia. After the war he worked at Radio Free Europe in Munich, where he also edited and directed Viktor Fischl's *Conversations with Jan Masaryk* for broadcast to Czechoslovakia. He died in Munich in 1954.

The author and playwright František Langer (1888–1965), who was born into an assimilated Czecho-Jewish family from Prague, was one of the founding members of the Friday Group. He studied medicine and worked as a doctor in the Czechoslovak legions and subsequently in the Czechoslovak Army. He was also a literary advisor at the Vinohrady Theatre in Prague. Jewish themes are scarcely touched on in his literary output, apart from passing references and episodic characters. After the Nazi occupation, he left via Poland for France, and then England, where he again served in the medical corps of the Czechoslovak Army in exile. When he returned to Czechoslovakia after the war, his works were rarely performed and published, as he was not among the supporters of the Communist regime.

Julius Firt (1897–1979), described by Klimek as "a member of the Castle's wider team", was one of the group who exercised a crucial influence over publishing and culture in the First Republic, and particularly the management of the pro-Castle *Lidové noviny*.

Firt was born into a Jewish family at Sestrouň near Sedlčany, and studied at a commercial school. He became a director of the Borový publishing house, and later, from 1936, of the *Lidové noviny* newspaper. He emigrated via Poland to France and then England, where he served in the Council of State and Foreign Ministry of the Czechoslovak government-in-exile. On his return to Czechoslovakia, he was elected to the National Assembly for the National Socialist Party and was appointed director of the Melantrich publishing house. After the Communist takeover in 1948, he emigrated once more, this time to the United States. He also served as a director of Radio Free Europe, and died in Munich.

Firt is best known nowadays in the Czech Republic for his book *Books and Destinies*, published by the exile publishers Index in Cologne in 1972, and subsequently in Czechoslovakia in 1991. The book captures the intellectual and cultural atmosphere of the First Republic and includes profiles of many Czech writers, publicists and politicians. An entire chapter is devoted to Karel Poláček and others, and the book also contains much valuable information about the Friday Group. He contributed two articles to a German book about "the Castle" *(Die Burg)*, one about the *Přítomnost* magazine, the other about "The Castle" from the point of view of a contemporary and survivor.

The group also included Dr Karel Kraus (b. 14. 9. 1891), a teacher from the Gymnasium in Truhlářská Street in Prague, who was introduced to the Čapeks' regular meetings by his friend Ferdinand Peroutka. He was a German scholar and authority on German literature, and, above all, an admirer of the works of Lion Feuchtwanger. He was also an English and Romance specialist, and a foremost translator of American, English and French prose.[290]

Most of the *Pátečníci* with Jewish backgrounds exercised a major influence on the cultural life and public opinion of the First Republic, and some of them directly helped frame "the Castle's" policies. Their status and activity are evidence of the high degree of Jewish assimilation, and the Jews' close involvement with the Czech nation, and with its ups and downs.

Masaryk died on 14 September 1937. Peroutka wrote about him: "And we live in much more complex times than Masaryk did. And we have to answer the questions that Masaryk did not answer, because they did not yet exist. In fact Masaryk died at the right time. To a certain extent his death was a blessing for him, as it spared him the need to struggle with forces he had never confronted in his life, and were unknown to him."[291]

---

290) In 1941 Karel Kraus was deported with his wife and two daughters to Łódź, where they all perished at an unknown date. Cf. V. Kaplický. *Hrst vzpomínek z dospělosti*. Praha, 2010.
291) F. Peroutka. *Deníky, dopisy, vzpomínky*. Praha, 1995, p. 167.

9. Masaryk's visit to Palestine in 1927[292]

However, where I see a difficulty is the fact that the Jews will hardly ever be in the majority in that country. I think it unlikely that anything can ever be done about the numerical superiority of the Arabs.
T.G.Masaryk in the *Prager Tagblatt*, 1927

Palestine was a favourite destination not only for simple pilgrims, believers, voyagers and researchers, but also crowned heads, such as emperors Franz Josef or Wilhelm II. After World War I, it was visited by democratic politicians, including Winston Churchill, then Colonial Secretary, who, in 1921, established the Emirate of Transjordan in Jerusalem. Nevertheless, T.G.Masaryk was the first president of a democratic state to visit Palestine, which he did, albeit unofficially, in 1927.

There were several motives for Masaryk's visit. First and foremost, there was Masaryk's deep attachment to the Orient, which was reflected in his instruction to set up an Oriental Institute in Prague in 1920.[293] Moreover Masaryk naturally had a wish to see Egypt, one of the cradles of civilisation, with his own eyes, and as a very devout Christian, for whom the Bible was the first book, he wanted to visit sites in the Holy Land linked to Jesus's ministry. Last but not least, there was Masaryk's lifelong interest in Jewish issues, and his lasting sympathy for Zionism.

T.G.Masaryk undertook his journey to Egypt and Palestine in the spring of 1927. The political situation at home was tense, and a presidential election was imminent, fixed for 27 May. Maybe it was to ease the situation by his absence that he went abroad for

---

292) The original version of this chapter was published in the collection *Hilsnerova aféra a česká společnost 1899–1999*. Praha, 1999, pp. 138–142.
293) See P. Poucha. *T. G. Masaryk a jeho vztah k Orientu*, pp. 142–143.

over two months, and was out of the country from 9 March to 25 May.[294] He was accompanied by his daughter, Dr Alice Masaryková, the Marquise Giuliana Benzoni (the former fiancée of Milan Rastislav Štefánik, first Minister of War of the Czechoslovak Republic), Dr Mladějovská, his personal physician Dr Maixner, the diplomats Vladimír Hurban and Frič, his secretary, Dr Kučera, and four others (bodyguards and valet). For part of the journey he was joined by the American John Crane. The party travelled via Switzerland to the south of France, and from there by ship to Egypt and Palestine, returning via Greece, France and Switzerland. Masaryk travelled under the name of T.G.Marsden.[295] Masaryk was in Egypt from 22 March and 7 April 1927; he visited Alexandria, Cairo, the pyramids at Giza, and Luxor, and sailed along the Nile and the Suez Canal to El Qantara in Ismailia, where he boarded a train for Jerusalem. Although Masaryk's trip was unofficial, he was received everywhere "at the highest level", as a head of state, and he was described as such in reports.

Masaryk's guide in Palestine was the philosopher Dr. Hugo Bergmann (1883–1975), originally from Prague, where he was a librarian at the University Library from 1910 to 1919. Bergmann had emigrated as a Zionist to Palestine in 1920 (from 1928 he would teach at the Hebrew University in Jerusalem, of which he was dean in the period 1936–1938). Bergmann wrote a lengthy article in the daily *Haaretz* welcoming Masaryk.[296] In it he explained Masaryk's significance for Czech society, scholarship and politics, and dealt at length with the chapter in Masaryk's *Social Question* devoted to Judaism, and with Masaryk's criticism of Marx's failure to understand the Jewish question; he also emphasised Masaryk's role in the Hilsner affair. Similar articles appeared in the other Hebrew-language newspapers *Davar* and *Ha-galil*.

The presidential party arrived in Jerusalem in the morning of 8 April.[297] In Egypt the party had been joined by the Czechoslo-

---

294) For more detail see A. Klimek. *Boj o Hrad*. Vol. 2. Praha, 1998, pp. 120–135.
295) Account of the visit according to the *Archive of the Office of the President of the Republic*; File: The President's Trip to the South, 510/25; File: Prezident T. G. Masaryk, D 8500/37.
296) *Haaretz, 7. 4. 1927.*
297) There is a discrepancy between the dates in official telegrams and newspaper reports. It was probably 8 April.

vak ambassador in Cairo, Vladimír Hurban, and was met in El Qantar by Dr. Frič the Czechoslovak consul in Jerusalem (the consulate had been established a year before Masaryk's visit). The entire party was housed in the Franciscan hospice, Notre Dame de France. Masaryk was "mildly indisposed" after his journey and almost spent the entire day resting, apart from receiving the Latin Patriarch Barlassina at 11 o'clock in the morning. The following day, 9 April, he entered the Old Town through the Jaffa Gate (the wall was breached in in 1898 in preparation for the arrival of German emperor Wilhelm II), where he was welcomed by Col. George Symes on behalf of the British High Commissioner and the Mayor of Jerusalem, Nashashibi. Masaryk viewed the Church of the Holy Sepulchre before proceeding to the Temple Mount, where he was welcomed by Jaber, the director of the Islamic museum and visited the Dome on the Rock and Al Aqsar mosques. Masaryk then left the group for a while to view on his own the mosques, the Garden of Gethsemene, the Kedron Valley and the Hills of Moab. He was then received by the representative of the supreme Muslim council, Qasim Pasha, and the mufti Hadj Amin al-Husseini (who returned the visit in the afternoon). Masaryk spoke with them in French, and mentioned that he had studied Arabic in his youth.

In the afternoon Masaryk drove to Bethlehem in a motorcade. He viewed the basilica of the Nativity, where he was accompanied by a Polish Franciscan monk, Professor Bulik. Masaryk also visited the Milk Grotto and the Shepherds' Field Chapel. The Franciscan monastery provided hospitality. The return trip to Jerusalem was via Solomon's Pools and Rachel's tomb.

The next morning, 10 April, Masaryk visited the National and University libraries in the New Town of Jerusalem, where he viewed the Goldziher Islam and Middle East Collection with its wealth of Arabic and Hebrew manuscripts, as well as the medical and mathematical departments. Masaryk was interested in the letters of Jewish socialists and photographs of Jews who had taken part in various revolutions. He read a letter from Heine to his friend Moser about Heine's conversion to Christianity. He conversed with Hugo Bergmann about Zionism, Hebrew literature and Jewish immigration to Palestine. Masaryk enquired whether any world literature had been translated into Hebrew and whether the university managed to publish textbooks for young people, and he was also interested in the country's investments and revenues.

After visiting the library, Masaryk moved on to Mount Scopus where he visited the Hebrew University. He was welcomed in English by its Chancellor, Judah Magnes, and visited a number of institutes – Chemistry, Microbiology and Jewish Studies, as well as the construction site of the Wolffssohn Library, which was completed in 1929. Masaryk looked out towards the Dead Sea from the amphitheatre. His morning appointments continued with the laying of a wreath at the British war cemetery, where he was welcomed by the British High Commissioner, Plumer. (Masaryk and the consul, Dr. Frič, then called on the High Commissioner, who returned their visit at the Czechoslovak consulate in the afternoon at Rachel Imenu Street in the New Town.)

Masaryk also visited the mosque of the Ascension and the Russian Church and Convent of Mary Magdalene on the Mount of Olives, where he conversed with the abbess of the convent in Russian.

At four o'clock in the afternoon there was a visit to Jerusalem's Czechoslovak Jewish community in the Mea Shearim neighbourhood, where he was greeted enthusiastically by people in the streets. A banner in Czechoslovak national colours with the words "Long Live the President" in Czech and Hebrew hung from the community building. Inside, in a hall decorated with Czechoslovak flags, Masaryk was welcomed in German by the 79-year-old Rabbi Chaim Sonnenfeld, a native of Slovakia, who prayed for Czechoslovakia (also in German), presented Masaryk with the text of the prayer on a parchment, and offered him hospitality. British and Jewish flags were also flown in addition to those of the Czechoslovak Republic. Masaryk was also greeted by the five hundred pupils of the Talmud-Tora school.

Afterwards Masaryk drove in the company of the Chairman of the Jewish Agency, Colonel Kisch, to the Great Synagogue, where he was greeted with a speech and a prayer by Jerusalem's Chief Rabbi Kook and introduced to representatives of the Jewish National Fund and the Foundation Fund. There followed a visit to the Jewish quarter in the Old Town, and the Ashkenazi Hurva Synagogue, where he was welcomed by Rabbi J. Chasid, and greeted by many representatives of Jewish Palestine, who wanted to be introduced to him.[298] In the evening Masaryk returned to the hospice.

In the morning of 11 April, Masaryk left Jerusalem with his entourage and drove via Bethany to the Dead Sea, the River Jordan (where they collected water), and to Jericho.

The next day, 12 April, the president and his entourage visited Rishon Letzion (the first agricultural settlement in Palestine, founded by Russian Jews in 1882), and at 4 p.m. they all arrived in Tel Aviv, still accompanied by Colonel Kisch. They were welcomed at the City Hall by Mayor Bloch (who was originally from Lithuania, but knew Prague, because he had studied there). In a conversation with the mayor, the President asked about social issues, the level of unemployment, support for the unemployed, social welfare, school fees, spiritual life in the city, etc. At the Hotel Palatin (on the corner of Ahad Ha'am and Nahalat Binjamin streets), opened in 1925, a group of some forty Jews from the Czechoslovak Republic and Dr. Grünwald, the Czechoslovak vice-consul in Tel Aviv awaited him. Masaryk asked them about the problems of life in Palestine and relations between orthodox and secular Jews, and he said he was pleased to hear that the city had a theatre and an opera house. On his way from the City Hall to the hotel, he was given a tour of different parts of the city, and he visited the local cemetery, where he laid a wreath on the graves of the Zionists Max Nordau and Ahad Ha'am. Masaryk had a particular liking for Ahad Ha'am's concept of cultural Zionism, about which he had written in *Naše doba* and *The Spirit of Russia*. (Max Brod was subsequently buried at the same cemetery.) That evening a large reception was held at the Hotel Palatin in honour of Masaryk.

On 13 April, President Masaryk and his party set off northwards for Galilee via Shechem (Nablus). After lunch in Afula, they reached the kibbutz of Heftziva, which was founded by Czech and German members of the Tchelet-Levan (Blau-Weiss) movement on land at Beit Alfa. Here he was welcomed by chaver (comrade) Wien. Masaryk asked Wien and other members of the kibbutz, including František Lederer, detailed questions about the principles of the kibbutz movement, the division of la-

---

298) According to Y. Jelinek. "Prezident Masaryk a Židia." In *T. G. Masaryk, idea demokracie a současné evropanství*, ed. E. Voráček. Praha, 2000, pp. 372–373.

bour, the success of the harvest, the religious life of the kibbutz members, the reasons for the *aliyah*[299] of Jews from the Czechoslovak Republic, etc. He was also welcomed to the kibbutz by the General Secretary of the Foundation Fund, Leo Herrmann (a native of Bohemia). Masaryk made a thorough visit of the children's home and asked about the school and its problems. Two years prior to Masaryk's visit the kibbutz had been visited by Alma Mahler and Franz Werfel during a two-weeks' trip to Palestine."[300]

After passing through Beit She'an, Masaryk arrived at the Degania Alef kibbutz, which had been founded in 1910, where he was greeted on behalf of the Jewish National Fund by its president Menachem Ussishkin. Masaryk toured the whole kibbutz, including its facilities and kindergarten, and spoke with the poet Irma Singerová from the Czechoslovak Republic.

Masaryk left the Degania Alef kibbutz on the south bank of the Sea of Galilee and travelled to Biblical Capernaum (Kfar Nahum) and from there via Tiberias to Nazareth, where he spent the night at the hotel Casa Nuova.

On 14 April he arrived at noon at Nahalal, the first *moshav*[301] in Palestine, founded in 1921. Leading Zionists – Ussishkin, Motzkin, Pick, Kaplansky, Leib Jaffe, Harzfeld, and Kisch (who was still accompanying him) – were gathered there to welcome him. Masaryk replied to them in English, saying inter alia: "I believe in your work. Work is a condition for happiness and I can see that you understand work. I hope you achieve your goals, and I wish you happiness and freedom." He then took lunch at the agricultural school for girls. (General Moshe Dayan's father was one of the founders of the moshav, and he himself is buried there.)

From Nahalal, the President continued on to Haifa, where he lodged at the German hospice and climbed Mount Carmel. (There is no evidence in the archive of a planned visit to Technion and the workers' settlement of Bibrach, so it probably did

299) From a Hebrew word meaning "ascent", aliyah is the term used for the immigration of Jews from the diaspora to Israel.
300) A. Mahlerová-Werfelová. *Můj život*. Praha, 1993, p. 162.
301) *Moshav*: a type of Israeli town or settlement, in particular a type of co-operative agricultural community of individual farms pioneered by the Labour Zionists during the second wave of aliyah (Wikipedia).

not take place, possibly because Bibrach was still under construction.) On 15 April, Masaryk left Haifa for Egypt.[302]

Masaryk's trip was widely commented in the local Hebrew and Arabic press, as well as in the Czechoslovak newspapers.[303] On the President's return, the Czech anti-Semitic and clerical press launched a campaign of slander, claiming that Masaryk had only visited Jewish monuments in Palestine. Dr. Josef Schieszl of the Office of the President was obliged to make an official statement in *Tribuna* explaining that the President had also been at Christian sites, a fact totally ignored by the so-called Christian press.

Masaryk's impressions of his trip to Palestine were positive overall. He expressed them during his journey in various speeches. Nevertheless he voiced some doubts regarding co-existence with the Arabs, stating in the *Prager Tagblatt*, for instance: "It is both interesting and imposing what Jews are undertaking there, and it has every prospect of success, since they have not only enthusiasm, but also plenty of resources to hand. However, where I see a difficulty is the fact that the Jews will hardly ever be in the majority in that country. I think it unlikely that anything can ever be done about the numerical superiority of the Arabs."[304]

As mentioned earlier, in honour of the President's birthday (7 March 1930), a forest named after him was ceremonially inaugurated on 21 April 1930 near the Sarid kibbutz in Galilee, in the presence of the Czechoslovak consul in Jerusalem and the vice-consuls from Tel Aviv and Haifa, as well as representatives of the Jewish Agency (Col. Kisch), and the Jewish National Fund. By the end of 1930, 13,000 trees had been planted. The entire project was the result of a decision at the 9th Congress of Czechoslovak Zionists, who collected 600,000 crowns, which they sent to the Jewish National Fund. Since then a forest has been planted nearby dedicated to Václav Havel.

On the occasion of Masaryk's 85th birthday in 1935, he was named an honorary citizen of Tel Aviv by its first mayor, Meir Dizengoff. At the mayor's request, a copy was made of the portrait

---

302) The description of the journey draws largely on H. Bergmann. "Masaryk in Palestine." In *Thomas G. Masaryk and the Jews.*

303) Including *Selbstwehr, 15, 22.* and 29. 4. *1927; Prager Presse, 9,* 11., 15. and 16. 4. 1927; *Prager Tagblatt,* 12 and 13. 4. 1927.

304) According to H. Bergmann. *Masaryk in Palestine.*

of Masaryk by Braun to be placed in the mayor's parlour. The former City Hall now houses the Tel Aviv municipal museum, where they have a number of photographs of Masaryk's visit. I was unable to discover what had become of Masaryk's portrait. A number of streets and squares in Israel are named after Masaryk, one of them coincidentally just a few hundred metres from the Czech embassy in Tel Aviv. There is also a kibbutz named after Masaryk – Kfar Masaryk – which was founded in 1940; current members still include Jews from the former Czechoslovakia. It has a small museum and miniature library dedicated to Masaryk. Due to lack of funding (neither the government of the Czechoslovak Federal Republic, nor the government of the Czech Republic were able or willing to contribute), a proposed Masaryk research or memorial institute was not realised. President Václav Havel visited Kfar Masaryk during his historic trip to Israel in April 1990.

The Israeli historian Yehoshua Jelinek had access to letters written to addressees in America by the Czechoslovak ambassador Vladimír Hurban and his wife during Masaryk's visit. He also used a translation of several sections of Giuliana Benzoni's memoirs, which were published in 1985. Both writers betrayed certain anti-Jewish sentiments in their descriptions of kibbutz life (collectivism, etc.), and in matters relating to Zionism. It is claimed that Masaryk spoke disparagingly about the communes in Palestine in a conversation with the German envoy Koch in 1928, and during his trip he had shared with Irma Singerová his misgivings about the non-religious atmosphere that prevailed in the kibbutzim. Masaryk would seem not to have grasped the spirit of the kibbutz movement, and did not entirely believe in the victory of Zionist ideology and its ability to settle Palestine.[305]

It is claimed that in private Masaryk admitted that his trip to Palestine had not made a great impression on him.[306]

Similar claims are made by Jaroslav Pecháček in his publication *Masaryk, Beneš, Hrad*, by reference to Hugo Bergmann: "'It is possible,' Professor Hugo Bergmann, native of Prague and first dean of the Hebrew University in Jerusalem, wrote in a publication in 1972, 'that Masaryk returned from Palestine with doubts about the prospects of Zionism's success in establishing

---

305) See Y. Jelinek. "Prezident Masaryk a Židia", pp. 376–377.
306) Cf. A. Gašparíková-Horáková. *Z lánského deníku 1929–1937*, p. 104.

its own state. That emerges from an interview he gave to Gershon Swet, in which he expressed his doubt that Zionism would succeed, and that Hebrew would be revived. Swet deduced from it that Masaryk had not defended Hilsner out of love for the Jewish nation, but rather out of his hatred for the Habsburg monarchy.'"[307] As we know, neither was true.

During his trip Masaryk wrote to Švehla: "Both Egypt and Palestine are very interesting, but tiring, because I am new to them; all our learning is based on Antiquity: we know so little about the Egyptians, the Jews and the Arabs."[308]

CONCLUSION

A number of important works on T.G. Masaryk have been published in recent decades. First and foremost there is Roman Szporluk's *The Political Thought of Thomas G. Masaryk* (New York 1981), in which he writes about Masaryk's attitude to the nation (pp. 118–121).

Masaryk regarded Jews as a nation on the basis of their religious faith and historical tradition, which corresponded to his view of the Czechs as a nation. He did not believe that the emigration of Jews to their historical homeland was a condition for their enjoyment of national rights. He felt that the mass emigration of Jews to Palestine would give rise to many practical problems. He supported the efforts of Jews to be recognised as an ethnic group in Austria. He was not in favour of Jews' acquiring Czech or German nationality if they retained the Jewish religion; it was not possible to be a Czech and also a religious Jew, but he did not rule out religious conversion. In this respect he acted in accordance with the tradition of Karel Havlíček Borovský. Hence, in the midst of a Czech-German conflict, it

---

307) J. Pecháček. *Masaryk, Beneš, Hrad. Masarykovy dopisy Benešovi.* Mnichov, 1984, p. 95. The most recent work on Masaryk's voyage to Palestine is A. Macková. "Čeští cestovatelé v Egyptě v letech 1918-1938. Cesta prezidenta T. G. Masaryka na Blízký východ." In *Cestování Čechů a Poláků v 19. a 20. století.* Praha, 2008, pp. 65-76.

308) This rather surprising comment from the letter to Švehla is cited by J. Kovtun. *Republika v nebezpečném světě,* pp. 497-498. Cf. *Korespondence T. G. Masaryk – Antonín Švehla,* ed. Eva Broklová, and Vlasta Quagliatová. Praha, 2012, Doc. No. 65, p. 110.

behoved Jews to choose their own Jewish nationality and not become Czechs or Germans. Consequently he had little sympathy for the Czech-Jewish movement. His attitude was not shared by his own Realist Party, which, in 1912 came out in favour of a Czech-Jewish solution at a time when it was possible to remain a Jew by religion and a Czech by nationality.

T.G. Masaryk is also dealt with extensively by Michael A. Riff in his article "The Ambiguity of Masaryk's Attitudes on the 'Jewish Question'". In: *T. G. Masaryk (1850–1937)*. Vol. 2. Thinker and Critic. Ed. by Robert B. Pynsent. London 1989, on pp. 77–87.

In his criticism of Marx in *The Social Question* Masaryk supports the Zionist position: although the Jews had abandoned Hebrew as their spoken language, they were a nation like any other, because language, in his view, was not the only sign of ethnic identity. Masaryk laid greatest emphasis on the moral regeneration of the Jews as being more important than their emigration to Palestine. It was up to the Jews themselves to improve their situation. Unlike Herzl's Zionism, the Zionism of Aron David Gordon and Ahad Ha'am did not focus on the poverty and oppression of the Jewish masses. Masaryk's appeals for the regeneration of the Jews had the sympathy of a minority of Czech intellectuals who accepted his rejection of anti-Semitism. This did not mean that those appeals were free of anti-Jewish prejudice. Riff observes that the Jews regarded Masaryk positively because of his stand against anti-Semitism and his support for Zionism, and tended to view him as a philo-Semite. Nevertheless Masaryk "was not free of some of the prejudices generally underlying anti-Semitism". He was more concerned about the betterment of the Jews than combatting anti-Semitism. "For the Czech Jews, Masaryk's position on Zionism was very disturbing." When he spoke about assimilation he had in mind "assimilation of the blood", against which there still existed legal and religious barriers. For him only cultural assimilation was justified. Jews had the possibility to assimilate as individuals, but their reception into the Czech nation was conditional and limited to individuals.

Riff considers Masaryk's views to be deeply embedded in his national philosophy. Following the Romantics and Herder, he believed that membership of the Czech nation was based on ethnic criteria. Right ethnic identity was a prerequisite for membership of the national community, which also involved the acceptance of certain common principles and values. If a Jew or German did not have the right ethnicity, he or she could not become a Czech. "Masaryk's national philosophy addressed itself solely to members of the Czech 'ethnic' nation". However, insofar as it embraced universal religious and humanitarian principles, "it appeared in some respects non-nationalistic".

Hence Masaryk saw Zionism as the only proper solution "not only because it offered the prospect of moral rebirth amongst the Jews, but also because it recognised the well-established complex nature of ethnic identity". Jews could continue to live amongst the Czechs, but only as associate members.

Masaryk's support for Zionism during the First Republic had positive consequences, including official recognition in the construction of the Yishuv. In Masaryk's republic Zionist developed with the official support and the Jews enjoyed a degree of national autonomy and recognition unique in Europe.

At the end of the chapter "Masaryk and Czech Jewry: The Ambiguities of Friendship" in his book *Languages and Community. The Jewish Experience in the Czech Lands* (Berkeley – Los Angeles – London 2000) Hillel Kieval states that: "Masaryk's attitudes [to the Jews] turned on the dichotomy between his affective, or emotional disposition and his rational, ideological convictions. Emotionally, Masaryk never completely overcame the mistrust and suspicion of the Jews he had learned as a child. Similarly, his intuition that the Jews constituted a distinct national element in the larger social body stemmed from a naïve reading of his early social-cultural environment. This does not negate the fact, however, that in Masaryk the village boy and the university professor, the Moravian Catholic and the Enlightenment rationalist, were constantly at odds. It was this struggle that produced the creative tension in Masaryk's life and work. It was the reasoning ideologist of political democracy and the enemy of cultural backwardness who defended the right of Jews to enter Czech society as equal members. And it was the critic both of Marxism and of Western liberalism, the theologian of national renewal, who discovered in Ahad Ha'am and the Zionist movement the spirit of Hus and the 'oil of the prophets'".

10. Masaryk and notable Jews

HENRI BERGSON (1859–1941)
French philosopher and writer, recipient of the Nobel Prize for Literature in 1927. Born in Paris.

Henri Bergson was introduced to Masaryk on 22 June 1918 at the residence of the French Ambassador to Washington, Jusserand. In the course of conversation, Bergson recalled his pre-war lectures in Paris, which were also attended by Edvard Beneš. Bergson was politically active during the war and pushed for intervention in Russia. Masaryk's reaction to him was that he "knew little", by which he was referring to his political knowledge.[309]

In an interview for *Les Nouvelles Littéraires* of 21 October 1923, when asked for his opinion on Bergson and Bergson's theories, Masaryk replied: "I consider that the elan, evolution and energy that he posits are a very interesting factor. Of course similar tendencies are to be found in German philosophy, particularly that of Schopenhauer and Nietzsche, but it is more precise in the case of Bergson. It is emotion and the will in contrast to intellectualism, positivism and criticism. Bergson is a great philosopher but I would express the matter differently. I would tend to adopt the expression 'inner experience', which the author of the work *Matière et mémoire* himself uses frequently."[310]

In *The Making of a State* in Section 34 on French culture, Masaryk refers to Bergson's intuition in philosophy as an attempt to overcome the abstract intellectualism of the positivist legacy and scepticism. He also mentions Bergson's élan vital etc.[311] Else-

---

309) See S. Polák. *T. G. Masaryk. Za ideálem a pravdou.* Vol. 5, p. 292 and note 5 on p. 495.
310) T. G. Masaryk. *Cesta demokracie.* Vol. 2, p. 451.
311) T. G. Masaryk. *Světová revoluce*, p. 88.

where in the same book he notes that he and Bergson had met in America.[312]

Masaryk also mentioned Bergson in his conversations with Čapek: "After all you will find belief in revelation in different variations in the works of outstanding modern philosophers: what else are James's exceptional experiences, or Bergson's intuition, or the irrationalism that is currently being propagated?"[313]

In an article in *Masarykův sborník X*[314], the French historian Alain Soubigou, author of an extensive biography of Masaryk,[315] mentions the Czech philosopher Milič Čapek, who indicated that Masaryk and Bergson "shared several common positions, particularly in their criticism of Kantism and neo-Kantism".[316]

EDUARD BERNSTEIN (1850–1932)
German journalist, writer and socialist politician; a theorist of revisionism in the German social democratic movement. Born in Berlin.

As early as 1905, in an article about Lassalle in *Naše doba,* Masaryk wrote the following about Bernstein: "At the same time as Oncken [Hermann Oncken: *Lasalle. Zwischen Marx und Bismarck*, trans.] a new edition of Bernstein's articles was published ; it is a coincidence, but the two books complement each other so superbly (Ed. Bernstein, *Zur Theorie und Geschichte des Sozialismus,* 4th ed. Berlin 1904). I don't need to say much about the Bernstein, because his *Abhandlungen* are simply conclusions that complement and expound his main, well-known work. Not a definitive revolution resulting from the impoverishment of the masses, as Marx taught, but increasing cultural demands and political education will bring about socialism – that in a nutshell in the basic idea of revisionism, as formulated and defended by Bernstein.... Bernstein, Jaurès and many others (perhaps I shouldn't

312) Ibid., p. 185 a p. 186.
313) K. Čapek. *Hovory s T. G. Masarykem*, p. 180.
314) A. Soubigou. "T. G. Masaryk a Francie." In *Masarykův sborník*. Vol. 10. Praha, 2000, pp. 199–211.
315) A. Soubigou. *Tomáš Garrigue Masaryk. Praha* – Litomyšl, 2004.
316) Ibid., p. 204. In note 14 on p. 210 of the article in question Soubigou cites Čapek's article Masaryk's personalism. In *Our Masaryk,* ed. J. Novák. Amsterdam, 1988, pp. 157–187, in particular p. 168.

mention Millerand) can claim Lassalle as their own; however, Bernstein's opponents, the orthodox, will also lay claim to Lassalle..."[317]

Bernstein and Masaryk lived in the same historical period, from 1850 to the 1930s. Masaryk concerned himself with Bernstein in articles in *Naše doba* at the end of the end of the 1890s, and he refers to him many times in *The Social Question* and *The Spirit of Russia*.

He chiefly presented Bernstein's critical opinions of Marx's *Capital:* "the first volume simply serves up new unbounded generalities [...] Marx's law of value only applies to the beginnings of the modern capitalist economy [...] goods are exchanged not for the value but for their production costs", etc.[318]

In another article – on the Stuttgart congress of the German Social Democratic Party – Masaryk reports on the proceedings and Bernstein's statement, which was read out at the congress by August Bebel. In the statement, Bernstein noted that the situation was not developing in accordance with Marx's predictions in the *Communist Manifesto* and *Capital*. Marx's crisis theory was not being fulfilled, the numbers of the wealthy were increasing and the middle classes were not disappearing, etc. Bernstein's critique was opposed by Bebel, Kautsky and Wilhelm Liebknecht, but Masaryk criticised their arguments as weak. Masaryk concluded that the proceedings and conclusions of the Stuttgart congress were a sign of the Marxism's longstanding crisis. The issues raised in Bernstein's statement were crucial in his view. Masaryk summed up Bernstein's main theses as follows:

1. The social crisis is not as big and all-encompassing as Marx stated;
2. the middle class is not declining as Marx described;
3. there are and will be no periodical crises ushering in a universal catastrophe;
4. communist society will not be established.

---

317) T. G. Masaryk. "Studie o Lassallovi", *Naše doba,* 12, 1905, pp. 565 and 567.
318) T. G. Masaryk. "Vědecká a filosofická krise současného marxismu", *Naše doba,* 5, 1897–1898, No 4, pp. 289–304. Published in German in the journal *Die Zeit* under the title Die wissenschaftliche und philosophische Krise des gegenwärligen Marxismus in 1898.

By formulating the basic questions, Bernstein was doing the greatest possible service to the party. Everything required the theorists of Marxism to revise Marx's teachings. This must be done openly, and the party must adopt theoretical progress. Marxism was in crisis which required a serious and immediate analysis of its causes.[319]

In a continuation of the article, Masaryk addresses Bernstein's book *Die Voraussetzungen des Sozialismus und die Aufgaben der Sozialdemokratie,* [The Prerequisites for Socialism and the Tasks of Social Democracy], 1899. (In it Bernstein does not mention Masaryk's *Social Question*, which was published in a German edition the same year, whereas Masaryk, in the *Social Question*, makes use of Bernstein for his critique of Marxism.) "Bernstein's book totally confirms my judgement of Marxism," Masaryk wrote. In it Bernstein spoke out against revolution; he wanted the Marxists to be a party of social reform. The party's main task was the creation of economic cooperatives. In politics it called for the greatest possible democracy. Bernstein had abandoned Marx's theory of value, and he regarded the theory of the disappearance of the middle class as groundless, and the same applied to the theory of the concentration of capital, and thus the doctrine of catastrophe and crises no longer applied.

In so doing, Masaryk maintained, Bernstein was abandoning the main theories of Marxism. Bernstein's book did not touch on the philosophical bases of Marxism, however.

Kautsky and Mehring had spoken out against Bernstein.

Masaryk's last article in *Naše doba* deals with Kautsky's relations with Bernstein. Kautsky had already come out against Bernstein in his articles in *Neue Zeit* and in *Vorwärts.* "Now he has published a book: *Bernstein und das sozial-demokratische Program. Eine Antikritik.* Stuttgart 1899, VIII, 195 pp., in order to end his discussion with Bernstein before the Hannover congress of social democracy that ended on 14 October 1899. The main topic of debate at the congress was the controversy between Bernstein and Kautsky."

In the introduction to his article, Masaryk is critical of Kautsky's book, and particularly what he considers to be the shallowness of its analysis. Kautsky had contributed nothing in

---

319) (M): "Ke krizi marxismu", *Naše doba,* 6, 1898–1899, No. 4, pp. 249–258.

relation to Marxist methodology (the materialist concept of history – dialectics – value). If the fundamental questions of Marxism were being debated then action must be taken on them too. Kautsky totally failed to fathom the foundations of Hegelian dialectics.

In his book, Kautsky dealt more thoroughly with issues of the economic development of modern capitalism, noting the problem of concentration in German agriculture and industry. In order to accept findings about that issue Kautsky broadened Marx's teaching in a non-Marxist fashion. According to Kautsky, Marx maintained that the working class and the big bourgeoisie expanded fastest of all, while the middle strata declined relatively. Masaryk protested that Marx's law on development had to be taken literally. Marx had also declared that the middle class would disappear absolutely, not relatively. But the statistics given destroyed Marx's theory. Kautsky also altered Marx's teaching on the decline of capitalism, and opposed Bernstein's statistics about the growing numbers of owners, which did not tally with Marx's theory of decline.

Kautsky almost violated Marx and affirmed Bernstein. The entire treatise was simply "transparent anti-Bernstein innuendo". Masaryk came to a single conclusion from the entire polemic: Marx was in need of additional work and correction, but any criticism of him was rejected. At least Marx's supporters needed to hear what was regarded as incorrect and questionable in the system.

The controversy between Kautsky and Bernstein was the main item on the agenda of the annual congress of the social democrats in Hanover in October 1899. The conclusions of Bernstein's and Kautsky's books confronted each other. The outcome of the entire "duel" was a partial acceptance of Bernstein's views. There were calls for Bernstein's expulsion from the party, but this did not happen in the end. The main speaker opposing Bernstein was Bebel, who failed to distinguish between Marx's teaching and the party's programme. Bebel took Kautsky's line and ended his speech with a "party resolution". According to Masaryk, Bernstein could draw satisfaction from it. The Bernstein camp held the high ground throughout the three days of debates. The official resolution was passed by 205 to 34, Liebknecht and his followers voting against. Kautsky "seemed" to have been disappointed by the outcome of the congress, Masaryk opined.[320]

T.G.Masaryk dealt with Bernstein in the course of his *Social Question*, where he states, for instance: "Bernstein was the one who most resolutely and definitely abandoned Marx's teaching. In his articles in Neue Zeit he sets out quite a penetrating critique of Marx [...] In the matter of historical materialism he firmly rejects materialism as a whole. 'Historical materialism as a whole does not dispose of the fact that people make their own history, that people have brains and the disposition of brains is not such a mechanical thing that they could be controlled by the state of the economy.' That statement is all the more significant in that Bernstein recognises ethical and ideological forces in general. The fact that he acknowledges morality as a positive and autonomous social and economic force [...] totally abandons Marx's concept of ideology."[321] Later in the book: "Bernstein got things moving for the last time when he declared that what is generally understand as the 'final goal of socialism' has very little sense and is of no interest. For him, that goal, whatever it is, means absolutely nothing to him: the movement was everything; by movement, however, he means the general movement of society, i.e. social progress, and the political and economic campaigning and organisation designed to realise that progress."[322]

Reacting to the contradictions in the theory of surplus value between the third and first volumes of Marx's *Capital*, which Bernstein acknowledged, Masaryk declares that "Bernstein's assessment of Marx's teaching is correct. Volume III contradicts Volume I in far too comprehensible language. Let the reader take a look at the book himself."[323] Masaryk goes on to state (with approval) that on the basis of German statistics Bernstein counters Marx's teaching "that capitalism will collapse under the weight of its own contradictions", and that Bernstein recognises the fallacy of "Marx's theory of catastrophes and their effects on the living standards of the working class".[324]

---

320) (M): "Ke krizi marxismu III – final part", *Naše doba*, 6, 1898–1899, No. 9, pp. 675–676.
321) T. G. Masaryk. *Otázka sociální*. Vol. 1. Praha, 2000, p. 110.
322) Ibid., p. 197.
323) Ibid., 227.
324) Ibid., pp. 253 and 258.

Concerning the question about when communism will happen Masaryk presents the notions of Kautsky, Marx and Engels, and concerning Bernstein he declares: "Not even Bernstein believes that communism will be introduced soon. Bernstein's scepticism about communism in the future can be inferred from what he has said about the social ideal; judging by his latest speeches, he has already totally abandoned communism."[325]

At the end of Volume II of *The Social Question* Masaryk addresses the problem of revolution in relation to Marx and Engels' successors: "What prompted Engels's opposition to revolution was a lively discussion about this question. Kautsky also does not come out in favour of revolutionary tactics in his exposition of the Erfurt Programme; in separate articles setting out the social-democratic catechism (1894), he started to use arguments against revolution that would soon be taken up by Engels. But Kautsky's statements are not definite enough. It is Bernstein who most resolutely and overtly rejects revolution and justifies his veto by rejecting Marx's catastrophe theory. Bernstein also calls for compromise. In opposition to those who demand intransigent tactics, Bernstein concludes that the social-democratic party can and must compromise, where necessary. [...] ...the German social-democratic party itself was the fruit of compromise [...] and it is deceitful to maintain that socialism eo ipso means radicalism." Bernstein even cites Marx in support of his assertion, Masaryk concludes.[326]

T.G. Masaryk also mentions Bernstein in the second volume of *The Spirit of Russia* in connection with the state of Marxism in Europe at that time, and particularly German Marxism. He speaks explicitly about a crisis of Marxism. He regards Marxism's historical materialism as outmoded both philosophically and sociologically. Marxism is basically modifying its positions. Marxist social democracy in Germany and Austria has revised its teaching about involvement in political and parliamentary activity. However, revisionism lacked "an outstanding theorist like Marx – revisionism was the fruit of political praxis". Masaryk continues in his critique of Marxism which is disproved by praxis and theory and states that "socialism can only be justified ethically". This brings him to Bernstein, who "does no more

325) T. G. Masaryk. *Otázka sociální*. Vol. 2. Praha, 2000, pp. 14–15.
326) Ibid., pp. 182–183.

than give expression to an admitted truth, when he desires to establish socialism subjectively not objectively; ethically, not historically. Socialism is an ethical problem."[327]

The relationship between Masaryk and Bernstein was dealt with by Karel Hrubý in *Sociologický časopis* in 1998. Masaryk and Bernstein, both critics of Marxism, were born in the same year, 1850, and in the introduction to his article Hrubý gave basic biographical details about Bernstein and listed his most important works. Masaryk knew Bernstein's articles from *Die Neue Zeit* and used his arguments when criticising Marxism in *The Social Question*. "There can be no doubt that with his articles in *Die Neue Zeit*, Bernstein furnished Masaryk with a number of incentives. The sociological and economic analysis of contemporary capitalism, based on statistical studies, as well as the critique of the theory of surplus value, and his serious objection to the catastrophism of Marx's theory, provided Masaryk with welcome (and amply cited) arguments that fitted his own criticism."[328] In his seminal work *Die Voraussetzungen des Sozialismus und die Aufgaben der Sozialdemokratie* of 1899 Bernstein does not mention Masaryk. Bernstein could have known Masaryk's pamphlet *Die wissenschaftliche und politische Krise des gegenwärtigen Marxismus,* which came out in *Die Zeit* in 1898 and Masaryk pointed it out to Kautsky, who could have told Bernstein about it. In a letter 18 May 1898 Masaryk asked Kautsky for Bernstein's address.[329]

Masaryk and Bernstein, Hrubý continues, each criticised Marx from different positions, Masaryk from "theistically conceived social synergism" and Bernstein from "anthropocentric humanism". They both criticised Marx's materialism, Marxist dialectics and their application to historical materialism. In addition they both rejected violent revolution, catastrophism, and the theory of the dictatorship of the proletariat. They both regarded the Russian revolution as a political revolution. Masaryk criticised Marx from philosophical, psychological and sociological positions, Bernstein from economic and political positions.

---

327) T. G. Masaryk. *The Spirit of Russia. Vol. 2*, p. 324.

328) K. Hrubý. "Masaryk a Bernstein", *Sociologický časopis, 34,* 1998, No. 4, p. 449.

329) "Karel Kautsky a Československo." A selection from the publication: *Karl und Luise Kautsky Briefwechsel mit der Tschechoslowakei 1879–1939,* ed. Z. Solle, and J. Gielkens. Praha, 1995, pp. 155–156.

The critique of both of them warned of the results of Marxist radicalism.[330]

ÉMILE DURKHEIM (1858–1917)

French sociologist, the first professor of sociology in France. Born at Epinal.

Masaryk and Durkheim never met. One of his seminal works concerned suicide. Masaryk's *Suicide* was published in German in Vienna in 1881 *(Der Selbstmord als soziale Massenerscheinung der modernen Civilisation)*, Durkheim's *Le Suicide* in Paris, in 1897.

According to Giddens, Masaryk's conclusions influenced Durkheim's formulations.[331] Durkheim mentions Masaryk, and Masaryk mentions Durkheim on several occasions in his works, but not in the sense that they wrote about the same topics or that Masaryk had precedence in it. Their approach to the topic of suicide and their conclusions are very different, including their view of religion, to which each of them had a different attitude: Masaryk's was personal while Durkheim's was scholarly; or of consciousness, which Masaryk regarded as solely personal, while Durkheim recognised both individual and collective consciousness.[332]

Durkheim is mentioned by Josef Král in his study on Masaryk's *Suicide*. He refers to his work *Le Suicide* and writes that Durkheim compares two types of suicide: egoistic versus altruistic, and anomic suicide at times of economic and marital crisis. The more religious a society is, the lower the incidence of suicide. Durkheim gives society as a whole priority over the individual.[333]

Masaryk first mentions Durkheim in *Naše doba*: "The author is a professor of sociology at the University of Bordeaux. He considers suicide to be the result of the moral crisis of our times and as a gauge of that crisis. He shows that modern rate of suicide is closely related to the various grave issues of the day and how he

---

330) See K. Hrubý. *Masaryk a Bernstein*, pp. 437–451.

331) A. Giddens. "Introduction." In *Masaryk, Thomas Garrigue. Suicide and the Meaning of Civilisation*. Chicago – London, 1970.

332) For a detailed comparison of the two see M. Petrusek, and N. Narbut. "Jak znal Masaryk své sociologické současníky?" In *Masarykův sborník*. Vol. 14. Praha, 2009, pp. 348–355.

333) J. Král. *Na okraji Masarykovy sebevraždy*. Bratislava, 1927.

it calls for systematic reformist social work. The statistical data are exhaustive and up to date. The book is a great contribution to the study of this grave historic and social problem."[334]

Masaryk's comments on Durkheim in his own writings are as follows: "Modern sociologists supporting this realistic and overtly materialist attitude to history based on Comte and also partly on Spencer, include Durkheim (who considers the division of labour to be the main motive force of development), Loria (a supporter of Marx's historical materialism), and also Labriola, as well as Tönnies and others, in a certain sense."[335]

Masaryk also cites Durkheim's rejection of Engels' view on the origin of the family, particularly as regards the question of promiscuity and group marriage, in *La prohibition de l'inceste et ses origines* (L'année sociologique, 1898).[336]

"Interesting is Mihailovkii's[sic] relation to Durkheim, who, following Comte, regards the modern division of labour as the most important factor in recent history and as the foundation of social solidarity. The division of labour compelled Mihailovskii to revise and supplement his formula. Durkheim's *De la division du travail social* was published in 1893. Criticising the work in 1897, Mihailovskii wrote, in definite opposition to Durkheim, that the social division of labour must be conceived as involving class differences and class contrasts. But it is open to question whether the emendation can save the formula or free it from ambiguity."[337]

"Postkantian philosophy had made so thorough a study of psychology and sociology, and above all of the philosophy of history, that, despite certain new attempts à la Durkheim, we can quietly ignore the mass consciousness talked of by Marx and Engels. The discussion concerning the nature of history has been so diligently and so persistently conducted that we are further in a position to discard Marx's conception of history and his purely would-be-objective historism. The historical dialectic

---

334) (M.). "Émile Durkheim, Le Suicide, Étude de Sociologie, 1897, " *Naše doba*, 5, 1897–1898, p. 283.
335) T. G. Masaryk. *Otázka sociální*. Vol. 1. Praha, 2000, p. 155–156 and note 2 on p. 247. (From the sociological standpoint Comte is is still of importance, Cf. E. Durkheim. *De la division du travail Social. Etude sur l'organisation des sociétés supérieures*. Paris, 1893.)
336) T. G. Masaryk. *Otázka sociální*. Vol. 2. Praha, 2000, p. 33, note 2.
337) T. G. Masaryk. *The Spirit of Russia*. Vol. 2, p. 152.

(200)

which was transferred from the 'Hegelian dialectic' has no real existence."[338]

In an article on Masaryk's sociological theory, the sociologist Jiří Musil mentions Durkheim, one of the founders of modern sociology, as a contemporary of Masaryk. Both Masaryk and Durkheim concluded that the period they lived in was a crisis of European society. However, Masaryk did not concern himself with Durkheim in his sociological theory; he addressed himself to four intellectual schools: sociological objectivism, social Darwinism, psychological evolutionism and the Russian school of sociological subjectivism. Musil argues that by positioning himself between sociological objectivism and sociological subjectivism, Masaryk criticised not only historical materialism (Marx), but also Durkheim's ideas on collective consciousness.[339]

Another Czech sociologist, Miloslav Petrusek, in his afterword to the Czech translation of Durkheim's *Sociology and Philosophy*, addresses the relationship between Masaryk and Durkheim. They were contemporaries but Masaryk preceded Durkheim with his treatise on suicide, which had a direct and indirect influence on Durkheim. Petrusek cites Anthony Giddens in his introduction to the English edition of Masaryk's *Suicide*, who states that, "The dramatic success of Durkheim's work in the respect has tended to overshadow Masaryk's contribution. However, although it is more systematic and sophisticated than Masaryk's work, Durkheim's *Suicide* shares a number of broad theoretical similarities with it, and Masaryk's conclusions no doubt influenced Durkheim's formulation of his own ideas."[340]

Petrusek notes that Masaryk did not become the "Austrian Durkheim", because he left Vienna for Prague and abandoned the academic trajectory that began with *Suicide*. Masaryk never reacted directly to Durkheim's book, *Le suicide*, and he does not even mention him in *Modern Man and Religion*. He tends to refer to Durkheim only marginally. In *The Social Question* he regards Durkheim as a supporter of "the realistic and materialist attitude to history" that overestimates the role played by the di-

---

338) Ibid., pp. 322, 323.
339) J. Musil. "Masarykova sociologická teorie: co je z ní stále živé." In *Masarykův sborník*. Vol. 8. Praha, 1993, pp. 89–100.
340) A. Giddens. "Introduction." In Thomas G. Masaryk. *Suicide and the Meaning of Civilisation*, p. xii.

vision of labour. In *The Spirit of Russia* Masaryk is disparaging about Durkheim's notion of collective consciousness, which he compares to Marx's concept of social consciousness.

Petrusek's afterword also lists the Czech sociologists who dealt with Durkheim, including Josef Král, Edvard Beneš (who was a student of Durkheim's in the period 1905–1907) and Jan Sedláček (who authored the only Czech monograph about Durkheim in 1979).

Petrusek cites an American work on sociology: "At the peak of scientific and industrial progress, Durkheim broke through into the intellectual world of the twentieth century and its deepest problem: the nonrational foundations of rationality."[341]

Petrusek concludes, "Durkheim also ranks among Veblen and London, among Schopenhauer and Hermann Hesse, among Simmel and Proust, among Baudelaire and our Masaryk."

Vladimír Pazderník is another sociologist who compares Masaryk to Durkheim in respect of their interpretation of suicide. He deals at length with the two books on suicide and gives an overall assessment of them both. Masaryk regards suicide as "the supreme crisis of modern society", while Durkheim "considers suicide essentially to be a social phenomenon, determined by social consciousness...", hence they have different attitudes to solving the crisis. Masaryk wants to bring about "a new religion" while Durkheim's posits a "well-functioning corporation". Both refer to transcendence, religious in the case of Masaryk. For Durkheim transcendence is social – an idea derived from Comte – and he sees humanity as the instrument for overcoming the crisis of modern society. Durkheim values religion as a significant factor in the moral renewal of society. Whereas Masaryk takes a position of critical realism, Durkheim propounds sociologism, which rejects psychology and emphasised the importance of social facts.[342]

---

341) M. Petrusek. *Durkheimův návrat do Čech*, p. 166; after R. Collins, and M. Makovsky. *The Discovery of Society*. New York, 1972, p. 81.
342) V. Pazderník. "Masarykovo a Durkheimovo pojetí sebevraždy." In *Masarykův sborník*. Vol. 10. Praha, 2000, pp. 56–73.

SIGMUND FREUD (1856–1939)

Austrian psychiatrist and neurologist; the founder of psycho-analysis. Born at Příbor (Freiburg) in Moravia.

Masaryk did not accept Freud and his teachings. This is evident from all extant statements by Masaryk. In *The Making of a State*, he says of the English novelist D.H. Lawrence "he seems to have got his decadence from reading Freud". And later: "The English and the Americans [...] have managed to spoil their minds with modern theories, [...] and even with Freud's ridiculous psychology. Take for instance Mr. Lawrence..."[343]

Masaryk says later in the book about Czech writers: "Just lately one-sided decadent Freudism has confused many men and women writers – and not only in our country..."

Masaryk dealt with Lawrence subsequently in a review of his short story *Glad Ghosts* in the magazine *Přítomnost* where he writes: "...Lawrence has written a psychoanalytical study; in his novels he follows Freud, sometimes crassly..."[344] Masaryk expressed the difference between himself and Freud in an interview with the *New York Times* in 1930, when asked whether at the age of eighty he was a pessimist like his contemporary, Professor Freud, and whether he rejected all faith, religion and higher goals: "I am decidedly not a pessimist, but neither should I care to proclaim myself an optimist, for I do not think the truth can be thus bifurcated. As for religion, I accept it as I accept art and science. I do not accept its enforcement. [...] I never could share those liberal or free-thinking ideas which are the absolute negation of religion. I have never been an atheist. I think the life of man and humanity and the existence of the universe has some meaning. There is an idea behind it and that brings me to believe in – well, call it God."[345]

Masaryk's view of Freud was also recorded by Ferdinand Peroutka: "... [Masaryk] also had a large library of psychological works, although I don't think he read them. He never mentioned Freud. Only once, in some debate, he suddenly said: 'the subconscious doesn't exist!' It was like one of his decrees! So

---

343) T. G.Masaryk. *The Making of a State*, p. 119.

344) T. G.Masaryk. *Cesta demokracie*. Vol. 3, p. 223.

345) "Masaryk. At Eighty, Toils On At His Task", *New York Times*, March 2, 1930, pp. 3 and 14.

I don't think he gave too much thought to Freud... [...] When I asked him once what he thought about Freud's psychoanalysis, Masaryk said to me: 'If I were to accept Freud's subconscious, I could no longer be a gentleman.'"[346]

HEINRICH HEINE (1797–1856)

German journalist, poet, writer, and satirist; the greatest German lyric poet of the 19th century. Born in Düsseldorf.

When Masaryk speaks in *The Making of a State* how he developed "from Goethe to Heine", he says about the latter: "Heine interested me a lot, but more in a political way. I'd add to that Börne and the young German radicals in general."[347]

Masaryk wrote most fulsomely about Heine in his book *Modern Man and Religion*: "I begin my remarks with Heine. (Really only remarks, no literary history!) I could not say that one work of Heine's satisfies me more than another, but as a whole they have considerable significance.

I do not mean only his literary revolt against bourgeois philistinism, but his whole world-view, and still more his Mephistophelian temperament, breaking out in a strange mixture of Voltairean classicism, redolent of the aridity of Talmudian sophistry, of sentimental Byronism, rising by degrees to cynicism, and of decadent anarchism.

Like Faust, Heine leaves the heights of idealism and throws himself into the lowlands of sensualism – sensualism not only out-philosophized but instinctively racial, Semitic. In Heine we can study the man of the new age, how step by step he becomes disillusioned – in love and in art, in politics and finally in philosophy. His heart betrays him first, his head follows – what, anyhow, would the head be without the heart for the modern man? Heine, like many others, also rejected all culture in the end. ('Vizli-Puzli'!).

Hegelianism made of Heine not only a Titan, but a god. As a god he behaved like Goethe's god in the poem, *The God and the Bayadere*, but very soon there was no money or health for all that. The Godliness wore off (the reader will see that I am keep-

346) F. Peroutka. *Deníky, dopisy, vzpomínky*. Praha, 1995, pp. 144 and 274.
347) T. G. Masaryk. *Světová revoluce*, p. 284.

ing to Heine's self-analysis), until it finally perished. Heine was cured of apotheosic illusion and even of liberal atheism.

'*als der Atheismus anfing, sehr stark nach Käse, Brantwein und Taback zu stinken: da gingen mir plötzlich die Augen auf, und was ich nicht durch meinen Verstand begriffen hatte, das begriff ich jetzt durch den Geruchsinn, durch das Missbehagen des Ekels, und mit meinem Atheismus hatte es, Gottlob! ein Ende.*'[348]

Titanic aristocratism is really very hard to get rid of. Heine in his strange hostile-friendly relation to Goethe did not fall in with Faust on this matter. To repent during illness and from fear is not to solve the problem. I do not know whether, having become a Christian in his own old way even on his death-bed, that strange delight (*Wollust*) in suffering troubled him – I, at least, despite all his literary repugnance towards romanticism, do not believe that that repentance was very deep, even though it was to blood. The poor fellow became a Lazarus (*Lazarus*), but still without real, strengthening hope. And so his Faustian-Byronic revolutionism, despite all its intensity of feeling, did not contribute to the solution of the problem of the times. Heine was not altogether genuine.

Of Faust's convictions there can be no doubt. Heine's revolutionary sentiment was always more negative; for positive reform he lacked heart and real faith – his insensitivity to Boern (to a certain extent even toward Platen) clearly shows that he could talk about the period of action which was to follow philosophizing, but that he was not capable of being a safe leader of it. But he comprehended the social movement of the age, and Saint-Simon had quite a marked influence upon him, but not a deep one. Lassalle seemed to him to be the expected Messiah of the nineteenth century! That is characteristic of Heine and it is not contradicted by his later idealization of Judaism and his delight in Rothschild. And, in the Jewish way, Heine never forgot all the humiliations and woes which in his youth he had to suffer both from Christians and from Jews. That hatred, breaking the shackles of prejudices thousands of years old, spoke a language

---

348) "… when atheism began to stink of cheese, brandy, and tobacco – then my eyes were suddenly opened, and that which I had not comprehended through reason, I now learned through my olfactory organs and through my loathing and disgust. Heaven be praised! My atheism was at an end." This translation from Heine's *Confessions*. In *The Prose Writings of Heinrich Heine*, Read Books, 2015.

comprehensible to all the oppressed and humiliated – but it was not the language of love, but of violence..."

"Heine journalized his Titanism – in this was his strength but also his weakness."[349]

There are occasional references to Heine throughout Masaryk's writings. For instance, whenever he writes about the Hegelian left (in *Karel Havlíček*), or Heine's influence on Neruda (in *Our Present Crisis),* and in *Jak pracovat* [How to work]: "Modern man enjoys hardship and being miserable. Inner calm – however rewarding – is not enough for him. For instance it is like when Heine talks about Christianity, the way he describes its sentimental component, and all that martyrdom that its dogma confronts one with."[350]

Masaryk returns to Heine several times in the *Social Question*. When Masaryk writes about the spirit of the new philosophy in Germany deriving from Kant, which penetrated literature and art, he mentions Goethe and after him Lenau arriving along with Faust: "...Heine had already fired his titanic, revolutionary, anarchic verses at the masses. Heine soon became a friend of Marx and later an admirer of Lassalle. He saw in this philosophical agitator the expected messiah."[351]

"Marx, like Heine and other Germans in the forties, was attracted by French politics and relative freedom, by the Revolution and French radicalism; but this passed."[352]

In the chapter on Marx and the Jewish question, Masaryk states: "The century of human philosophy and the Enlightenment, the century of the Rights of Man could not ignore this question. In Germany Lessing wrote his *Nathan* to no avail. In the spirit of that ideal Jew, Mendelssohn, himself a Jew and a pupil of Lessing's, started to work on the emancipation of the Jews – and Christians; he contributed [...] considerably to the German Jews becoming Germans. [...] Heine is the best-known representative of Judaic-Christian syncretism for the era of Marx."[353]

"The attachment to socialism of many Jews is understandable – its revolutionary aspect is agreeable to people who are

349) T. G. Masaryk. *Modern Man and Religion*, pp. 292–294.
350) T. G. Masaryk. *Jak pracovat*. Praha, 1947, pp. 20–21.
351) T. G. Masaryk. *Otázka sociální. Vol. 1*, p. 35.
352) Ibid., p. 51.
353) T. G. Masaryk. *Otázka sociální. Vol. 2*, pp. 113–114.

socially and politically oppressed. In Germany, Heine wrote for the proletariat and extolled its revolutionary spirit; Lassalle and then Marx became leaders of German socialism, and almost of socialism as a whole. Heine saw in Lassalle the Messiah. He definitely felt himself to be a Messiah, like Marx – that's a Jewish trait; but Marx's messianism suffers from the fault that he himself ascribes to the Jews – Marxism is too practical, too objectivist, too materialist."[354]

At the time of Marx's ascent in Germany, Masaryk assigns to Heine the leadership of political and social literature. In his description of Marx, he has the following to say about Heine: "To me it seems significant that Marx liked Heine and his works, especially since Marx himself was serious in temperament, while Heine is more reminiscent of Lassalle. Heine thought of Lassalle, not of Marx, as the messiah. I consider Marx's fondness for Heine evidence of that special bitterness, of that partly anarchistic mood. Marx is totally devoid of humour, but he has a generous allowance of Schopenhauer's anger."[355]

Equally there are references to Heine in *The Making of a State* – chiefly regarding the influence of young Germany and the literary influence of Heine on Russian philosophical literature, and on Young Rus. Heine had an "Emancipatory influence" on the Russian revolutionary democrat D. I. Pisarev, who ranked him alongside Shakespeare, Dante, Byron, and Goethe. Heine and his acerbic criticism has pride of place in the genealogy of nihilism.[356]

Masaryk expressed his interested in Heine during his trip to Palestine in 1927, when, on a visit to the Hebrew library, he asked to be shown Heine's letter about his conversion to Christianity.

MOSES HESS (1812–1875)
German utopian socialist and Zionist, born in Bonn.

Masaryk mentions Hess briefly in his *Social Question:* "In his article in *Neue Zeit*, Struve [Pyotr Struve, Russian political economist, philosopher and journalist – author's note] tries to demon-

---

354) Ibid., p. 119.
355) Ibid., pp. 332–333.
356) Masaryk's attitude to Heine is also dealt with in K. Polák. "Masaryk und Heine", *Germanoslavica*, 3, 1935, 3–4, pp. 15–240.

strate that in the years 1844–1868 Marx critically came to grips with the Babel-like tangle of socialist systems and after abandoning utopian socialist laid the bases for scientific socialism. Previously, according to Struve, Marx and Engels had been adherents of the "right-wing socialism" of K. Grün[357] and Hess, a utopian and Feuerbachian ethical socialism, i.e. 'humanism'".[358]

In the second volume of *The Social Question* Masaryk virtually repeats the same.[359]

EDMUND HUSSERL (1859–1938)

German philosopher, the founder of phenomenology. Born in Proßnitz (Prostějov).

Masaryk made the acquaintance of Husserl, nine years his junior, during his studies in Leipzig in 1876. They attended a number of lectures together[360], as well as the Philosophical Society. Masaryk advised Husserl to study the main representatives of modern philosophy: Descartes, the English empiricists and Leibniz. Husserl, for his part, introduced Masaryk to higher mathematics. Masaryk influenced Husserl by what he told him about Brentano, so that Husserl eventually went to study under him in Vienna.[361] It was under the influence of Masaryk that Husserl started to study the New Testament and converted to Protestantism.[362]

Husserl's attitude to Masaryk is explained in his 1935 letter to Professor Janák in Prostějov.[363]

After their acquaintanceship in Leipzig in 1876–1877, they associated with each other in Vienna, where Husserl attended Brentano's lectures at Masaryk's urging. Then they went sepa-

357) Karl Grün (1817–1887), German philosopher of Feuerbachian leanings, historian, publicist and liberal democratic politician.
358) T. G. Masaryk. *Otázka sociální*. Vol. 1, note 1 on p. 47.
359) T. G. Masaryk. *Otázka sociální*. Vol. 2, p. 74.
360) K. Čapek. *Talks with T.G.Masaryk*, p. 104
361) Z. Nejedlý. *T. G. Masaryk*. Vol. I.2, p. 254.
362) Similarly V. K. Škrach. "Edmund Husserl a T. G. Masaryk." In *Masarykův sborník*. Vol. 3. Praha, 1929, pp. 367–368.
363) The letter survives only in Czech. See J. Patočka. "Husserlova fenomenologie, fenomenologická filosofie a 'Karteziánské meditace'." In E. Husserl. *Karteziánské meditace*. Praha, 1968, pp. 162–163.

rate ways. In 1900 Husserl travelled to see Masaryk, but missed him. At the end of 1901 he sent him his work *Logische Untersuchungen* [Logical Investigations] and a letter with the news of his appointment as *extraordinarius professor* at the University of Göttingen, where he intended to stay and not return to Austria, because "what was sowed at White Mountain" continued to exert influence there. Masaryk thanked him in a letter, in which he also announced his intention to spend some time in America.[364]

Masaryk's reception in Austria is dealt with by Dalibor Truhlář. In a wide-ranging article he states that "Masaryk introduced Husserl to Brentano and thus more or less contributed to the emergence of phenomenology". The motto of phenomenology *"Zu den Sachen selbst!"* is in character with Masaryk's realism, as well as his opposition to historicism. There is a line from Masaryk to Husserl, and then to Patočka and Havel.[365]

Husserl reached the age of seventy in April 1929. On that occasion he received a letter of congratulations from T.G.Masaryk dated 14 March, in which Masaryk recalled the time they spent together in Leipzig at lectures by Zöllner and Wundt, and at the meetings of the Philosophical Society. Masaryk also mentioned how Husserl had helped him cope with higher mathematics.[366]

Husserl called Masaryk his "first tutor".

In August 1934 Edmund Husserl was invited to attend the international philosophical congress in Prague. Jan Patočka also tried to arrange a speaking tour for Husserl in Prague and Brno. During Patočka's visit to the Husserls' at Christmas 1934 they spoke a great deal about Masaryk. Husserl had to postpone that trip, but he eventually travelled to Prague later the next year, lecturing at the German and Czech arts faculties on 14 and 15 November 1935 about the crisis of European sciences and psychology, as well as at the *Cercle linguistique* about the phenomenology of language. He was also invited by the Brentano Society and Professor Utitz to take part in the discussion at Utitz's seminar

---

364) See S. Polák. *T. G. Masaryk. Za ideálem a pravdou.* Vol. 4, pp. 91–92 and notes 61, 62, where Husserl's letter is cited in German, with a Czech translation of Masaryk's reply.
365) D. Truhlář. "Masaryk v Rakousku – dnes." In *Masarykův sborník*. Vol. 9. Praha, 1997, pp. 133–150.
366) I. Blecha. *Husserl.* Olomouc, 1996, p. 105.

at the German University. Husserl's lectures were also attended by his Viennese friends and Oskar Kokoschka.[367]

Husserl was too exhausted to make a planned trip to Moravia. It is said that he read Čapek's conversations with Masaryk in German translation at Christmas 1936, and they revived memories of his birthplace and old homeland.[368]

Masaryk's and Husserl's notions of the spiritual crisis of European humanity were compared by Jan Patočka.[369] Masaryk's thought deals primarily with society and the human individual. He was a civiliser and organiser. European humanity was undergoing a major spiritual crisis, the roots of which went back to the beginnings of modern thinking. The spiritual crisis is "a mass social phenomenon of modern civilisation". The disintegration of life and the modern tendency to suicide were symptomatic of it. Masaryk accepted Comte's principle of the philosophy of history: ideas are the decisive driving force of historical and social processes. Masaryk's sociology and philosophy of history are an analysis of the impact of ideas on the individual and society. Symptomatic of the critical state is irreligiosity that Masaryk accounts for through his analysis of the suicide tendency.

In contrast to Masaryk, Husserl was a logician and metaphysician, and "was the last great contemplator in the West European metaphysical tradition." Husserl's concept of spiritual crisis was that in crisis, logic was the most rigorous of all sciences. "Husserl sees the crisis in a lack of clarity at the foundation of the sciences, and his critique is already an attempt at its systematic reconstruction. The way out of the crisis is subjective. To solve the crisis it is necessary to solve the question of a single foundation of philosophy and science. The solution to the crisis is a rebirth of Europeanness out of the spirit of radical theory. "The European spirit is the great rationaliser of all ideals." Husserl draws on Weber's idea of "a European rationalising impulse, which does not stop short at religion". In the process of idealisation

---

367) Ibid., pp. 116–117.
368) Ibid., p. 131. For more detail about the relationship of Husserl and Masaryk see I. Blecha. *Edmund Husserl a česká filosofie*. Olomouc, 2003, pp. 26–33.
369) J. Patočka. "The Spiritual Crisis of European Humanity *in Husserl and Masaryk*." In *On Masaryk: Texts in English and German*, ed. J. Novák. Amsterdam, 1988.

God becomes "the bearer of the absolute *logos*." For Masaryk and Husserl, emerging irreligiosity is the symptom of a state of crisis. Husserl supports this with his conception of religion as a metaphorical grasp of the ultimate metaphysical mysteries.

What constitutes the profound unity of their perception of the problem of crisis? Patočka asks. Although Masaryk and Husserl were in agreement that irreligiosity was a symptom of the crisis, they differed about what was the essence of religion. "For Masaryk, religion is primarily a feeling of trust and love in a dedication to the world and to one's task [...] (i)n short, for Masaryk religion is the support of an active life lived in a positive relation to all that is. Wherein, though is the positivity of this relation grounded? Here Masaryk answers unambiguously: in religious objectivism, in the conviction that an all-knowing and all-powerful God, the creator of the world, cares about us. 'Religion, essentially authoritarian, is objectivistic. Theism opposes an excessive religious subjectivism.'"

There is a subjective and objective component to Masaryk's conception of religion. Husserl might possibly have accepted this but not Masaryk's theological conception.

Husserl never expressed himself unequivocally about the essence of religion. "Religion remains for him an entirely emotional and conceptually inadequate version of profound philosophical motifs." Religion was a form of effective idealism.

Masaryk and Husserl were agreed on the causes of irreligiosity, namely, that modern scepticism, deriving from subjectivism, was the origin of the spiritual crisis. Patočka continues: "Radical subjectivism makes him recoil as a blasphemy because it virtually superordinates the subject to God." "Since Husserl's time, we have known that modern scepticism is brought about precisely by bad naturalistic subjectivism."

"The problem that flows from the confrontation of Husserl's philosophy with Masaryk's is one of personal faith in the context of radical subjectivism [...] without addressing this question we cannot resolve the problem of the spiritual crisis." And Husserl's intellectual optimism was not enough.

Eight of the German letters that Masaryk sent Husserl from Vienna and Prague in the years 1878–1930 have survived. In them Masaryk successively informs (his dear friend) that he became engaged to Charlotte Garrigue (1877); that he has applied for habilitation, and fully shares Husserl's enthusiasm for mathematics (1878); that he has been studying Laplace's *Essai philosophique sur les probabilités* (1878); that he plans to move to America, because "*hier kommen die Impotenten besser fort*", and asks about the situation in Berlin, whether it was better than in Austria (1879); that he remembers the time they spent together in Leipzig; that he is devoting himself to sociology, ethics and religious philosophy; that he has four children, and planning a trip to Chicago (1902); that he is following developments in philosophy in Germany; that he is in contact with Professor Kraus in Prague, and with Ehrenfels from the German university; that since 1914 his attention has been focussed on politics (1922); that he sends Husserl birthday greetings, is following his philosophical career, and again recalls their time together in Leipzig (1929); that he once more recalls Leipzig, and is working on a second edition of *Concrete Logic*; that he wants to finish his chronicle about Russia, which will be a critique of Russian writers (1930). In later years he started to address Husserl as "*Herr College*".[370]

FERDINAND LASSALLE (1825–1864)
German writer and politician, founder of the first German workers' party; German working-class leader. Born in Breslau (Wroclaw) in Silesia.

In 1905 Masaryk published his *Studie o Lassallovi* [Study on Lassalle], an extensive review of H. Oncken's *Lassalle,* published in 1904. The following does not include all of Masaryk's objections to or agreement with Oncken's propositions, and is limited to just some of Masaryk's main arguments:

"...Balthasar's words to Sickingen in Lassalle's Franz von Sickingen are the psychological key to Lassalle's character and his politics. Sickingen was simply a self-portrait of himself, and in analysing his hero, he analyses himself. In one letter to Marx and his friends, Lassalle wrote an excellent analysis of Sickingen-Lassalle, where we read 'cunning where it concerns an idea', and being sincere with his friends, admits fairly obviously '*mutato nomine de nobis fabula narratur und ewig so*'.

---

370) See J. Jirásek. "Masarykovy dopisy Husserlovi." In *Sborník prací Filosofické fakulty brněnské univerzity. Řada filosofická (B)*, 19, 1970, B 17, pp. 164.

All praise to Oncken for making that 'cunning' the basis of his analysis of Lassalle, albeit this analysis would benefit from greater psychological and particularly historical depth.

Historically speaking Lassalle was confronted by a political problem: Revolution. He himself had lived through 1848 (as a twenty-two-year-old) and realised that 1848 was simply a continuation of the Great French Revolution, whose theory and practice enthralled him. Everywhere, even in Germany, and particularly Prussia, revolutionary democracy had an impact on the old aristocratic and monarchistic social orders. Socialism detached itself from democracy as a radical movement.

It wasn't just the political events of that time that categorically demanded a solution to the problem of revolution, but also the theories, particularly philosophy and literature that were Lassalle's starting point: Kant, Fichte, Hegel – they were all compelling him to come to a decision. His closest associates in the Hegelian philosophical school were evolving towards radical socialism or ultra-individualism (Stirner), and the entire younger generation in general were on the trail of revolution, whether literary and philosophical, like Feuerbach or Strauss, or political like Marx and Engels. Before 1848, liberalism was already imbued with the spirit of revolution and republicanism (Rotteck, Welcker).

Opposing revolution, on the other hand, were the state, the church, capital, and in terms of theory – the politicians, the state and legal philosophers of the historical school, including Stahl and the conservative and reactionary thinkers in general. In their midst stood intermediaries of every possible and impossible hue, and combination of revolutionary and conservative thinking and tendency.

And it wasn't only Germany and Austria that confronted thoughtful observers and active politicians with this situation and practical problem, but the very same existed in France and Italy, and the whole of Europe in general. Paine and Burke were already in confrontation during the French revolution, and not long afterwards not only de Maistre, but also Comte were writing against revolution, while the socialists spoke in favour of it.

We need to look to literature to get the best picture of how revolution was occupying minds everywhere. What was the

German *Sturm und Drang* – Schiller and Goethe himself in his younger days – calling for, if not revolution? Do I actually have to cite Byron and his enormous effect on European literature as a whole? And what else for Lassalle were the younger German writers like Heine, Börne et al? And wasn't Lassalle also influenced by Schiller?

The excellent parallels to Lassalle's 'Franz von Sickingen' published in the early 1830s by the great Polish poets Krasiński – in the 'Un-Divine Comedy'– and Mickiewicz – in his 'Konrad Wallenrod' show clearly just how topical the issue of revolution was. Lassalle's 'cunning' was expressed by the Machiavellian 'bisogna essere volpe e leone'. Russian literature is still trying to solve the same problem, if it is seeking to solve the problem of nihilism in the special circumstances of the Russian revolution – Lassalle stands like a politician, philosopher and poet at the centre of the great and powerful movement of his day; the problem of revolution forcefully intrudes on his thinking and conscience.

Bearing this in mind, it is easier to understand Lassalle both as a person and as an individual. Because Lassalle was driven not only historically but also personally – in an intimate sense – to revolt against the status quo; we can see in the Hatzfeld trial a precocious Jewish youngster in powerful revolt: 'I, a young powerless Jew, rose up against the most dreadful of powers', Lassalle rightly declared at a more mature age about his own resistance, which was not the first. Oncken gives little detail about Lassalle's personal circumstances and his early development, which is a pity; the psychological critic corrects the meagre details supplied by Oncken, especially in ethical terms, in terms of character, and particularly in view of the strong language resorted to in the course of the book, such as 'sophist', 'unmanly revenge', 'diabolical trait' – in order subsequently to rectify, and sharpen the contours.

All we can do now is imagine what it meant before or after 1848, to decide in favour of revolution, or against it. It was necessary politically to consider the balance of forces, and estimate the consequences of victory or defeat. Whereas the experiences of 1848, just like the experiences of earlier revolutions, counselled caution, political hatred and enthusiasm, a desire for revenge for defeats suffered, and last, but not least, a philosophical passion for consistency, all urged renewed revolution. Essentially polit-

(214)

ical struggle was confronted with the ethical question of conscience: do you want to sacrifice your own life, and the lives of your enemies and of your friends? Do you have to kill? Are you permitted to kill? An awful responsibility for anyone who, out of democratic zeal, opposes violence and brutality. Marx's 'power is truth' was easier to say, than to believe or feel.

Confronted with that dilemma Lassalle said neither a definite yes nor a definite no. He was in two minds, broken in two, a revolutionary and a conservative in one. The souls of thinking people suffered the very deep contradiction of that time. As a Hegelian, Lassalle increasingly shifted theoretically from violent revolution to gradual evolution, but, after all, Hegel was over-concerned about sudden contradictions, so his formula failed very often. So at one moment Lassalle is suddenly enthused with organic progress, and the next moment is preaching revolution. And thus he oscillates between social republicanism and monarchism, between violent revolution and didactic evolution. Within him there appears a rift that split the Hegelians into right and left. The outcome of Lassalle's historical and political ideas are an attempt to unite organically what was historically inherited with what is being newly created. In his 'System of Vested Rights' Lassalle dares theoretically to merge natural and historical law. The attempt suffers from the same duplicity as 'Franz von Sickingen'; the 'System' is indeed merely a legal commentary to 'Sickingen'. In practical politics, and above all in political speeches, this organic synthesis fares even less well: revolution usually emerges victorious. Hence those corrections in many defensive speeches that are characteristic of this man. Overnight the enthusiastic – or rather would-be enthusiastic – revolutionary turns into a cold advocate, apologist and sophist.

I don't think Oncken is right in thinking that a politician cannot show any originality. But there are politicians and politicians: political novelty does not consist solely in implementing old ideas, but in creating a new political life, and in politics the saying that you don't pour new wine into old wineskins applies. Lassalle was not that kind of politician, although I also share Oncken's view that he was a very excellent politician. However, such creatively active personalities are few and far between. In all events Lassalle's character never achieved philosophical and ethical unity. He was a political Faust – and moreover a Faust without the other part. Lassalle was too much of a politician to be a politician of great style. Lassalle was too taken up with the moment, as we can observe in particular in his attitude to religion (about which Oncken says almost nothing).

Bernstein is absolutely right to draw attention to Lassalle's caesarism (Oncken fails to lay enough stress on it) and to criticise him for gambling with the working class; Oncken dresses up the latter by saying that Lassalle did not sympathise with the workers, he simply thought for them. Lassalle remained more a revolutionary than a democrat – a leader of masses fighting for progress through political action is unable to extricate himself from the manners and habits of aristocratic leaders of the past. Lassalle called his political intellectualism the dictatorship of reason."

"Lassalle's duplicity is evident in his most intimate relations with people. In his amorous relationships, passionate and rapturous love are combined with rhetorical calculation, and throughout his life his friendships were two-sided. He sought out Marx, but also Bucher[371] and sought them both out honestly out of real need. And in just the same way we should judge ethically and psychologically his relationship with Bismarck. He found not only in Marx, but also in Bismarck congeniality, matching talents, and like-mindedness, more so perhaps in the case of Bismarck than that of Marx.

More is written about that relationship than is necessary, because it really was only one instance out of many. However, what is interesting about this case is that for his part, and in his situation, Bismarck negotiated with revolution, as he admits in his 'Gedanken und Erinnerungen'. The half-heartedness that Lassalle succumbed to was and is a general political ailment, and it can be observed not only on the left but also on the right. And revolution in particular supported and pursued it, and continues to do so, not only from bottom up, but also from top down. The principle of legitimacy that Stahl and the conservative philosophers of the state and law promoted so vigorously definitely did not find in Bismarck a radical advocate, because how could the new German empire rise up? 'The German empire arose

---

371) Adolf Lothar Bucher (1817–1892), Prussian liberal politician and journalis, friend of Ferdinand Lassalle from 1861.

'in a thoroughly unconservative fashion', Naumann says in his book, 'the idea of legitimacy is not an old-Prussian idea'. What Lassalle called 'cunning where it concerns an idea,' Bismarck expressed in a conversation with Lassalle by saying that it amounted to which of the two of them was capable of 'eating cherries with the devil'.

The deceptive stance vis-à-vis Bismarck that Lassalle ended up in, can be observed throughout his political career, from the very beginning. The biographers lay special emphasis on Lassalle's volte-face in respect of Bismarck, but in reality Lassalle's entire struggle against liberalism and in favour of democracy is precisely so false, albeit from another aspect. Depending on what position they are coming from, they emphasise one aspect or another, they criticise or acknowledge this or that, but psychologically and ethically Lassalle strove from the very start to be clever in important matters. Admittedly, only later did Lassalle realise everything about himself and his situation – the fact is his character and his tactics essentially remained unchanged.

Part of Lassalle's 'cunning' is what Oncken refers to as sophistry in respect of him. Lassalle also studied Machiavelli and quite frequently made use of means available to him, without hesitation or qualms of conscience. That is something that Lassalle shares with many people and is not so characteristic of him as his sceptical cleverness and even precocity, which would have definitely been the death of him if a Wallachian hothead had not cut short his life's prospects.

Mehring rejected the legend that Lassalle indirectly committed suicide by duelling out of fear of meeting with Marx and Engels. I believe Mehring that Lassalle was not anxious in any way about meeting his friends. It doesn't matter, what is important is that Mehring himself indicates that his premature death was a self-inflicted death, or indirect suicide, when he says that he 'gave preference to' a quick death over a lengthy illness. Lassalle very definitely tempted fate, when he, a theoretical opponent of duels, made himself a target for the bullet of a stranger with no political interests. In the very same way he gambled with the workers, he gambled with himself, with his life. It could not have been a fairer gamble.

Duelling is the sign of an aristocrat, a Titan, who wants to introduce democracy himself, as a hero in government. Lassalle was not made for small-scale activities in favour of democracy, for workers' education. Oncken quite properly notes that Lassalle, like many statesmen, allowed inner politics to determine external politics, and Oncken approves Lassalle's opinion. But yet again there is the fateful contradiction between Lassalle's aristocratic and democratic tendencies, regardless of whether this opinion is actually correct.

The fact that he felt the yearned-for revolution was a lie and a deception does not make that contradiction in Lassalle any less tragic. What Marx, and particularly Engels and the more recent revisionists later taught, Lassalle had started to understand much earlier.

If we read the preface to Marx's Class Struggles, which Engels wrote in the year he died (1895), we will understand why Marxists now acknowledge Lassalle with greater warmth, alongside Marx and Engels. On many questions Lassalle's judgement was better than Marx's. He realised very soon what was wrong with the socialist revolutionary programme, which is why in his policies he drew the same theoretical conclusions from the demand for universal suffrage that Engels drew from practice thirty years later.

A new edition of Bernstein's discourses were published at the same time as the Oncken. It is a coincidence, but the two books complement each other excellently. I don't need to say much about the Bernstein, because his *Abhandlungen* are simply conclusions that complement and expound his main, well-known work. Not a definitive revolution resulting from the impoverishment of the masses, as Marx taught, but increasing cultural demands and political education will bring about socialism – that in a nutshell in the basic idea of revisionism, as formulated and defended by Bernstein.... Bernstein, Jaurès and many others (perhaps I shouldn't mention Millerand) can claim Lassalle as their own; however, Bernstein's opponents, the orthodox, will also lay claim to Lassalle, and particularly his – 'cunning'."[372]

Lassalle is referred to several times in *The Social Question*. "There is something like messianism in socialism, and that element was replanted into it from Judaism by Lassalle and Marx.

---

372) T. G. Masaryk. "Studie o Lassallovi", *Naše doba*, 12, 1905, pp. 513–517, 564–567.

There is a growing awareness of solidarity (class consciousness) in socialism, leading to enormous sacrifices – which are religious characteristics."[373]

"Lassalle was right in a way when he said of the German classics that they are *volkstümlich* [popular, trans.] only because the people don't understand them properly."[374]

"Marx himself was serious in temperament, while Heine is more reminiscent of Lassalle. Heine thought of Lassalle, not of Marx, as the messiah."[375]

"It is impossible to condemn all revolution on ethical grounds. Lassalle went too far when he promised absolute legality and peace. Revolution, like necessary self-defence, can at times be inevitable. "[376]

Masaryk's book *The Spirit of Russia* also contains minor references to Lassalle.

EMIL LUDWIG (1881–1948)
Austrian writer and journalist born in Breslau (Wrocław) in Silesia.

Ludwig visited Masaryk several times in the 1930s, and their conversations formed the basis for the book *Duch a čin* [Spirit and action], which was published in 1935 and re-edited many times in later years, most recently in 1996 with an afterword by Milan Machovec. Masaryk studied the German manuscript carefully and made corrections. Several details about Ludwig's visits to Lány and Topoľčianky were recorded by Anna Gašparíková, including the fact that during his visit to Topoľčianky on 8 October 1930, Ludwig interceded with Masaryk on behalf of Trotsky, asking Masaryk to grant Trotsky political asylum. "The President said a definite 'nein'. The reason he gave was that it would be impossible to guarantee sufficiently his safety. [...] The President spoke with Ludwig, and told us later that Ludwig did not interest him."[377]

373) T. G. Masaryk. *Otázka sociální*. Vol. 2, p. 213.
374) Ibid., p. 246.
375) Ibid., p. 347.
376) Ibid., p. 333.
377) A. Gašparíková-Horáková. *Z lánského deníku 1929–1937*, pp. 52–55.

At Lány, Masaryk expressed the view that "Ludwig is becoming a literary Schöngeist [aesthete, trans.]", and he found it unpleasant.[378]

Gašpariková also mentions an episode when Ludwig and Masaryk were reading Hitler's *Mein Kampf*. Masaryk "...shared some of his funny recollections about Jews from his childhood. He went even more deeply into the Jewish question and ended by saying: 'I didn't like them very much at first. You know what they did against us Slavs at the time of Austria-Hungary. But when I want to be fair in general, I can't be against.'"[379]

KARL RAIMUND POPPER (1902–1994)
British philosopher, born in Vienna.

Karl Popper referred to Masaryk on several occasions: "Masaryk has been described sometimes as a 'philosopher king'. But he was certainly not a ruler of the kind Plato would have liked; for he was a democrat. He was very interested in Plato, but he idealized Plato and interpreted him democratically. His nationalism was a reaction to national oppression, and he always fought against nationalist excesses. It may be mentioned that his first printed work in the Czech language was an article on Plato's patriotism.... Masaryk's Czechoslovakia was probably one of the best and most democratic states that ever existed; but in spite of all that, it was built on the principle of the national state, on a principle which in this world is inapplicable. An inter-national federation in the Danube basin might have prevented much."[380] "Fichte's and Hegel's ideas led to the principle of the national state and of national self-determination, a reactionary principle in which, however, a fighter for the open society such as Masaryk sincerely believed, and which the democrat Wilson adopted."[381] Popper also described Masaryk as "one of the greatest of all fighters for the open society".[382]

Karl Popper was in Prague several times before World War I, as well as during it, but did not come back there again until

---

378) Ibid., p. 118.
379) Ibid., pp. 176–177.
380) K. R. Popper. *The Open Society and its Enemies*. Chapter 12, note 53.
381) Ibid., p. 284, note 2.
382) Ibid., p. 49, note 3.

1934. He returned to Prague once more sixty years later, in 1994, to receive an honorary doctorate from Charles University. On that occasion, he gave a lecture to the 3rd Faculty of Medicine of Charles University in which he spoke about Masaryk as follows: "...Sixty years ago, there lived in the Hradčany Tomáš Garrigue Masaryk, the great founder of the Republic of Czechoslovakia, and its Liberator President. I deeply admire Masaryk. He was one of the most important pioneers of what I have called, one or two years after Masaryk's death, the Open Society. He was a pioneer of an open society, both in theory and in practice; indeed, the greatest of its pioneers between Abraham Lincoln and Winston Churchill. Of the successor states of the Austrian Empire, now defeated and impoverished, Masaryk's creation, the Czechoslovak Republic, was the only successful one. It was a financial, an industrial, a political, an educational and a cultural success; and it was well defended. Never was a new state – after all, the result of a revolution – so peaceful and so successful, and so much the creative achievement of one man. And all this was not due to the absence of great difficulties; it was the result of Masaryk's philosophy, his wisdom and his personality in which personal courage, and truthfulness, and openness, played so conspicuous a role. He described his own philosophy as a critical realism. This is indeed what it was. But humanism, or humanitarianism, also played a dominant role.

Masaryk's extraordinary life has, I expect, been closely studied by historians. Nevertheless, I have come to Prague in the possession of two stories, or anecdotes, that are, very probably, quite unknown to all his biographers. Both stories may, I believe, still be testable, at least partly, by someone interested in researching the documents that may still be extant. The first is the story of the strange circumstances under which I first heard Masaryk's name mentioned, in the winter of 1915–16, during the First World War, when I was 13 years old. My father was a lawyer in Vienna, and a family by the name of Schmidt, with their three sons and a daughter, were close friends of our family. One son was a professional army officer, another, Dr. Karl Schmidt, then in his late twenties, was a lawyer; and the third, Oscar, was a pupil in my class at school. Dr. Karl Schmidt frequently came to see us, and he often stayed for dinner. On one of these evenings, dressed in his war-time uniform of an officer of the Austrian Imperial Army, he told us that his present duty in the army was to investigate cases of high treason and prepare for the military court proceedings against the traitors. He told us of a most interesting case which he was then pursuing: the case of a Professor of Philosophy at the University of Vienna, Dr. Tomáš Masaryk, then 66 years old, currently in England or in the United States, one of the main leaders of the Czech and the Slovak Movement for National Independence and, most obviously, a man guilty of high treason. But, he continued in strictest confidence, a wonderful man. Schmidt told us that he was reading Masaryk's book, especially a book about Russia's relations to Europe, which he found most impressive. Warming to his subject, Schmidt gave us a lecture on this incredible traitor, a man of the highest learning and culture, a leading philosopher, a teacher of ethics, a great liberal, and a man prepared to risk his life to achieve the freedom of what he regarded as his people. Schmidt later told us also of the Czech Army which Masaryk was organising against Austria and Germany with Czechs living abroad, in France, England, Russia and the United States, and also from Austrian Czech soldiers who had become prisoners of war in Russia.

This was an extraordinary experience, and it is vividly before me after 78 years. It could have happened, I now think, only in Austria. Imperial Austria was then at war and ruled by a law that applied to special conditions that made parliamentary control impossible. It was ruled by its prime minister, Count Stürgkh, who exerted dictatorial powers, under martial law. And yet, the liberal atmosphere of the pre-war period was still alive in Vienna. Here was a lawyer, at the same time an army officer, appointed to pursue treason – and he was, obviously, committing treason himself by telling us, ordinary civilians, in confidence, on each of his occasional visits, about the progress of his investigations, and about his admiration for a traitor! Yet he had, clearly, no fear at all. He knew he was safe: safe in spite of the dictatorship and the state of martial law. What a difference from the situation that started a year later in Russia and that led to that horrible thing that we may now call 'modern dictatorship'! So this happened in 1916, in Vienna. But locally in some of the provinces, in the regions of Austria in which the state authorities were facing irredentist nationalism, state terror ruled. The bureaucrats, the pocket dictators, were unaffected by the liberalism of the cities – and they were afraid. They ruled by secret terror, and even torture: and I learned it all from the same extraordinary source, from the recurring visits of Dr Karl Schmidt. Schmidt told us all about the movements of Masaryk, his hero against whom he was preparing a legal case that was bound to lead to Masaryk's execution, should victorious Imperial Austria ever get hold of him. But by 1916 it had become clear even to me that this would never happen: that the central powers had lost the war.... What I did not know was that even members of the Government of Austria wished to give in, and that Austria continued with the war largely for fear of a German invasion. This is the end of my first story.

Almost twenty years later, when Chancellor Schusnigg was the dictator of Austria, I happened to hear again something very personal about Tomas Masaryk. At the University of Vienna I had been a pupil of Professor Heinrich Gomperz, the Greek scholar, and we had become friends. After the murder of Chancellor Dollfuss by a troop of Austrian National Socialists, Schuschnigg had taken over, and had demanded from all persons employed by the state, or by local governments, including all teachers and professors, that they join an organization which he called the Patriotic Front, an organization that admitted as members only people who signed a declaration that they were opposed to the Anschluss, the unification of Austria and of Germany. Germany was then under Hitler's dictatorship. All university professors signed, (and especially those who were Nazis). There was only one exception: Professor Heinrich Gomperz whose family came from Germany and whose cultural background and Greek scholarship made him partial to a union with Germany where Greek scholars abounded. He himself was of Jewish descent and he was well aware of Hitler's terroristic ethnic theories – and his terroristic practices. But he had faith in the high civilization of Germany, and he looked upon Hitler as a political freak, certain to disappear soon. Gomperz, I think, found it below his dignity to take much account of Hitler. In most of this, Gomperz was sadly mistaken. However his failure to sign up with Schuschnigg's Patriotic Front led to the dismissal of Gomperz from his professorship with total loss of his income: and censorship prevented this from ever getting into the papers. Nobody heard of this dismissal. No rumour reached me, until one day he rang me and we met. Then he told me what had happened and that after his dismissal he had decided to emigrate to the United States. But he had not the money to pay for the costly journey. So he went to Prague, to ask his old colleague and friend Masaryk for a loan. Masaryk gave him the money from his own personal savings as a gift, rejecting a loan and explaining to Gomperz that he did not wish to use any kind of official funds for this purpose because the political element in it might make it look as a pro-German act, and even as pro-Hitler... And Gomperz told me how wonderful and moving his meeting with Masaryk had been.

Ladies and Gentlemen, I have always admired Masaryk as one of the two great statesmen and heroes of twentieth century Europe: I mean Masaryk and Churchill.

Masaryk's Czechoslovakia was, I do not doubt, the most open of all societies ever to develop in Europe. It lasted for only twenty years. But what difficult and what marvellous years! In the shortest time, this open society had built a solid economy and the most solid military defence system in Europe. Then Masaryk's Czechoslovakia was destroyed by the two older of the European open societies – by Britain and France, under the governments of the appeasers, who co-operated with Hitler in destroying Czechoslovakia. And we might speculate that, had Masaryk still been alive, it is improbable that the appeasers could have helped Hitler in the destruction of Czechoslovakia. Hitler was still bluffing, and Masaryk, I believe, would have called the bluff.

[...] And now, when we are again suffering some of these setbacks, we must think of our very latest success: South Africa. And we must keep fresh before our memory such incredible achievements of the spirit of freedom, openness and humanity, as that of Churchill's seemingly hopeless resistance to Hitler, after the fall of France, and of Masaryk bringing back his valiant soldiers, an army of 60,000 men, through Siberia and Vladivostok, and across the Pacific Ocean and the American continent in order to found a great republic, an open society, strong enough to rise again after many a violent death."[383]

383) *Karl Popper Lecture* (Prague 1994), https://www.lf3.cuni.cz/3LFEN-255 .html.

GEORG SIMMEL (1858–1918)

German philosopher, sociologist and historian, born in Berlin.

The relations between Masaryk and Simmel have been the subject of study by the Czech sociologist Miloslav Petrusek.[384]

There are passing references to the name Georg Simmel in Masaryk's writing particularly in *The Social Question* regarding the "close association between sociology and socialism".

Masaryk felt no great affinity with Simmel. He read Simmel's *Sociology* "as an academic sociologist conditioned by the times" and criticised Simmel for what he would criticise him later, namely: "a not entirely successful attempt to define sociology specifically as a science 'about the social forms of association.'"

Petrusek notes that Masaryk and Simmel had at least three things in common:

1. When Masaryk makes an attempt at academic sociology (like Simmel in his "formal sociology"), he is unconvincing and sociologically uninspiring. He is convincing in his book *Modern Man and Religion*, which was published in 1898; Simmel's seminal work *The Philosophy of Money* came out in 1900.
2. Masaryk and Simmel were both analysts of modernity and perceptive diagnosticians.
3. Both Masaryk and Simmel established a new style of expression that Georg Lukács would call "sociological impressionism", which was the beginning of shift in sociology towards a "non-scientistic, non-quantitative and non-experimental" sociology.

According to Petrusek there is a deeper connection between Masaryk and Simmel, but it remains to be found.[385]

Miloslav Petrusek also described Masaryk's review of Simmel's *Sociology*. "Masaryk's review praises sections of the work that he considers a 'ponderous book', criticising the confusing ordering of the material, and the imprecise use of terminology. There are other digressions in the ten chapters, which make it difficult to read. The index is incomplete. Although the book contains some very good and valuable reflections, such as regarding the process of socialisation, superiority and subordi-

---

384) M. Petrusek. "Simmel a Masaryk. Na okraj jedné neznámé Masarykovy recenze", *Sociologický časopis,* 33, 1997, No. 3, p. 367–376.
385) Ibid.

nation, controversy, etc., 'sociology as a whole and a system is absent from the book.'"[386]

BARUCH SPINOZA (1632–1677)

Dutch philosopher born into a family of "crypto-Jews", i.e. those who forcibly underwent Christian baptism in Spain. The d'Espinoza family came to Portugal after being expelled from Spain and then moved to Holland, where Spinoza was born in Jodenbuurt, Amsterdam.

Masaryk rejected Spinoza, which is already evident from his *American Lectures*, where he says of pantheism: "First of all, as far as theism is concerned, nowadays maybe the majority of philosophers and even many more progressive theologians reject a personal God, but people who now speak about God think of God as impersonal, and conceive of Him pantheistically. Pantheism states: God is within us and in the world; God and the world are one. The word pantheism means worship of many gods. Pantheism is often called monism. Monism means: oneness, singleness. Monism is very modern – people yearn for oneness and are opposed to dualism (duality); they don't like the world and God being dissimilar, or the body and soul, or spirit and matter being totally different. They therefore want a single principle.

"I cannot be a pantheist, because I see numerous things, I see numerous people, and I have my own restricted knowledge. Pantheism is, I believe, an unjustifiable hypothesis. The mere fact that pantheism admits to desiring a simpler world and society, and that it does not accept the old view of the church concerning a God totally separate from the world."[387]

In his book *Modern Man and Religion* Masaryk says the following about Spinoza's ideas: "...as far as scientific thinking was concerned, it put an end to the conflict between the human and the divine; After Spinoza, all European philosophers worked with this end in view, until Kant, by making a religion out of morality struck off the shackles of revelation from religion..."[388]

---

386) "Sociologie Georga Simmela od profesora dr. T. G. Masaryka, člena rakouské říšské rady v Praze. Soziologie. Untersuchungen über die Formen der Vergesellschafung. Leipzig 1908," *Sociologický časopis,* 33, 1997, No. 3, pp. 377–382.
387) T. G. Masaryk. *Americké přednášky,* p. 63.
388) T. G. Masaryk. *Modern Man and Religion,* p. 174.

The Social Question and *The Making of a State* contain many references to Spinoza, who is presented alongside Jeremiah and Jesus as an epitome of the Jewish nation. Masaryk saw Spinoza's method in Marx, and maybe even his character. Masaryk thought that Chernyshevsky, Solovyov and Bogdanov were influenced by Spinoza. Masaryk mentions several times J. Stern's *Die Philosophie Spinozas,* whose second edition was published in 1896.

LEON TROTSKY (1879–1940)
Real name Lev Davidovich Bronstein; Marxist theorist, Russian revolutionary and Soviet politician. Born at Yanovka (Ukraine) in the Russian Empire.

Trotsky consciously distanced himself from his Jewishness, but, as a revolutionary and public figure, he had to come to terms with it. He regarded himself first and foremost as a revolutionary and a Russian, and he was firmly grounded in Russian culture. His knowledge of many languages, and the fact that he lived abroad for many years before the revolution and after his expulsion from the USSR, meant that he was truly a citizen of the world.

There is only one reference to Masaryk in Trotsky's memoirs; it relates to Trotsky's hasty departure from Vienna for Switzerland after the outbreak of World War I: "Behind us, we had left the ties of seven years, and books, papers, and unfinished writings, including a polemic against Professor Masaryk on the future prospects of Russian culture."[389]

It would appear that Masaryk and Trotsky never met in Vienna, although they both lived there prior to 1914: Trotsky from 1907, and Masaryk also, after he was elected to the imperial parliament that year, and again after his re-election in 1911, although he shared his time between Vienna and Prague. Masaryk makes only one reference to Trotsky in his writings, and namely in his *New Europe* in the chapter about Prussian Germany, where he speaks about Prussian political materialism and described Prussian policies "which never were honest and generous (see for example the dishonourable peace with revolutionary Russia:

---

389) L. D. Trotsky. *My Life: An Attempt at an Autobiography.* New York, 2012, p. 236.

William makes agreement with Trotzky [sic] – the super-legitimate monarch with a revolutionist, and, what is more, a Jew, who in William's army could not be promoted to be an officer."[390]

Trotsky wrote an extensive negative review of Masaryk's *The Spirit of Russia*,[391] in which he bitterly criticised the book. The review was also published in Czech.

In the introduction to his review, Trotsky states that Masaryk was trying to create the problem of Russian history "from inside Dostoyevsky", before suddenly discovering that "even on paper the immense substance of Russian history cannot be squeezed into Dostoyevsky's moral and philosophical schemata". According to Trotsky, Masaryk admitted his failure and this "failure really means a total collapse of the misconception that derives Russian history from its 'philosophy of religion' and then embodies it in a randomly chosen person".

Trotsky goes on to label Masaryk as a Kantian, whose task is limited to "the moral-philosophical foam of historical developmental processes". Masaryk uses Kant's normative philosophy for the "philosophical and moral 'assessment' of the individual epochs and individual representatives of the development process of Russian society".

Masaryk, says Trotsky, deals with religious philosophy emerging out of human history, but does so without any method, and he appears simply as "an uncritical compiler, helpless and confused. [...] He lacks both historical intuition and monistic theory". Trotsky also criticises Masaryk for alleged "numerous errors, anachronisms and misunderstandings".

Trotsky claims that the underlying theme of the book is that "Europe has reached where Russia wants to go", i.e. Russia is theocratic and is struggling against that theocracy. This "basic idea" is rejected by Trotsky. "Masaryk's concept of theocracy lacks all political and historical content. He expresses this concept psychologically, and every state that relies on a religious consciousness, on a myth, is theocratic in its eyes." Trotsky proceeds to give his own explanation of the developmental difference between eastern and western Europe, which "lies in the far

---

390) T. G. Masaryk. *The New Europe: The Slav Standpoint*. London, 1918, p. 40.
391) Leo Trotzki. "Professor Masaryk über Russland", *Der Kampf, sozialdemokratische Monatschrift*, 7, 11–12, 1914, pp. 519–527.

less favourable material and cultural conditions of the East." He cites factors such as soil, climate, and the heritage of Roman culture, which were all more favourable in the West than in the East, subject to incursions by Asian nomadic tribes. In the East, the state emerged in oppressive conditions, the church was weak and had to submit to the state and become bureaucratised. Trotsky continues with his description of development in Russia, explaining that the church could not enrich itself with the legacy of classical civilisation, and did not adopt Latin; the adoption of a Slavonic language by the church was "the expression of the country's cultural poverty". Russia also knew no Reformation. "In contrast to the countries of Catholic culture, the liberated personality in Russia broke the myth without fierce internal struggle and placed itself on the ground of realism." There was nothing of the Titanic subjective tragedy about this break as Masaryk supposed, based on his reading of Merezhkovsky.

According to Trotsky, the Russian intelligentsia is largely non-religious, and Russian liberalism is indifferent to religious matters. The workers were abandoning the church even more painlessly than the intelligentsia: "Materialist socialism is for them in general the first form of subjective existence – existence per se." By transforming the real social and state order of Russia into a supra-historical theocracy, Masaryk comes to the erroneous conclusion that "it is precisely the religious question that has brought about the crisis of the revolutionary movement." According to Masaryk, Trotsky says, "the revolutionary movement has failed because of the problem of God", whereas in reality the opposite was true: "the revolutionary crisis brought on by deep social causes induced a mysticism reflex in some circles of the intelligentsia." Masaryk had no idea of the materialist dialectic, Trotsky declares at the end of this section of his review.

Most of the second volume of Masaryk's book was given over to Russian Marxism. According to Trotsky the second volume "must, for the most part, be considered completely unusable." Trotsky devotes a whole page of his review to factual errors that he claims Masaryk made in expounding the history of Marxism in Russia. Essentially, Masaryk reiterates the same thing he once published about the crisis of Marxism, but now he applies it to Russian Marxism also. "According to Masaryk, theoretical Marxism has long since been surpassed. [...] But how does this explain that the influence of Marxism is not diminishing, but increasing?" Trotsky asks. According to Masaryk, Marxism is "... the scientific formulation of revolutionary socialism". In other words, says Trotsky, "Marxism continues to satisfy the practical needs of the working class movement", although Masaryk maintains that Marxism's revolutionary nature has also been surpassed. So what maintains it, Trotsky asks, and replies caustically: "Probably only the good nature of our Prague professor". In the history of Russian Marxism, he says, "Masaryk sees a new and effective refutation of Marx's historical materialism". According to Trotsky, Masaryk fails to answer the fundamental questions: why the Russian intelligentsia adopted Marxism, and in what form, and why it abandoned it en masse, etc. Trotsky gives his own explanation of the evolution of the Russian intelligentsia, and why its left wing adhered to Marxism. Masaryk's idealism prevents him from seeing the historical reality, and he fails to see the social roots of the Russian world of ideas.

Trotsky concludes by acknowledging Masaryk's sympathy for the emancipatory movement in Russia, but declares that he ought to moralise less and have greater mental clarity, political insight, and – a better writing style.

Illustrations

1. T.G.Masaryk and his wife Charlotte in 1905, shortly after the Hilsner Affair.

2. T.G. Masaryk in New York, 1918.

3. Representatives of the Jewish National Council meet President Masaryk, January 1922.

4. A walk in Jerusalem, 9 April 1927.

5. President Masaryk and his entourage, Jerusalem, 9 April 1927.

6. In the streets of Jerusalem, 9 April 1927.

7. T.G.Masaryk in the Mea Shearim district of Jerusalem, April 1927, in the company of Slovak-born Rabbi Sonnenfeld.

8. T.G. Masaryk with Hugo Bergmann in Jerusalem, 9 April 1927.

9. A visit to Bethlehem, 9 April 1927.

10. Arriving at the Dead Sea, 11 April 1927.

11. The President and his entourage at the Dead Sea, 11 April 1927.

12. By the River Jordan, 11 April 1927.

13. T.G.Masaryk in Tel Aviv, 12 April 1927.

14. President Masaryk visits the Rishon Le Zion settlement on 12 April 1927. To his right, Alice Masaryková.

15. At Rishon Le Zion, 12 April 1927.

16. Welcome at the Beth Alfa kibbutz, 13 April 1927.

17. President Masaryk among the settlers at Beth Alfa kibbutz, 13 April 1927.

18. T.G.Masaryk in the streets of Nazareth, 14 April 1927.

19. President Masaryk at Capernaum, 14 April 1927.

20. At Nahalal, 14 April 1927. T.G.Masaryk at far right; Alice Masaryková is fifth from right (in a hat).

21. Zionist leader Nahum Sokolov in talks with President Masaryk, 16 December 1927.

22. Copy of Rudolf Braun's portrait of T.G. Masaryk.

Afterword
Converging destinies in the thought and life of Miloš Pojar

PETR PITHART

I kept track of the author's life from childhood until his death – the two of us started primary school together in the same class in the Bubeneč district of Prague – so I am now not only an attentive reader of his book about Masaryk and the Jews, but I can say I was a witness to the career that led up to its creation in the course of his remarkable life.

His life had a clear goal and that goal had an undisputed meaning. Miloš Pojar achieved his goal and fulfilled his life's purpose. Towards its end of his life, as a senior civil servant and author, he was able to address to a broad audience his appeal: Justice for the Jews! I know few contemporaries about whom one could say without hesitation that they found fulfilment by fulfilling their long held resolutions in the public sphere.

The title of the book epitomizes him, as if it were a testament containing the most important message for the future: let us cherish Masaryk and his concern that justice be done to the Jews, and let us beware of doing them wrong or treating them unjustly! Masaryk demands our esteem in particular because his struggle with anti-Semitism was a personal issue. Masaryk was no admirer of the Jews. He was convinced that they themselves had to make efforts to better themselves .

Even as a child, Miloš Pojar showed signs of a kind of premature adulthood. His first interests were animals and geography, and then history, particularly the history of the Czech lands, and their Hussite and Reformation past, with its great heroes. Later still he became more and more interested in the Jews. He himself was a so-called "half-Jew", but he accepted the fate of a full Jew, of that entire sorely-tested nation. So an encounter with Tomáš Garrigue Masaryk was inevitable. He then spent many years enhancing and cultivating his attitude to Masaryk in lengthy conversations with his guru, the philosopher Milan Machovec. In latter decades I was also part of those conversations. We would consider from every angle the controversial issues of Czech history, including, therefore, the Jews, the Germans – and T.G.Masaryk.

One day in 1980, in light of the fact that the last Masaryk anthology was published during the First Republic (No. 6, *Leader of Generations,* edited by Vasil Škrach in 1930), we decided to compile a new anthology – No 7. – to mark the 130th anniversary of Masaryk's birthday. We entitled it *TGM and Our Present Situation.* It was published in samizdat, of course, but with great care, and it was almost technically perfect. The three of us edited it and also contributed articles. We were very demanding as editors, and treated the manuscripts as if they were for a normal publication, whereby we revived Masaryk scholarship in the Czech lands, which had been disgracefully curtailed. Our anthology was subsequently re-edited as a conventional publication by the Academia publishing house in 1992, since when publication of the anthologies has continued.

I recall how very proud we were of that publication in those days – the fact that we'd had the courage to undertake it, and succeeded. Our objective, one which we were not certain to achieve, was to open its pages not only to dissidents, but also to interesting thinkers who had managed to maintain their positions on the fringes of the official structures without compromising. Of particular pleasure were two contributions from Masaryk's grand-daughters, Anna and Herberta, as well as a hitherto unpublished text by Masaryk on correct social behaviour – such as not keeping coal in the bath because it made it difficult to maintain cleanliness...

In those days Miloš Pojar was no longer employed by the Academia publishing house as a philosophy editor, but only as technical assistant in charge of magazine distribution. For that reason his contribution, a Masaryk bibliography, appeared under the name of Josef Dubský. Just a few weeks after the three volumes were "published" in Prague in samizdat we listened to a report on *Voice of America* by Professor Jiří Kovtun), in which he informed listeners that the three-volume anthology (which weighed over five kilos) had already been acquired by the Library of Congress in Washington, where he was then working. That was the sort of experience that I would wish on every author whose works are readily available in bookshops. Even we thought it better not to have a copy of the anthology at home because of the risk of its being found during a house search by those who had never bought a book like it in their lives...

Pojar's contribution to the anthology was probably one of the building blocks of the present book. Miroslav Horníček's observation that "books have destinies of their own" was probably even more valid then than now. And the authors who were also editors had their destinies too: in those days words were more important because of the risks involved – when one wrote them, copied them, turned them into books, and distributed them.

...

But the history of Miloš Pojar's connection with the Jews and the state of Israel does not end there, however. On the contrary! In February 1990, just a few months after the Velvet Revolution, Miloš's friends recommended him to the newly-appointed Foreign Minister, former dissident Jiří Dienstbier, as ambassador to Israel, with which the new regime was planning to renew diplomatic relations. And it happened – as things did at that time. We had some very distinctive ambassadors around the world in those days! I've never managed to find out who recommended Miloš, but a number of names come to mind.

An utterly improbable dream became a reality. A well-concealed interest turned into an opportunity: an offer to assume top-level political responsibility. How was it possible? In those days a lot depended on the trust of people who knew each other from dissident circles, and from the "grey zone", which consisted of hundreds and thousands of people without whom the dissidents would have been even more isolated from society than they actually were. Miloš was a typical "warrior" of the grey zone – and I don't know why the term has started to acquire a pejorative undertone nowadays. Following his appointment as ambassador, and before he left Prague, he welcomed the Israeli deputy Prime Minister (and future President) Shimon Perez to the Czech Republic. Shortly afterwards he flew to Tel Aviv, where the building of the Czechoslovak embassy was derelict, since it was abandoned in 1967. He was housed in a hotel, where he prepared for an official visit by President Václav Havel – no easy task.

Having once written a detailed account of Masaryk's visit to Palestine, the future territory of Israel, as the first international statesman to travel to those parts (as early as 1927), Miloš Pojar now accompanied the president of his country also on his first visit, but to the state of Israel this time...

Yes, such things happen too, when people have a lifelong awareness of their duty and responsibility.

His tour of duty completed, Miloš Pojar worked at the Foreign Ministry as a deputy to the Director General, where his brief included Holocaust commemoration. His subsequent appointment as director of the Educational and Cultural Centre of the Jewish Museum in Prague was therefore a natural progression. He also published a number of books on the topic of Czech-Jewish relations, and was deeply involved with the issue of Czech-German relations (as a member of the Czech-German Fund for the Future). In later years his son Tomáš was also appointed Ambassador to Tel-Aviv.

In spite of recent rapid and surprising changes in the Czech Republic, a sympathetic attitude towards the State of Israel and Jews in general remains the norm in this country, in spite of anti-Semitic sentiments that are still to be found here as everywhere else.

At the official level, sympathy is reflected in the special relationship between our two countries. The Czech Republic is exceptional among member states of the European Union (and also of the United Nations) in defending Israeli interests, a position that is frequently acknowledged publicly by Israel.

At an unofficial level, it is hard to gauge people's sympathies, but without deluding ourselves, I think one may say that Czech anti-Semitism is fairly timid in nature, and its public manifestations are immediately the subject of sharp condemnations from educated sections of the population, and rare attempts to blacklist Jews attract public ridicule...

In this afterword to a book about Masaryk and the Jews one cannot help but ask the question whether Masaryk and his achievements have some bearing on present-day attitudes. They certainly do, but to what extent it is hard to say. The present book outlines the various factors affecting our attitudes to Jews and Israel, but the author was also unwilling to make any final judgement. This is not to its detriment, however. There are certain matters between heaven and earth that are hard to define or assess.

The Hilsner Trial and Masaryk's commitment to the struggle against anti-Jewish prejudice certainly attracted great attention at the time, but I am not sure whether, in the final analysis, this was of benefit to the Jews; after all, Hilsner was convicted, and after World War I the prosecutor in his trial became a popular mayor of Prague. In *Making of a State*, Masaryk's account of the efforts undertaken abroad by himself, together with Beneš and Štefánik, to promote Czechoslovak independence, Masaryk emphasized the assistance he received from Jews around the world. The Constitution of the first Czechoslovak Republic was the first in the world to recognise the Jews as a separate nationality. With government support, three international Zionist congresses took place in Czechoslovakia (1921, 1923 and 1933). It is likely, however, that Karel Čapek's extremely popular "Conversations with Masaryk" are what chiefly influenced public opinion in this country. In them Masaryk freely admitted to having from childhood deep-seated feelings of anti-Semitism, including prejudice about ritual murders, and the sober, cautionary way he comments on how those attitudes evolved is very convincing. It's hard to say, but cautionary words are probably no cure for anti-Semitism... On the other hand, word of caution from someone who himself was "not without sin", and had to overcome his own prejudice is certainly more effective than intellectual moralizing. That was precisely Masaryk's case.

I also think that our sympathy for the Jews derives from our pride at having rendered them active assistance after World War II, not only by supporting the creation of the Israeli state in the UN, but also aiding the resettlement of Jews to Israel after the proclamation of independence in 1948. But Czechoslovakia's main achievement was helping to arm Israel and train the members of its army and air force.

That official post-war military assistance (the supply of arms, particularly aircraft, training of air crews and other military personnel), which was kept secret as possible, and which surprisingly continued until the first months of 1949, was promoted by Tomáš Masaryk's son Jan, who was Foreign Minister until his death in suspicious circumstances in March 1948. I think we are particularly proud of that help as "friends in need" because our country acted independently, and we even supplied weapons in defiance of the UN's declared embargo – albeit they were paid for by Israel.

At the same time it was a case of "one good turn deserves another", in a certain sense. After all, there had been a large proportion of Jews in our military units that fought with the Allies on all fronts in World War II. Sometimes they constituted a third of combatants, and in some cases they were in the majority. This was still public knowledge after the war, but was then officially expunged from the national memory for many decades.

By now it is impossible to assess and gauge the significance of all those factors that favoured our special relationship with Israel. Indeed it was certainly partly due to Moscow's post-war illusions of making the Jewish state one of its satellites. And the support for resettlement and arms sales was not only promoted by President Beneš and Jan Masaryk, but also by the Communist leader Klement Gottwald.

The enforced breaking-off of diplomatic ties with Israel after the "Six-Day War" in 1967 was viewed negatively by the public, partly because it was imposed by the Soviet Union, and also because a large number of people in this country secretly identified with Israel – seeing it as a sort of David against Goliath. It's what we would like to have been – in 1938, for instance...

The outcome of that suspension of diplomatic relations was an abandoned and derelict embassy in Tel-Aviv. And it was Miloš Pojar, as the first ambassador in twenty-three years, who unlocked its doors and peopled it once more. The breach was mended.

Masaryk's influence on the Czech public's unusual attitude to Jews and the state of Israel is manifested with absolute clarity in the life and work of Miloš Pojar. Indeed he was a convincing embodiment of that influence. In his person, Tomáš Garrigue Masaryk posthumously "found" his disciple, who would continue and implement his ideas. Masaryk's interest in the "Jewish Question" and Miloš Pojar's involvement with the fate of the Jews converge like a vanishing point in his book.

Books indeed tend to have "destinies of their own", but equally some remarkable human destinies have their books – and this is one of them.

Petr Pithart
(dissident, historian, former Czech prime minister
and president of the Senate)

Acknowledgements

Miloš Pojar's *T. G. Masaryk and the Jewish Question* developed over a great deal of time, often through discussions and conditions that were anything but academic. The text was prepared posthumously by the Masaryk Institute and Archives of the Czech Academy of Sciences, namely by Richard Vašek, from the author's estate, lecture notes, and his earlier drafts for the book. The photographs were selected and the accompanying captions composed by the editor with help from Dr. Helena Kokešová of the Masaryk Institute and Dr. Klára Woitschová from the National Museum. I am incredibly grateful to them for their painstaking work.

The occasional repetition or omission is a result of being unable to intervene in the author's work and complete his ideas. I trust that these deficiencies are more than made up for by the strengths of the book: its wealth of information and its impressive selections from the writings of Masaryk – many of which have never before been published in English.

I owe sincere thanks to Rita Spiegel, David Hercky, Hugo Marom, Avraham Harshalom, the Israel - Czech Republic Friendship Association, and the Forum 2000 Foundation. Without their generous support, the English edition of my father's book would not have been published.

Tomáš Pojar

Index

(254)